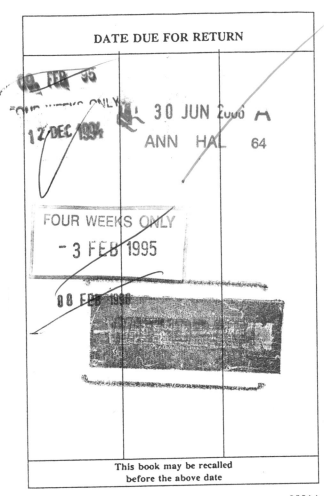

WILLIAM
TREVOR

A Study of the Short Fiction

Also available in Twayne's Studies in Short Fiction Series

Twayne's Studies in Short Fiction

Gordon Weaver, General Editor
Oklahoma State University

William Trevor. Photograph by James Paulson.

WILLIAM TREVOR

_____ *A Study of the Short Fiction* ____

Suzanne Morrow Paulson

Minot State University, North Dakota

TWAYNE PUBLISHERS • *NEW YORK*

Maxwell Macmillan Canada • *Toronto*

Maxwell Macmillan International • *New York Oxford Singapore Sydney*

Twayne's Studies in Short Fiction Series, No. 48

Twayne Publishers   Maxwell Macmillan Canada, Inc.
Macmillan Publishing Company   1200 Eglinton Avenue East
866 Third Avenue   Suite 200
New York, New York 10022   Don Mills, Ontario M3C 3N1

Library of Congress Cataloging-in-Publication Data

Paulson, Suzanne Morrow.
    William Trevor: a study of the short fiction / Suzanne Morrow
Paulson.
        p. cm. — (Twayne's studies in short fiction ; no. 48)
    Includes bibliographical references and index.
    ISBN 0-8057-0858-8 (alk. paper)
    1. Trevor, William, 1928– —Criticism and interpretation. 2. Ireland
in literature. 3. Short story. I. Title. II. Series.
PR6070.R4Z84 1993
823'.914—dc20   93-16606
                          1000045938   CIP

10 9 8 7 6 5 4 3 2 1

Printed in the United States of America.

For James

Contents

Contents

Preface

My sense of tragedy probably comes from childhood—the source, I think, of both tragedy and comedy. The struggle in Ireland—and the sorrow—is a good backdrop for a fiction writer, but it is not for me any sort of inspiration. . . . What seems to nudge me is something that exists between two people, or three, and if their particular happiness or distress exists for some political reason, then the political reason comes into it—but the relationship between the people comes first.[1]

William Trevor's reputation as a major modern writer is well-established in Europe but not in America.[2] No one has yet focused attention on his short-story masterpieces—lost, as they are, in an overwhelming amount of attention paid his numerous fine novels (14). This Irish storyteller and ex-sculptor of nearly 17 years considers his short stories his most important art, and most critics see the short story form as best suited to Trevor's genius.[3]

Trevor's short stories deserve much more critical attention than they have so far received. His short-story masterpieces belong on the shelf alongside those of Chekhov, Dostoyevski, Joyce, Conrad, James, Faulkner, and Flannery O'Connor. Brilliantly rendering the pain of adolescence, the agony of courtship and marriage in an emotionally barren terrain, and the narcissism of destructive parenting, Trevor continues a long tradition of British and Irish literature about men, women, and society. He writes a personal sort of fiction yet transcends the personal because his art encourages sympathy for even the most ridiculous of grotesques.[4]

The depth of Trevor's understanding of people is rare in this age of perpetual violence between nations and regions, within cities and within the family. Reviewers have acknowledged what Richard Eder calls Trevor's "prophetic power."[5] V. S. Pritchett has declared Trevor "the master of the small movements of conscience that worry away at the human imagination and our passions."[6] Ted Solotaroff points to Graham Greene's favorable comparison of Trevor and Joyce because "both Trevor and the early Joyce are geniuses at . . . the deeper realism: accurate observation turning into moral vision."[7]

This Irish shape-shifter deftly renders the perspective of an elderly woman worried about senility, a young wife betrayed by an unfaithful husband, and a middle-aged spinster/schoolteacher distressed when terrorists in Belfast murder a British army officer, decapitate the corpse, and send the head to the officer's wife in a "biscuit tin."[8] Focusing on the vagaries of personality and the more disturbing circumstances of modern life, Trevor, with his psychological and moral insights, individualizes his characters and dynamically depicts their struggles to endure personal hardship. He writes powerful prose because he masters the comic as well as the tragic impulse. His stories cannot be read indifferently, even when they make us laugh. Like other modernists he writes tragicomedy; his work renders the grotesque aspects of human nature under stress. R. Z. Sheppard rightly notes that Trevor "understands as well as any contemporary writer that the defeated, the shelved, and the slightly batty make [good] fiction."[9]

Regressively willful men, women, and children in Trevor's stories disrupt the lives of everyone around them. Tricksters victimize the vulnerable. Traumatized wives, sensitive men, and psychologically abused children suffer because they are at the mercy of cruel authority figures. A rush into a personal relationship meant to console a wounded heart somehow falls into the soundless abyss of indifference, miscommunication, and short-circuited good intentions. The ridiculous, contemporary Everyman/woman cannot overcome a terrifying sense of alienation from society and self. Yet few stories are tragic from start to finish.

The comic tales, such as "Mulvihill's Memorial" and "The Day We Got Drunk on Cake," appear at times more funny than tragic; like Trevor's other masterpieces, however, they encourage what J. Hillis Miller, Robert Scholes, and others designate as an essential experience of "intersubjectivity"—that is, a reading experience reaffirming our humanity and expanding our understanding of others.[10] When I interviewed Trevor in 1989, he declared that his primary interest is people, who, he said, "don't really change all that much." Later in the interview he said, "When you write about anyone—man or woman—there has to be some affection."

Trevor is at his absolute best in those stories expressing his sympathy for women, sensitive men, and adolescents who suffer from destructive stereotypes of feminine and masculine behavior. Whether set in urban England or rural Ireland, these stories depict women who seek autonomy but are forced to serve the interests of the farm, the country estate, or the commercial enterprise in communities demanding that men be aggressive, never nurturing, and that women be nurturing, never aggressively working to solve community and world problems.

There are exceptions, such as the aggressive wife Hilda in "Lovers of Their Time," who is far from nurturing; the nurturing fathers found in "Matilda's England"; Agnes's nurturing husband/father in "Teresa's Wedding"; and the holy father in "August Sunshine." For the most part, however, Trevor's wives, mothers, daughters, and sensitive sons are terribly limited by society and oppressed by patriarchal authority—sometimes yielding to insanity. The politics of gender is an important aspect of Trevor's art.

Confrontations between men and women in love are especially poignant when lovers struggle for meaningful relationships—for example, in "The Forty-seventh Saturday" and "Lovers of Their Time"—but meaning is measured in dollars and cents. Alert readers must sort out the authorial voice from that of the unreliable narrator, whose shifting moods and fuzzy perceptions serve as a window to the world; readers must sort out moments in the text when the discourse of business-as-usual promotes the materialistic values of advertising and the mass media.

Replete with slogans and jingles from radio, television, and movies, commerce diminishes love in these stories. Usually, however, Trevor resists the comic writer's temptation to be satisfied with caricature.[11] His short-story masterpieces in this vein treat with compassion those who struggle in the industrial wasteland. Anthony Glavin points out that Trevor makes "us care *about* people we don't especially care *for*,"[12] and Derek Mahon notes that his "severe [yet] compassionate judgments [are] handed down more in sorrow than in anger."[13] This sorrow is conveyed by masterful manipulations of style rendering inner landscapes or surrealistic dreams such as those found in "The Ballroom of Romance," "The Raising of Elvira Tremlett," and "The Blue Dress."

Nevertheless, the reader may feel revulsion given the vast range of human foibles so poignantly rendered in Trevor's stories. William Cole complains about what he sees as Trevor's "gloom, gloom,"[14] Robert Towers about his "gleeful misanthropy."[15] The criticisms that Trevor represents too much suffering in his stories may suggest the reviewer's confusion between the character's outlook and Trevor's.

✦

Trevor's short stories convey his wise bewilderment over life. He masterminds puzzles of experience that happen to be stories. Like Joyce and other modernists, he works almost entirely by indirection, understatement, and very subtle implication—sometimes relating horrific events in a deadpan tone, sometimes developing volatile perspectives that leap forward and backward in time and in and out of assorted characters' minds. While discussing reasons the Irish "have taken to our hearts the breathless gallop as opposed to the marathon," the short story rather than the novel, Trevor points to suffering owing to oppresion by the British and then declares that the "ability to slip effortlessly from mood to mood [is] . . . the hallmark of the real short story writer."[16] Trevor conveys an incredible range of moods—from tragic despair to comic hilarity.

A 1981 *Newsweek* review, however, calls Trevor a "Master of Malevolence." This is but one example of a reader equating the author's perspective with that of his less reliable narrators. These readers miss Trevor's humanity. John J. Stinson argues that critics assume compassion is lacking in the stories because they do not carefully sort out the many different "voices" in his work. Nor do they consider the modernist methods of the author's style and the modernist tendency to focus on the dark side of human nature. Stinson concludes that "Trevor's carefully controlled and deliberately understated stories are alive with implication. . . . Readers discover a slightly strange world full of eccentric personalities and small quirky events that remain, for all that, very much the world we know."[17]

Trevor in fact reveals the mindscapes of a plethora of eccentric characters.[18] Usually the reader can determine which character's mindscape is being represented—for example, in such first-person narratives as "Beyond the Pale"—because the passage focuses on that character, shown looking at a scene or pondering an idea. Maybe the reader is expected to identify who belongs to what stream of consciousness because it matches behavior established previously in the story as particular to that character. This latter case requires an extremely alert reader, especially when unreliable narrators reveal their own appalling natures.[19]

Trevor's fiction is indeed difficult when an unreliable or omniscient third-person narrator—with shifting moods and fuzzy perceptions—serves as the only window to a complex world. No critic should fail to heed M. M. Bakhtin's argument that modern fiction is "multi-voiced," reflecting sociocultural and historical contexts.[20] Besides being alert to differences between the narrator's and the author's voices, readers must sort out moments in the text when various community voices intrude—the voice of authority reflecting Catholic or Protestant church dogma; feminine communal voices rebelling against pub-crawling husbands and fathers; conforming voices of spinsters and bachelors; alienated schizophrenic voices of adolescents struggling for self-definition; and phallocentric voices of men training their sons to become farmers, auto mechanics, butchers, or various knights of industry (hotel proprietors, storekeepers, boarding school taskmasters, etc.). These voices invariably represent communal values determined by gender, class, and nationality—values that amount to powerful forces dramatically determining the course of a given life.

Trevor understands well the biological, psychological, and social forces that may undermine the best of human intentions—deterministic forces represented in the fiction of such English naturalists as George Eliot, Thomas Hardy, and Joseph Conrad—all writers Trevor mentions when talking about his work. To define Trevor's work as "naturalist" would not be inappropriate. Like both nineteenth-century naturalists and twentieth-century modernists, Trevor adopted a pessimistic attitude toward the industrial world, although his view is far less bleak than some critics suppose.[21]

Modernist writers' pessimistic questioning of God and human nature is best represented in double fictions. Trevor's fiction is not unlike that of E. T. A. Hoffmann, Kafka, Dostoyevski, Dickens, Conrad, Joyce, Poe, Melville, Hawthorne, Twain, James, Faulkner, and Flannery O'Connor—all writers depicting Jekyll-Hyde sorts of double figures, mildly or outrageously schizophrenic protagonists with uncertain identities and a hypersensitivity to suffering in a seemingly godless world. The fragmented self struggles for meaning, longs to communicate with others, and feels lost because it is unable to integrate the finite and the infinite, as the Christian philosopher Kierkegaard sees it; the id and the superego, as the agnostic psychoanalyst Freud sees it; the anima and animus, as the mystic Jung sees it.

Moral judgments in the modern age demand difficult choices independent of mindless conformity to religious doctrines—difficult choices that force us to be divided within ourselves and against one another. Neither Catholics nor Protestants have managed to stop the atrocities perpetrated by both sides in Belfast. Joyce criticized the Catholic Church because of disparities between doctrine and the practices of particular Church representatives—disparities that further shake the foundations of religious faith. In Ireland, of course, a particularly dogmatic and stern form of Catholicism was associated with the Christian Brothers' schools. The teacher-brothers lack humanity as Trevor depicts them in his stories—Trevor being, like Joyce, a modernist in his critique of the Church. Trevor did, however, declare in a letter to me that he believes in God. His stories certainly acknowledge spiritual emptiness, materialism, and alienation in the modern age, but they affirm the importance of community, the importance of "connecting" in the Forsterian sense—as husbands and wives, fathers and mothers, and members of society.

Trevor, then, must be considered modernist in terms of his style, his focus on the dark aspects of human nature, and his skeptical attitude toward some representatives of the Church. He should be related to the nineteenth century, however, when considering his emphasis on deterministic forces undermining human will and the ability to "connect." And let us hope that his compassion and humor prefigure the twenty-first century and a future when his tales will be more fully appreciated.

Most of Trevor's stories convey a genuine optimism and a love of people—a love based on a profound understanding of suffering, a sympathetic acceptance of human weakness, and shrewd insights into social hierarchies. His interest in the more ludicrous aspects of human nature, alienation, identity, and insanity are best expressed by tragicomedy, and his most brilliant short stories borrow from this genre. He writes an intensely poetic, understated, and ironic fiction—the hallmarks of the modern short story.[22]

What I mean to do here is spotlight representative masterpieces of human insight—masterpieces demanding that Trevor be recognized in America for his singular understanding of personality and his major contributions to the short-story form.

❖

The first chapter of Part 1, "Trauma and Talk: Suffering, Self-Defense, and Disinterested Bystanders," includes stories that amount to a study in the psychology of coping or failing to cope with trauma. In these stories Trevor positions distressed and compulsive talkers in various tension-filled social contexts: students share personal problems in a British boarding school ("A School Story"); a wife is abandoned by her husband and tries to cope during a cocktail party ("The Mark-2 Wife"); a husband and wife puzzle over mysterious and threatening phone calls to their suburban home ("A Happy Family"); men buy women drinks at various pubs ("The Day We Got Drunk on Cake"); a teacher in an Irish community school shares with her students her feelings about a politically motivated atrocity ("Attracta"); and a middle-aged suitor takes tea with the parents of his future young bride on the lawn of a country estate ("The Blue Dress"). Miscommunications are at the heart of these stories. Absurd telephone conversation promote misunderstandings. Jokes prevent meaningful moments of intimate sharing. And yet in the last two stories here, the protagonists retreat into a contemplative state of mind that inspires an epiphany—a complete understanding of the disturbing situation at hand.

Protagonists able to reach epiphanies, however, are rare. Most of Trevor's protagonists cope with pain by withdrawing into the self to remake the past according to narcissistic needs rather than adjusting to an immediate and disturbing change of circumstances. The stories addressed in "The Sins of the Fathers and the Destruction of the Alienated Child" are about narcissistic fathers who cannot understand themselves or their adolescent children. Since I believe that Freud's insights about the human psyche, sexuality, and the family are absolutely essential to sounding the depths of modern literature, I briefly discuss in this chapter such Freudian concepts as the Oedipus complex.

Psychoanalytic and gender critics have helped us to be more self-aware and have fostered a better understanding of modern fictions meant to be studies of human nature. "The Raising of Elvira Tremlett" and "A Choice of Butchers" are but two of many Trevor stories clarified by considering psychology and gender. In these stories sensitive adolescents face insensitive fathers discouraging their sons and daughters from becoming independent. "An Evening with John Joe Dempsey" portrays licentious community fathers whose behavior overwhelms an adolescent boy trying to understand his emerging sexual feelings. The presumed abstinence of one community father, Lynch, apparently contradicts the promiscuity of all the others.

This chapter ends with an outstanding example of a story about parents who lovingly care for their adolescent children. "Matilda's England" traces the development of Matilda, who rejects her compassionate mother for remarrying after her father dies in World War II. Despite a nurturing father and stepfather, Matilda loses her mental health as she narcissistically retreats into the past.

"Stories about Courtship: Bachelors/Spinsters, Fathers/Daughters" renders the suffering of adolescent girls, spinsters, wives, and mothers as they conform to destructive stereotypes governing proper feminine and masculine behavior. In various societies cultural codes denigrate the spinster, require the subservience of women to men, and encourage marriages based on economic necessity rather than love.

In "The Ballroom of Romance," for example, Bridie seeks to become a bride but fails to escape her crippled father, who depends on her to meet his most basic needs. This father-daughter relationship is destructive because of community pressures requiring Bridie's subservience and economic realities confining them both to an isolated farm. "Teresa's Wedding" clarifies differences in masculine and feminine attitudes toward sexuality—differences underlying the contrasting behavior of daughters and fathers, bachelors and spinsters, attending this wedding. "The Property of Colette Nervi" is a complex story, but the fear of spinsterhood is again important when a crippled young woman and her family accept a middle-aged bachelor, who proves himself to be a thief and a philanderer, as a suitor.

In "Kathleen's Field" a father too focused on providing for his son's inheritance unknowingly sacrifices his daughter's chances for independence by asking her to work as a servant so that he can repay a loan enabling him to purchase his neighbor's field. Finally, "The Wedding in the Garden" defines social pressures on an adolescent boy, whose family aspires to upper-middle-class status and disapproves when their son falls in love with the maid. Again, the son's inheritance is an issue, and economic arrangements determine the probable suffering of two women—the maid and the more appropriate Protestant maiden the son finally marries.

The last chapter of Part 1, "Commerce, Communication, and the Business Class," includes those Trevor stories most concerned with materialistic values promoted by advertising and the mass media. Love romantically glorifies commercial exchange and commercial settings in "Lovers of Their Time." In "The Forty-seventh Saturday," an unmarried mistress is faithful to her elderly lover, even though he callously offers only a bottle of wine for a meal and an afternoon of narcissistic sex.

In the centerpiece of this group, "Mulvihill's Memorial," Trevor indicts a commercial world that profits from pornography and advertising. And in "Broken Homes" he explores the suffering of an elderly woman worried about senility, alienated from her community because all her day-to-day dealings take the form of a commercial exchange with disinterested persons—the wheeler-dealer teacher who allows his adolescent students to destroy the poor woman's home; those who bring meals on wheels; and her overly solicitous, storekeeper neighbors, who so rudely undermine her dignity. Caretaking becomes big business.

Part 2 is a compilation of Trevor's comments on his art, his reader, and his community—comments derived from two interviews (my own and one conducted by Mira Stout for the *Paris Review*), from Trevor's introduction to the *Oxford Book of Irish Short Stories*, and from one of his reviews that reveals a great deal about his standards of literary excellence. Part 3 provides an overview of responses to Trevor's work and a brief gathering of articles and reviews published in America, Ireland, England, Canada, and France.

Notes

1. Mira Stout, interview of William Trevor, "The Art of Fiction CVIII," *Paris Review* 110 (1989): 118–51.

2. Graham Greene argues that Trevor's *Angels at the Ritz* (1975) is "surely one of the best collections, if not the best, since Joyce's *Dubliners*" (dust jacket). John Banville declares Trevor's work "among the most subtle and sophisticated fiction being written today" ("Relics," review of *Two Lives, New York Review of Books*, 26 September 1991, 29–30), and Stephen Schiff declares Trevor "the greatest living writer of short stories in the English language" ("The Shadows of William Trevor," *New Yorker*, 28 December 1992–4 January 1993, 158). Trevor is a member of the Irish Academy of Letters; has received the Royal Society of Literature Award, the Whitbread Award, the Hawthornden Prize, and the *Hudson Review* Bennett Award; and has been shortlisted for the Booker Prize. More than 30 of his stories have appeared as plays on British and Irish television. A film of his novel *Fools of Fortune* was released in 1989. His work has been translated into more than 15 languages.

3. Anne Duchêne observes that "the territory of unease, the sure-footed sinister prowl round the edges of pain, at which [Trevor] excels, is less easily handled in a novel than in short stories" (*Times Literary Supplement*, 18 June 1976, 731). Robert Nye argues that "the idea of Trevor as a novelist-in-miniature seems to me the wrong way of looking at his specific skill in the short story form. . . . He is more nearly a poet of brief fictions. . . . His stories have more *shape* than those of any other contemporary practitioner of the difficult art on either side of the Atlantic" ("Storyteller with a Poet's Feeling," *Christian Science Monitor*, 16 June 1976, 23). Lis Harris argues that Trevor's "novels, although well-written, are not on a par with the stories chiefly because they are overpopulated" (*New Yorker*, 28 January 1980, 99–101).

4. Daniel R. Schwarz observes that "great fiction is produced when personal problems are felt as moral problems whose significance transcends the limitations of ego" (*The Humanistic Heritage* [Ithaca, N.Y.: Cornell University Press, 1987]). More than one review has compared William Trevor with Flannery O'Connor (see Peter Goldsworthy, "Flawed Characters Collected," [Sydney] *Morning Herald*, 23 August 1986).

5. *Los Angeles Times Book Review*, 4 May 1986, 3.

6. *New York Review of Books*, 19 April 1979, 8.

7. *New York Times Book Review*, 21 February 1982, 7.

8. *The Stories of William Trevor* (London: Penguin, 1983), 593.

9. *Time*, 10 October 1983, 72.

10. See J. Hillis Miller, *The Ethics of Reading: Kant, de Man, Eliot, Trollope, James, and Benjamin* (New York: Columbia University Press, 1987), and Robert Scholes and Robert Kellogg, *The Nature of Narrative* (Oxford: Oxford University Press, 1966). A *Washington Post Book World* review notes Trevor's "endless sympathy for his characters" (Howard Frank Mosher, 25 May 1986, 6).

Preface

11. Complaints about characterization tend to focus on the early novels rather than Trevor's best stories. Paul Bailey in a review of *Elizabeth Alone* complains that Trevor's "is a world composed of types, not people" (*New Statesman*, 26 October 1973, 611). But Bailey then qualifies his complaint when he points out that "the scene in which the ugly Miss Samson tells Elizabeth about the agony of losing one's faith is the best writing Trevor has ever produced." Unlike those who complain that Trevor is gloomy, Bailey declares this scene is superb because "it hints at a world of despair and darkness [which] gives me hope that his next book will concern itself with [the] mysterious aspects of life." No critic addressing Trevor's masterpieces of the short story have been disappointed in this way.

12. *Christian Science Monitor*, 2 May 1986, B5; my italics.

13. *Times Literary Supplement*, 15 October 1971, 1247.

14. *Saturday Review Book World*, 9 February 1974, 42.

15. *New York Times Book Review*, 2 October 1983, 1.

16. Introduction to *David's Daughter Tamar*, by Margaret Barrington (Dublin: Wolfhound Press, 1982). Here Trevor provides three reasons "that the Irish possess what might be described as a genius for [the short story]: due to disaffection, poverty, and the confusion of two languages Ireland was unable to provide the emergent nineteenth-century novel with the leisurely, stratified society which it nurtured so fruitfully in Victorian England; that the Irish mood is psychologically better suited to the shorter form; that we have, as a people, so inordinate a passion for gossipy anecdotes that we are led quite naturally to the shorter form" (7–8).

17. See "Replicas, Foils, and Revelations in Some 'Irish' Short Stories," *Canadian Journal of Irish Studies* 11, no. 2 (1985): 17.

18. Gerard Genette calls this "focalization" in his *Narrative Discourse: An Essay in Method*, trans. Jane E. Lewin (Ithaca, N.Y.: Cornell University Press, 1980).

19. The methods of Robert Browning's satiric monologues (such as *Andrea Del Sarto*) might be compared with Trevor's treatment of the narrator in "Beyond the Pale."

20. M. M. Bakhtin, *Problems of Dostoevsky's Poetics*, ed. and trans. Caryl Emerson (Minneapolis: University of Minnesota Press, 1984).

21. Jacqueline Stahl Aronson reports that during an interview "Trevor spoke of himself as a person 'who was meant to be a pessimist but wasn't'" (*Irish Literary Supplement* 5, no. 1 [1986]: 7). Trevor has said that he sees his work as being more related to the nineteenth than the twentieth century.

22. In a review of Trevor's *Silence in the Garden* (1988) Elizabeth Tallent clarifies the author's gift for understatement: "The narrative style is so muted that tiny domestic details acquire vicarious force" (*New York Times Book Review*, 9 October 1988, 12). Robert E. Rhodes notes that "Trevor's canon of short stories is crafted with exquisite care; . . . the style is so understated as to be nearly elided" (*Irish Literary Supplement* 2, no. 2 [1983]: 28). Steve Connelly writes of Trevor as "a master of the resonant fact, the informational nugget which accretes meaning through implication" (*Eire-Ireland*, 20, no. 2 [1985]: 144).

Acknowledgments

I am especially grateful for the hospitality of William Trevor and his wife, Jane, during my visit to Shobroke Mill. The author thoughtfully offered corrections and promptly granted permissions. Trevor's publisher, The Bodley Head, was very helpful, arranging for me to study the files at the University of Reading in 1989—not to mention allowing a busybody critic to puruse the files in its London office. Professor Edith R. Farrell translated a BBC review, enabling me to include a French critical perspective on Trevor's work.

I appreciate very much the help and financial support given by various administrators and committees at Minot State University. Don Wharton, vice president of academic affairs, awarded me research appointments in 1989–90 and 1991–92. Dean of Arts and Sciences Dale Elhardt, Chair of Humanities George Slanger, and the Minot State Research Committee provided research assistance, equipment, and partial funding for trips to Ireland, England, and France. A Bush Foundation Grant also allowed me to travel in Ireland.

My colleagues at Minot State University have been understanding when this project demanded time I might have spent helping to row the English Department and university boat. Humanities Division Chair George Slanger deserves special recognition for sharing the throws of a difficult project, offering encouragement, and suggesting revisions. Cornell University Professor Daniel Schwarz was generous with his time during and after a National Endowment for the Humanities summer seminar on modernism and literary theory. Gladyce Romine, the division administrative secretary, offered important help as I was juggling teaching and writing tasks. Larry Greenwood, director of the Gordon Olson Library, and other librarians—Susan Podrigula, Jane laPlante, Steve Kirby, George Clark, Martha Williams, and Jim Millhorn—devoted a great deal of time and energy sending for materials and helping as I developed the bibliography. Donna Weishaar proved to be an outstanding computer specialist.

My teaching assistants, Joy Currie and Walt Runyan, and my research assistants, Wendy Knudson and Ellen Greene, relieved me of numerous tasks, organized an enormous amount of background material, helped with proofreading, and pointed to areas in need of clarification.

Gordon Weaver, the series editor, wrote letters of good cheer, offered wonderful ideas for cuts and changes and patiently tolerated last-minute revisions. I appreciated the editorial expertise very much. Chester Anderson, Joyce scholar and professor of English at the University of Minnesota, Minneapolis, deserves credit for introducing me to Trevor's work and for nurturing me through both my master's and doctoral degrees. Ryan Lahurd, Augsburg College, provided important support by encouraging my son Craig during a difficult period of his junior year.

My husband, James, and my sons, Mark Forrest and Craig Alan, have shared many burdens and steadfastly offered love.

Acknowledgments for permission to reprint the articles and reviews excerpted in Parts 2 and 3 appear on the first page of each piece. I am very grateful for the cooperation of permissions editors of various publishing houses, journals, and newspapers—not to mention the generosity of critics and reviewers whose work I am proud to include in the brief gathering of critical excerpts in Part 3.

Part 1

THE SHORT FICTION

Trauma and Talk: Suffering, Self-Defense, and Disinterested Bystanders

William Trevor's special interest in people under stress finds its clearest expression in his many stories about obsessive characters trying to master a crisis by talking to various bystanders, who usually respond with indifference. The protagonists in these stories talk through the trauma, exactly the sort of process the psychiatrist encourages. But lines of communication that might heal the wounds from tragic loss fail to develop. The stories in this vein amount to studies of apathy in the face of suffering, the inadequacy of talk to comfort those in distress, the impotence of language, and the vulnerability of victims confronting a crisis. An Irish writer like Trevor would naturally be interested in trauma and would ponder how indifference to suffering could develop on a mass scale. How could British landlords watch children starve in eighteenth-century Ireland? How can terrorists in Belfast today plant bombs that kill innocent children? Curiously, in only one story of those focused on trauma and talk do the Troubles emerge as a critical factor.

In "Beyond the Pale"[1] public troubles jeopardize personal relationships. The female narrator (a traitor to her own sex) carries on an affair with the husband of her friend Cynthia. On a holiday at an Irish resort the betrayed wife hysterically expresses her misery in an emotional outburst—a flood of talk released because she has just witnessed a man's suicide after listening to his life's story. Far from being an indifferent bystander, Cynthia apparently had listened intently as this man told her his own tragic love story. He murdered his lover because he was repulsed by her involvement with IRA atrocities. Cynthia understands this stranger's despair as it relates to her own despair and, most importantly, to the despairing history of Ireland: "people starved or died while other people watched. A language was lost, a faith forbidden. Famine followed revolt."[2]

Cynthia's outburst is witnessed by her wayward husband, his mistress (her friend), a roustabout bachelor (supposedly her "partner"), and various other guests at the resort, all indifferent bystanders who think her insane.

3

The resort owner chastizes her: "This talk is most offensive" (708). "Beyond the Pale" is indeed an important story that might be understood in terms of the Troubles, but the most important insights to be gleaned from Trevor's stories about trauma and talk are those that help in understanding people under stress and the psychology of suffering, rather than insights into political intricacies.

These stories assume *destructive* and *constructive* forms. In some stories talk has the destructive tendency to occur in a context of self-defense ("A School Story"), empty social gesture ("The Mark-2 Wife"), desperate symptom ("A Happy Family"), and comic coercion ("The Day We Got Drunk on Cake"). In other stories—some of his best—he explores the constructive tendency for talk to occur in a context of communion or intersubjective sharing (e.g., "Attracta" and "The Blue Dress").

Most of Trevor's traumatized protagonists in fact do recollect past trauma, obsessively repeating the details of their worst nightmares, but they do not really gain mastery over their experience. They develop an illusion of mastery. The retelling of past experiences distorts present perceptions. New events are measured according to old forms. Characters are lulled into apathy.

Trevor's style takes on the rhythm of a metronome in the stories about trauma and talk: storytelling, ritual, ceremony, and daily routines calm the frenzied soul.[3] The calming effect of mindless repetition and an overdependence on the past, however, prevents us from perceiving experience in its immediacy. Traumatized protagonists suffer because laconic, indifferent bystanders formulate evasive responses when confronting someone else's suffering.

"A School Story": Talk as Aggressive Self-Defense

"A School Story" is the most dramatic example of a traumatized victim and indifferent bystanders. Here Trevor presents a bewildering instance of motiveless malignity in the "unhealthy personage" of Williams, the boarding school student/bystander who victimizes his friend Markham and finally drives the boy insane. Complicated interactions develop between a trio of "friends": the disturbed adolescent Markham, who compulsively tells the story of his mother's death and later suffers the death of his father and stepmother; the true friend, the narrator, who frets over Markham's desperate struggle and tries to help but finally succumbs to the apathy all around him; and the false friend, Williams, a sadistic adolescent who convinces Markham that he is responsible for the death of his father and stepmother.

At this boarding school "every night after lights-out there was a ceremonial story-telling" during which the boys shared spooky or intriguing tales. The nameless narrator's friend, Markham, is encouraged by his dormmates to repeat "again and again" (100) the story of his mother's death. Obviously, Markham is struggling to gain mastery over his own tragic circumstances—struggling to discharge despair. The storytelling in the dorm staves off the "gloom" (98). Markham's gloom and his story about the death of a parent fascinates the other students because it represents a crisis they themselves will someday face. His story is "real"—much better than the "trite" stories involving stereotypes of "the Englishman, the Irishman and the Scotsman," for example. Markham's audience is more than "satisfied" with his story even though he reenacts the past over and over again without developing "anything new." The story reassures bystanders of their own imperviousness; someone else is suffering; disasters always happen to someone else. Moreover, the students here are reassured to see someone apparently master a traumatic death by talking about it.

Trevor's ingenuity peaks when he presents a nameless narrator who tells the story of Markham, who retells to his dormmates his father's story about his mother's death due to a hunting mishap. The nameless narrator judges Markham's character as innocent; Markham judges his father a liar telling a "story" about his own gun firing accidentally and killing his mother. The reader in turn hears the "story" of a student/narrator who is disturbed by the victimization of his friend Markham but is finally indifferent enough to look the other way while his friend is condemned to the madhouse. In fact, this story-within-a-story and parallel recurrences of storytelling diffuse the sense of guilt.

Markham and the nameless narrator in "A School Story" are emphatically superior to the other characters because they do not evade guilt; rather, they assume responsibility. But even though the narrator is compassionate toward his friend and willing to assume responsibility for others in his life, he finally fails Markham. And guilt is exactly the burden that drives Markham mad. He claims to be "sharp as a knife" (98) while explaining his aggressive feelings toward his father. Markham mercilessly condemns his father for covering up what he believes to be his mother's murder. Markham's certainty that his father killed his mother and his own subconscious guilt over his aggression toward his father intensifies his resolve "to wipe out [his parents] with a couple of swoops of a butcher's

5

knife" (98). And yet despite Markham's rampage against his father, the widower seems to deserve sympathy. In fact, he asks his son to imagine a husband's suffering from guilt for accidentally being "the instrument of [his] wife's slaughter" (98). Apparently Markham's father compulsively reiterates "how beautiful she'd been," boring the son who interrupts "when [he] could get a word in." Markham then hurries his father toward an explanation of the mother's death—the sort of thing Markham's dormmates do when eager to hear his gory story. Indeed, the father's compulsive talk reveals his love for his wife, Markham's mother.

Unjustifiably, Markham wishes to kill his father. Yet lest we judge the son too harshly, the narrator points to his friend's gentle nature, explaining that "people liked him." In fact, during the morbid storytelling the narrator says that Markham "seemed to be speaking outside his role." Markham's hasty condemnation of his father is only human given his grief over losing his mother—grief complicated by a repressed wish to "kill" his father. This wish represents a return to the stage of infancy when the son wants the mother's exclusive love. The desire for exclusive love of the (m)other/self and the intolerance of all other rivals is a regressive tendency we usually outgrow as we learn to be self-giving rather than possessive and jealous. Markham seeks relief from guilt for his aggressive wish to murder his father. Thus he repeats that he is "right" (99)—reaffirms that he is absolutely "correct" (100), as he puts it—while sharing his past.

Usually such proclamations of innocence *do* reveal guilt. The basic irony of this story, however, depends on the fact that Markham does finally assume responsibility for the murder of his parents, even though he is actually not guilty—or guilty only in that we all harbor death wishes against parents during childish moments of rage.

Markham's Oedipal rage, then, is revealed by his storytelling, his attitude toward his father, and his incapacity for maintaining more than one friendship. Moreover, the narrator defines his association with Markham and Williams as "an odd kind of triangle" (101)—an unhappy love triangle of a most destructive sort. The narrator realizes that "there was something wrong" with Markham, but he and his friends at the age of 15 "scarcely analysed [their] feelings," much less their Oedipal feelings.

Despite Markham's rage against his father and his conviction that it is "right" for him to "dream at night of the sharpening of the knife," this outraged son is not the true villain in this story. His impulses are regressive, but they pale when compared with those of the "dreaded Williams" (103), who in the course of the story "is transformed from a cunning nonentity into a Satanic figure of mystery and power" (101), "a fit candidate for

[hell]" (105). Epitomizing the aggressive potential of children, a recurring motif in Trevor's fiction,[4] Williams intrudes on the friendship between the narrator and Markham. This uncanny figure exerts a remarkable degree of control when he woos his victim into a friendship that excludes all others, then drives him to madness.

When Markham joins the narrator and Williams in order to smoke a cigar and toast bread in the school's boiler room, the three boys share their life's ambitions: Williams declares that he will become a lawyer and Markham that he will "hang quite soon for the slaughter of [his] father" (100). Williams's asking Markham to postpone the murder until he can defend the would-be avenger seems harmless enough, but it soon is apparent that the would-be defender is Markham's destroyer. The guilt-ridden, masochistic boy wants to take responsibility for his crime. Williams taunts Markham by declaring him "a bloody madman," and the reader suspects this Satanic young adolescent has fathomed his friend's vulnerability. Markham's desire for being "correct" in "hatching schemes of vengeance" masks a terrible, self-destructive drive owing to feeling "guilty already" (100). When Markham's father and stepmother are butchered by Mau Mau in Kenya, Williams exploits Markham's guilt until he indeed behaves like "a madman" (100, 101, 102).

Misquoting Hamlet's famous soliloquy about "the slings and arrows" of fate (a hackneyed phrase), Headmaster Bodger announces at the start of the fall term "the sudden and violent death of Ian Markham's father and stepmother." The students had been expecting an announcement about the usual "items of school routine" (102)—necessary reminders after the summer break. The narrator and his schoolmates believe for a short time that Markham butchered his parents and not "a Mau Mau marauder armed with a heavy knife" (102), as Bodger puts it, and Markham reinforces their beliefs when he regresses to silence and befriends Williams, which amounts to an admission of guilt.

Nonetheless ever sympathetic to his friend, the nameless narrator judges it "unlikely" (102) that Markham butchered his parents and fully understands the his friend's suffering. The narrator concludes that Markham is "almost dead himself . . . [but] not a figure to inspire terror," puzzles over Williams's ability to attract Markham, and decides that the troubled boy's "crazy" need for Williams is due to the fact that "since he had no father to hate now, he was feeding on this unexplained hatred of himself" (103). Williams's hatred provides Markham with a means of self-punishment. The two boys form a sadomasochistic pair. The narrator, alarmed by this terrible development, decides to seek help from Pinshow, "a fat, middle-aged master who welcomed the personal problems of his pupils" (103).

When the narrator meets with Pinshow, the teacher confronts a crisis challenging his sensitivity to the suffering of others, but instead of discerning the complexities of the case, he offers a lame insight: "Out of the slimy mud of words . . . out of the sleet and hail of verbal imprecision, come approximate thoughts and feelings, words that have taken the place of thoughts and feelings, and the beauty of incantation" (104). "Incantation" fosters indifference to suffering, and even the narrator, who seems so very sympathetic as he struggles with his friend's deterioration, accepts the teacher as a model and parries hackneyed quotation for hackneyed quotation: "There is a land of the living and a land of the dead and the bridge is love" (104), a quotation Pinshow identifies as Thornton Wilder.

After this sequence of quotations seemingly irrelevant to the case at hand, Pinshow pointedly asks, "Love . . . or love? One sort or the other sort [Platonic? hetereosexual? homosexual]?" Trevor does not directly clarify what Pinshow means by his question, but Pinshow does report to the headmaster that Markham and Williams's relationship is "illicit" (105). The headmaster then confronts the narrator, grills all three boys, and tries to "shame" (106) Markham—a terrible irony given Markham's overwhelming burden of guilt and shame.

This story poignantly examines human indifference to the suffering of others—Williams's indifference and the indifference of the students who ask Markham to repeat his story of a mother's death (or possible murder) at the start and who later eagerly await "a new and gory story" (102), or better yet—when Markham's parents are butchered at the end—a murderer's confession. Indifference poses as compassion when the headmaster feebly announces the murders of Markham's parents, and also in a minor incident when the student Block recalls a joke while pretending to listen to the narrator express his worries over Markham. Block can only laugh, however, while the narrator compassionately observes his friend's "sad, lost looking face" (104).

Despite the narrator's compassionate nature, he too, like Pinshow, fails to help the lost boy. The story ends when the narrator confronts Williams because he knows that the "evil bastard" convinced Markham of his own guilt ("made him believe he did it" [107]). And he also knows the "right" (99) or "correct" (100) thing to do is to defend the helpless victim. But instead of explaining to the headmaster that "Williams had insidiously

The Short Fiction

played upon" Markham's "fears" (107), the narrator responds mechanically to "the urgent chiming of a bell."

The call to attend class destroys the call to conscience. When the narrator abandons his friend to madness he seems no longer a caring human being sensitive to the suffering of others but, as Trevor describes him, an automaton, "like the object of some remote control . . . [answering] the familiar summons" (107). Admittedly, the narrator's failure to help his friend may not seem as serious a crime as Williams's aggression, but this story about murder and madness clearly implicates bystanders who are indifferent to suffering as well as aggressors who actively harm others.

"The Mark-2 Wife": Talk as Empty Social Gesture

Whereas the sinister, ominous undercurrents in "A School Story" reveal Trevor's mastery of tragedy and "The Day We Got Drunk on Cake" affirms his mastery of comedy, "The Mark-2 Wife" and most of Trevor's other stories show him to be a virtuoso at tragicomedy. Despite the incidental hilarity that emerges from the cocktail party that circumscribes this story, it is ultimately a serious study of a wife who finds herself abandoned by her husband in a world that targets women as the title suggests. Anna Mackintosh apparently has been replaced by a would-be Mark-2 wife.

Anna's husband, Ed, had asked her to meet him at a cocktail party given by his business associate. Reluctantly attending the party, Anna finds that her husband has stood her up. Knowing no one at this party (not even the hosts, the Lowhrs), this timid wife repeatedly feels an uneasy urge to telephone her psychiatrist, Dr. Abbatt. An elderly couple, the Ritchies, who also do not know the other partygoers, notice Anna's discomfort, and Mrs. Ritchie declares to her husband, General Ritchie, "We should go and talk to her" (254), thus responding sympathetically to Anna's loneliness and grief.

Mrs. Ritchie's abilities to help the younger woman are unfortunately hampered by her own insecurities. She enjoys offering sympathy because rescuers have power over those who need help. This compensates for the fact that she and her husband, in their old age, expect the hostess, Mrs. Lowhr, to assume a condescending attitude toward the elderly couple. So with self-interest partly motivating her to action, Mrs. Ritchie strikes up a conversation with Anna. An awkward silence follows. This interested bystander is totally ineffective in helping Anna, the Mark-1 wife, who blurts out her fears that her husband has abandoned her because she is infertile.

9

Mrs. Ritchie unrestrainedly delights in telling Anna about her "dozen grandchildren" (257), which in effect bungles her cause given Anna's painful confession about being barren. It is true that Anna masochistically torments herself by asking Mrs. Ritchie to talk about her grandchildren, but still Mrs. Ritchie's natural pride in being a grandmother and her fear of being disrespected because "the elderly [exaggerate] things" (261) prevents her from understanding the childless wife.

Social tension then intensifies as Anna's behavior deteriorates from apparent neurosis—talking to an elderly couple about her personal woes as if she had "talked many hours" to her psychiatrist (256)—to apparent madness. She is obsessed by her infertility. She imagines in great detail the younger, more attractive, and infinitely fertile woman taking her place. Suspense builds as the reader wonders whether Anna's husband has in fact taken a mistress or whether Anna suffers a masochistic delusion. Convinced that her husband's mistress is responsible for her husband's delay, she imagines the woman's sudden appearance and a scene in which the Mark-2 wife demands that her husband leave his Mark-1 wife, who suffers from delusions of possessing prophetic powers: "I know precisely what's going to happen" (256). She imagines the future in vivid detail, the terrible pity she will suffer when the Lowhrs realize she has been "left all in the lurch" (257). Tragically absorbed in herself ("Look at me," she says), she feels totally abandoned.

When Anna compares acquiring a "Mark-2 Wife," a terrible "tragedy," with abandoning the use of a particular "gadget" for "more up-to-date models" (257), the reader is more than convinced of her instability. She weeps, drinks whiskey, uses her handkerchief to clear her nose, and feels that "there's not enough ventilation" in the room. Anna's conversation with the Ritchies becomes more disjointed and erratic "because it didn't seem to matter any more what words were spoken" (257). She transgresses the rules of etiquette governing party banter by demanding intimate knowledge from strangers, asking the General the embarrassing question of whether he ever wished for "a change" in wives.

For most of the story the disturbed wife seems totally irrational. Her fears had "on other occasions" (257) been groundless, merely fantasies, symptoms deserving psychotherapy. As might be expected given the usual response to unaccompanied women, the General feels from the start that "something was the matter with this woman who was on her own" (254).

Everyone in this story needs to talk to someone else, but no one offers meaningful comfort. Indeed, the hostess eventually does belittle Mrs. Ritchie for worrying over Anna, and this insensitivity of the hostess marks the only instance that inspires the General to support his wife in the course of a very stressful evening. He is unresponsive to Anna's *and* his own wife's needs. He laughs at his wife when she confesses having had similar neurotic fears regarding his fidelity. He soon finds "himself talking to nobody" (261), the central predicament characterizing the entire evening.

Even Anna's psychiatrist might as well be talking to himself. Unresponsive to the poor woman's grief, he suggests over the telephone that she has "been drinking too much" (263). She defines her therapy sessions as one-sided, with the doctor telling her "to face things" (264). He defines these same sessions as reciprocal and presumes to speak her mind for her: "*We* talked it out" (264; my italics), he says condescendingly. The collective pronoun "we," used by authority figures in Trevor's stories, infers that a woman has been deprived of autonomy. The horror of losing a husband is the horror of powerlessness—of losing a valuable identity determined by the marriage contract and celebrated by the community. Anna suffers a terrible loss of self-worth and declares through her tears, "I'm not myself" (257). The psychiatrist and her husband usurp this dismayed wife's identity.

Although victimized by others, Anna herself fails to respond sympathetically to the Ritchies' need for respect. She accuses them of "mocking" her by offering to help and then accuses them of enjoying her plight as "a good bit of gossip" (259). She complains that they will turn her plight into a story to tell their grandchildren. Rather than consider that in their old age they fear being "entirely useless" (263), she thinks of them as "scarecrows" (262) too old to understand. And yet the impotence of old age is actually closer to the situation of the woman abandoned by her husband than Anna realizes.

Anna's need for control over her life drives her to what she fears most. She decides she will "insist on a divorce," "taking matters into her own hands . . . rejecting, not being rejected herself" (265). She leaves the party feeling that she will determine her own fate. Amazingly, at the end Anna's husband does arrive with his Mark-2 wife. The Mark-1 wife's conviction that her husband has found a Mark-2 wife proves to be an exceptionally sane insight about her husband's infidelity. Her agony is not narcissistic and groundless but a normal reaction to a terrible loss. Her only "disease" is an overly active imagination and a heightened sensitivity to the fact that men use women as "targets" to challenge the masculine ego.

This tendency to "target" women is epitomized by the obnoxiously amorous bald man who gestures to Anna "without a word" to communicate his desire to dance with her. Rather than talk to Anna, he is silent as they dance, his lips playing "with a strand of her hair" (258). He responds with a shrug when she declares that her husband has been unfaithful. He manhandles her until she stops him. Without a word he abandons her. The Mark-1 wife seems infinitely sound when compared with some of the other partygoers.

Only when Anna seems to be leaving do the Lowhrs respond to her distress. The Ritchies speak with Anna's husband, Ed, and Mrs. Ritchie finally demonstrates sensitivity by remarking that Anna needs "a little time [to] feel she has a voice in her own life" (266). All of the conversations in this story are no more fruitful than the psychiatrist's long-distance telephone therapy during the crisis/party. The telephone functions well enough when lines are open, but in Trevor's stories it serves as a metaphor for being disconnected. It is also an important factor in "A Happy Family" and "The Day We Got Drunk on Cake"—two other stories about being disconnected during times of stress.

"A Happy Family": Talk as Desperation

Another story focused on a suffering wife, "A Happy Family" is narrated by a bystander-husband far less a culprit causing his wife grief than is Ed Mackintosh. A traumatized victim himself, this unhappy husband watches his wife's mental decline in horror. The husband suffers because he cannot fathom his wife's insanity, which seems to develop from early childhood imaginings (perhaps compensation for her father's insensitivity) and the stresses of lonely mothering, but as usual we cannot be absolutely sure when pointing fingers.

The narrator-husband appears at the start having just come home from work. His one-year-old "daughter," Bridget, looks at him "as if she had forgotten that [he] was closely related to her" (208). Her unresponsiveness is due to his. As she greets him, he asks if she is going to bed—his first words to her after the day's absence and an inappropriate question because the daughter "didn't look sleepy." Moreover, a one-year-old does not usually converse in the manner suggested by the father's question. This initial misunderstanding and the missed signals between father and daughter prefigure missed signals between a wife who cannot communicate with her husband and a husband who cannot recognize his wife's distress before it is too late, even though he earnestly tries.

Elizabeth Farrel, the narrator's wife and mother of two daughters and a son, suffers from schizophrenia. Elizabeth develops the feeling that her essential self is dead, having based her identity on being a wife and mother

When the Lysarths note that Terris's name is "odd," Trevor here intimates his protagonist's involvement with world "terror" and also infers that he is different from them—soothsayer up against liars. Ironically, when he meets the family and fully expects rejection because he is so much older than Dorothea, he does not feel like "an interloper," his more usual stance being that of the eavesdropping journalist, the odd man out. He is surprised that the family accepts him as a future regular of their croquet team. His prospective mother-in-law's affirmation—that his skill at croquet "will one day put [the family] all to shame"—suggests their acceptance but prefigures *his* rejection of them, because of a child so shamelessly ignored when they recall "other games of croquet" on the lawn once so sullied with blood. Twin Jonathan's denial—"Not that we're on the side of cunning" (717)—and Dorothea's cry—"What a family poor Terris is marrying into!"—reverberate with irony when we realize the "cunning" required to present murder as accident.

Finally, the investigative reporter encounters the ultimate coverup. His skill at exposing corruption is challenged by the "almost artificial" quality of their stylized and aristocratically conditioned conversations, the seemingly rehearsed "domestic scenes" that "belonged in the theatre" (717). Terris eventually participates in the "telepathy" between the members of this family behaving as if according to "practised theatre" (717), and this suggests his failure. Totally out of character, for a time he conforms "precisely [to] what was expected of [him]," succumbing to the Lysarths' script all too politely, all too easily.

Terris pinpoints his crisis as the moment Dorothea "confesses" the horror of her childhood; worse yet, she reveals that she became "furious" (718) with Agnes Kemp's behavior. His epiphany is centered on her ability to address so blandly the gruesome event and then immediately smile, proferring him a kiss. Dorothea's revelation haunts Terris while the indifferent family clusters for tea around a white table beneath the beech tree. They "smile in unison." He can only imagine "the spoilt child on the grass" (718). The reader shares Terris's "horror" at the family's indifference to the death of a child entrusted to their custody and care.

Terris rightly feels the odd man out as the Lysarth family smiles "in unison" to cover up what has been done, all "untroubled" (721). What drives him mad is that this scene also coalesces with his own family's apathy, the incident when his mother had told him not to be "troubled" by Miss MacNamara's suffering. This memory is followed by Terris's sense of alienation when judged "mad" by Charlotte, an accusation that then reminds him of his parents' "worry" apparently over the same possibility.

27

with no other means of confirming her self-worth. She cannot voice her sense of inadequacy from being totally dependent on her husband. Her essential self, then, takes the form of the "bad" Mr. Higgs, a regression to a childhood fantasy. This old, imaginary "familiar," who years ago comforted the little girl Elizabeth, reappears as a stranger making obnoxious telephone calls and voicing reservations about the mature woman's married life, now expressing her true but repressed feelings while her false self goes through the motions of being a "happy" wife and mother. It is interesting that her ``true" self takes a masculine form.

Elizabeth's husband of course wonders about this stranger harassing his wife, but he does not even remotely consider that she is maintaining regular conversations with her own self—a phenomenon that marks the concluding stages of madness. After a terrible struggle to solve the mystery of Mr. Higgs's disturbing telephone calls, the distressed husband learns the caller's identity from his mother-in-law. At the end of the story he faces his "goddess's" lunacy only when a psychiatrist appears on the scene and takes charge of his patient—much as is the case with Golyadkin in Dostoyevski's *The Double*. The family, especially the bewildered husband, is terribly distressed—an infant's worst fear being that of abandonment.

The lethargy of the first few paragraphs is striking when Trevor outlines the usual litany of "exchanges" and "conversations" that constitute the family's everyday routine. The entire family, not just the baby daughter "loitering" in the hall, has been in a drowse for some time. In the story's first sentence the narrator outlines his return home as if starting a journal or, as he puts it later, "a report sheet": "On the evening of Tuesday, 24 May 1962, I returned home in the usual way" (208). Then he reviews other "usual" daily activities: "I used to leave the house at half past eight every morning" (208). Looking back, he realizes his family was "neither happy nor unhappy": they visited the zoo and observed the animals "smelling of confinement." They planned birthday parties attended by "children . . . creatures who might have been bored." They went on "dawdling walks" (208). Even their arguments were uneventful, changing nothing and followed by "days when everything went well."

As the narrator then ruminates on how he "used to" imagine Elizabeth's "usual" day as she used to explain it, the same drowsy malaise overshadows the comings and goings of "ill-tempered children" and guests invited for tea or lunch in the garden—a malaise further suggested by the mother's nap—her "dozing" and "being woken up by Bridget" (209). In turn he remembers how "she would ask" about his day. He re-creates for us what he would say. Unlike the wife's many-peopled account, the husband

repeats three times the fact that Miss Madden (a shadowy character mentioned only here) left for Buenos Aires, while he imagines Elizabeth repeating the fact that she fell asleep in the garden. This surreal and imaginative daydream of what "would" usually happen abruptly ends by repeating what the husband had imagined was a regular part of his wife's day—Elizabeth "dozing" and "being woken up by Bridget" (209).

This rambling ménage of memories, dreams, and daydreams confuses sleeping and waking, past and present, sanity and insanity, appropriately introducing us to Elizabeth's immediate problem of "remembering all the details" about her conversations with Mr. Higgs. To confuse fact and fancy is a problem common enough to children but devastating to adults. When the narrator then envisions his wife's "beauty" and "contentment," he wistfully longs for an obviously inadequate past. His review of memories and dreams is detailed hypnotically. The husband's memories reveal a disjuncture between how he envisioned his wife and how she actually was—a disjuncture that results in paralysis.

Daydream, reverie, nightmare, madness, and heightened despair—various levels of consciousness—are here arrayed. The older daughter, so like her mother, asks her father how one can differentiate between sleeping and waking: "I could be dreaming" (211), she seems to query. This incident prefigures Elizabeth's declaration that she "was almost asleep" during a Sunday afternoon picnic in the woods—sleep being something she can now do "sitting upright" (212). In this way Trevor edges his way toward the bewildering revelation of Elizabeth's insanity.

Without the stimulating contacts of a life fully engaged with humanity's inordinate problems worldwide, women confined to the home lack a heightened awareness of others struggling with the same problems. Then talk becomes more and more meaningless. As this story progresses the exchange of talk is replaced by an exchange of money. The narrator considers Elizabeth's brother, Ralph, as possibly the culprit Higgs, although Elizabeth's father had bribed his wayward son to stay out of the country, fearing he would sully the family's reputation. Communication between this father-son pair amounts to an exchange of pain; the father complains that "most of the time you didn't know what he was talking about" (214). When the father dies Elizabeth continues the bribe.

An exchange of money also replaces communication and love in the case of Mrs. Awpit, the woman paid to take care of old Mrs. Maugham, Elizabeth's mother, who feels neglected "with no one to look after [her]" (216). Lines of communication and generational lines are severed between mother-daughter, father-son, brother-sister, father-sister, grandmother-

grandchild, and husband-wife. The terrible disjuncture between worried husband and distressed wife worsens when the wife refuses to discuss Higgs. The husband feels "some awful shaft between us" (215). He had equated his wife's "greater beauty" as she aged with "her contentment" (209). Mr. Higgs, however, articulates her discontent when he says, "You clean his house, you prepare his meals, you take his opinions. . . . You've lost your identity" (210).

When Elizabeth asks, "Do I know you, Mr. Higgs?" her basic problem emerges. She has not been living an active enough life to know herself. Those who can "explain" who they are do not need to cultivate a second self. Explaining Mr. Higgs would put him "out of business" (210). Elizabeth cannot remember who he is because she does not know who *she* is. Incapable of recalling her own childhood memories, she eventually cannot even remember the birth of her own children. This mother wishes to be defined as a separate entity of value apart from biological and socially acceptable functions—mother and hostess planning tea parties.

Nonetheless, Trevor carefully avoids casting blame in this story about the commonplace situation of an unfulfilled wife and an un-self-aware husband. He focuses on the pain of the situation without assigning blame, providing only a few hints alluding to several possible causes of Elizabeth's madness.

Elizabeth's father and brother could be implicated in Elizabeth's insanity. Parental abuse is intimated by her traumatic memory of her father demanding of her at age 10 to "tell us what you're going to do with yourself." When she "announced the trend of [her] ambitions" (210), her brother Ralph laughed, further undermining her self-worth. And society could be implicated in this disaster of a woman gone mad, especially given the social conditioning that promotes women as beautiful objects or "goddesses," as her husband here puts it—women being ornaments to inspire sexual desire in men.

Elizabeth may not feel "successful" because her sense of self-worth has been thwarted by being her "husband's instrument" (211). The alarmed husband claims that he is "not given to forcing [his] opinions on others," yet he remembers that "Elizabeth said [he] wasn't [forcing his opinion on others] either" (211). The wife's agreement with her husband may confirm the idea that he "does the thinking" (210) for them both.

Other possible causes flicker and fade: Elizabeth's insanity may be due to her husband's inability to imagine the stresses of mothering or Elizabeth's own incapacities. Elizabeth's dependence on her husband could be his fault or hers, the fault of her parents or all of the above. When the hus-

band ponders the possibility that Mr. Higgs is "someone like a window-cleaner to whom [Elizabeth] once perhaps talked of [her] childhood" and apologetically adds that he "can't see [her] doing it" (211), her failure to confide in anyone is implicated. Yet it is not clear whether the husband fails to be receptive or the wife fails to communicate.

It is true that Elizabeth's desire to communicate with someone may be inferred by her fantasy that the strange Mr. Higgs is the hired painter who read her diaries. The husband's inability to communicate may be due to a bad temper. He does reveal that he "was aware of considerable pique" during a conversation about Higgs (211)—the structure of this sentence again teasing the reader with possibilities: the "pique" could be Elizabeth's anger at herself or her repressed anger at her husband, who wants her to be a "goddess" well-suited to the god, himself. The "pique" could be the husband's anger at his wife, frustration with himself for failing to solve the mystery of Mr. Higgs, or anger at her tormenter, Mr. Higgs.

To complicate matters more, the willfulness of the children may have contributed to the mother's distress—willfulness only hinted at here and there. At the start the children are "talking loudly," apparently to avoid hearing their mother's orders to "wash themselves properly" (208); later we learn that they must be "told everything twice" (213), and at the end they are envisioned as failures and victims. Elizabeth imagines her son with a fallen woman who "[tortures] him with words." Then she imagines her daughter gone mad, counting "the words in telegrams" (218). What should serve to communicate is mindlessly counted. Each generation determines the fate of the next.

None of these possible causes of Elizabeth's madness are developed enough to establish with any certainty the cause of her mental deterioration. Given the complexities of mental illness, the uncertainty of these possibilities so tenuously posited seems exquisitely appropriate, however painful. When Higgs tells Elizabeth, "Soon it'll be your turn to take on the talking" (211), a painful contradiction obtains because the reader knows Elizabeth *is* exactly taking "on the talking" by imagining another self able to articulate her suffering—what she cannot overtly do without feeling guilty. Her guilt is all too thinly disguised, causing her to feel that Mr. Higgs must be a "wicked," "an evil man," "Mr. Gipe . . . guided from Hell" (211).

Elizabeth's terrifying withdrawal from her husband culminates when he realizes, as he puts it, "she didn't trust me" (215). He lies to his mother-in-law, Mrs. Maugham, by telling her the children miss their grandmother (216), who in turn "snappishly" scolds Mrs. Awpit. The son-in-law,

grandmother, and paid caretaker shout at each other. Absorbed in self-pity, the disinterested Mrs. Maugham claims not to know of Mr. Higgs until, as is often the case in Trevor's stories, her delayed message provides the turning point in the plot. After "a week or two" the cruel truth is revealed when Miss Awpit, the intermediary, relays the old woman's memories of her three-year-old daughter's imaginary "friend," Higgs—just like "Mambi," the imaginary friend invented by the narrator's daughter Anna, whom he "loved best of all . . . because she reminded [him] so much of Elizabeth" (211). The narrator's loss is redoubled by this revelation; his despair as he pleads with his wife, "We need a rest," is poignant given the ominous confusions between sleeping and waking, madness and sanity, Elizabeth and Higgs, self and other, we and you.

Everyone in this story suffers bewildering loss. The brother loses his "soul"; the daughter's imaginary friend, his "hair"; the wife, her mind; the children, their mother; the husband, his wife. There is no one to blame.

"The Day We Got Drunk on Cake": Talk as Coercion

The most comic of the stories in this vein, "The Day We Got Drunk on Cake," starts with the protagonist-narrator, Mike, claiming to suffer a "prevailing condition of emotional delicacy" (108)—a condition worsened because an old friend Swann de Courcey makes a surprise visit and talks him into spending the afternoon running the circuit of local pubs. Mike's response to this coercion is excessive: he claims to feel pain as if he were "under the surgeon's knife" (108). His response to what seems the root cause of his distress—losing Lucy, "the love of [his] life" (119)—is also excessive.

Talk in this story is a meaningless gesture between various communicants who never listen to one another because they are burdened by staid frameworks of the past and narcissistic concerns. Before leaving his office with his friend, Mike makes the first of eight phone calls that evening to Lucy. This would-be Romeo seems to enjoy playing the role of abandoned lover. Mike longs for a desired presence, Lucy, but is forced to converse with undesirable others (Swann and friends), a common pattern in Trevor's work (cf. "The Mark-2 Wife"). The narrator suffers the disinterest of his friends, but he himself becomes a disinterested bystander when he refuses to help the same friends, who also suffer from loneliness.

The comedy of the telephone conversations between the love-sick narrator and Lucy is complicated by conflations of time, conventions governing polite conversations, the expectations of courtship, and the etiquette of

telephone conversations. The absurdity of the first telephone call is evident when the conventions governing social discourse lead Mike to say that he is "very well," thus contradicting his previous claim to suffering. Then Mike drops an inappropriate line apparently taken from the early stages of his past courtship, "We must meet again soon." This is followed by the narrator's irrelevant news that "an old and valued friend has just transpired," this last word in this sentence an oddity since events, not people, transpire. What we have here is perhaps a play on "expire." In any case, Lucy's disjointed response of "That's nice" violates the mood of the suffering Mike. And Swann's idea of an evening out—a double date with advertising artists, Margo and Jo, hardly suits an amorous mood.

Mike obsesses over unrequited love while the foursome migrate from pub to pub to restaurant and finally to a private home near Soho. All sorts of contradictions undermine our hero's sentimental romanticism, however—not least the situation of two carousing men who envision the women of the evening as "pert shorthand typists . . . whose heads may easily be turned by the crisp jingle of money"—a definition better suited to prostitutes than "puritan maids" (109). The confusion of multiple and contradictory meanings throughout the story is conveyed by the playfulness of Trevor's diction.

Trevor's medley of pub conversations, vacuous banter, and telephone calls to Lucy is accompanied by mismatched moods, communication gaps, and the blasé indifference of all participants toward everyone else. The absurd nature of Mike's second telephone call is clear when he asks Lucy a question with an obvious answer ("What are you doing?" / "Talking to you on the telephone" [110]). Mike again asks, "Shall we meet sometime?"—meaning "Will you meet me sometime?"—and Lucy expresses her disinterest by mindlessly responding, "I'm sure we shall" (110)—meaning "This is a possibility I don't plan to pursue" (110).

Despite Lucy's indifference, Mike persists on calling her, periodically returning from the telephone to his friends, whose pub conversations likewise reveal distress. There Mike only half-listens, for example, to the distraught Margo, who questions her husband's sanity (Nigel's "mental") because he brings home elderly women to sit in a circle of silence ("Nobody says anything" [111]).

Out of tune with the other revelers, Margo totally misses Mike's humor in one instance when he sidesteps a continuing conversation about Nigel by feigning ignorance: "For all I know he may have an artificial stomach" (111). Margo takes everything literally and responds with a deadpan denial: "Nigel hasn't an artificial stomach, actually" (111), thus revealing a

literal-minded incapacity to understand linguistic or any other ambivalence.

Misunderstandings owing to literal-mindedness abound: Mike tells Lucy he is "feeling funny" (111), meaning metaphorically "sick" (118). Frank, Lucy's visitor/lover, sees Mike literally as "funny," which Mike denies ("I'm not being amusing"). And then Margo points out that her husband has "become funny" (111), meaning insane.

Most of the time Mike says nothing—"bored" (113) because Swann forces him to tell "the history of his life" (110), bored because Margo forces him to listen to her talk about her "talkative" husband, who "would tell you anything." Finally, while talking to Jo, Mike turns his back on Margo just when she starts to join the conversation.

Mike's ridiculous conversation with Margo culminates in a lie. Margo asks the narrator to serve as intermediary by calling her husband about the identity and purpose of bringing home elderly women. Mike leaves his cohorts again and pretends to call Nigel as promised, but instead he calls Lucy. When Mike returns, he explains that Margo's husband "was out" (116)—not much help for Margo here and not much help for Mike. Margo tells Mike he would "make a good husband." Mike wants only "to hear [Lucy's] voice" (110).

The potential for the human voice to offer comfort is circumscribed by self-delusions, pretense, miscommunications, jokes, and lies. Gaps in logic and incomplete sentences stand for a vacuum of weightless people unable to connect with each other: Swann says to the narrator, "I've got a couple [of women?] in a hostelry" (109); the narrator could care less. He does not even care that at last "Margo stopped [talking?] about Nigel" (110) in order to "leer" at Mike. Distressed over discovering a man in Lucy's apartment, Mike asks, "Who is he [to you?]"? and "What does he do [to you?]"? And during Mike's next to last call to Lucy, his ex-lover refuses to join him at a party because she says she is "doing things" (117), meaning "I'm busy" but interpreted by Mike to have sexual implications.

Indeed, conversations in this story do not mean much. Margo responds to Jo's success story (she published a children's book) with the wisdom, "Words . . . mean a lot to Jo. She has real sense" (109). Swann contradicts Margo's praise of Jo with a cliché: "She's bonkers" (109).

Throughout this story everyone is "pretending to listen" (117), but self-absorption distorts the message. Mike is disinterested in Margo's problems, and she apparently has been unresponsive when forced to listen to her husband, whom she considers a "God-awful bore." Jo is unresponsive when Mike wants to talk about the fact that Lucy "says unexpected things"

(111). And, contrary to Mike's desires, Jo wants to talk about Margo, exactly what Mike hopes to escape by turning to talk with Jo. Meanwhile, Margo and Swann sit in silence, not "even listening" to Mike and Jo. When Margo first singles Mike out as a partner who might share her intimate concerns over her husband and declares, "Nobody's to listen" (110), the reader senses the *potential* for a meaningful exchange of affection. Indeed, a sort of collective intimacy does develop when the pub-hopping group acknowledges Margo's problem with her husband by asking Mike to call Nigel, again asking Mike to serve as an intermediary who might explain Nigel's suspicious behavior. After each request for help, Mike demures but calls Lucy instead.

Most likely out of guilt, Mike then explains Margo's problem to Lucy, but "lucidity" gives way to drunken babble. Dejectedly, Mike returns to the group, but remarkably no one asks him what Nigel said, although Margo eventually does ask this question in a taxi on the way to a party. The delayed responses, the indifference to others, the lies, the use of intermediaries, the interruptions of the story line by Mike's telephone calls to Lucy, and the mismatched moods are carnivalesque, the comic dimensions intensified because none of the characters comprehend the humor intended by others. Mike sees no humor in Lucy's lover's joke (he claims to be a freight agent). Mike soberly suffers this "sample of Frank's humor" (117). Margo's deadpan stance in response to Mike's joke about her husband having an artificial stomach and Mike's inability to see humor anywhere prefigure the deadpan young woman philosophizing to Mike about love when the unhappy wanderers reach the last stop, a party at a private home.

This earnest philosopher on love mirrors Mike's sentimentality over his love of Lucy, but Mike does not respond to her exegesis on love's "extraordinary infection" (116). Love figures as disease in more than one Trevor story (cf. "The Ballroom of Romance"), and the lovesick romantic cannot be comforted. Mike's sentimentality over Lucy ironically prevents him from responding to someone else's sentimentality. Trevor here introduces an eavesdropping partygoer whose hilarious laughter exactly demonstrates the appropriate response to absurd philosophers of love and dejected romantics like Mike.

The inadequacy of Mike's responses to life is clear when he finally understands that he has lost Lucy. His last call at 2 A.M. finds Frank still at her apartment. Mike comforts himself by envisioning a future when he will remember this day as "rather funny" (119). The lovesick romantics sulking

in the shadows of Lovers' Lane in Trevor's stories do not "want to be cured" (119). The disease is self-love.

"Attracta": Talk as Communion

"Attracta" and "The Blue Dress" warrant special attention because both stories present the unusual case of compassionate bystanders who identify with victims so intensely that they reveal their own vulnerability. Attracta is a schoolteacher shocked into a better understanding of her past when she reads a newspaper account of IRA members in Belfast who had killed a British officer and then mailed his decapitated head to the victim's wife, Penelope Vade. The grieving wife's response was to affirm the rightness of her husband's politics by joining the Women's Peace Movement in Belfast, thus exposing herself to danger. The six murderers learned of her presence, found her apartment, and raped her. They apparently felt no remorse for the murder of Penelope's husband, not to mention for the rape and eventual suicide of Penelope.

Although not even a firsthand observer to this tragedy suffered by a stranger, Attracta is still nearly overwhelmed. She imagines Penelope's pain, which she relates to her own loss of her parents, also victims of nationalist fervor, and feels relatively fortunate. She decides "she had not suffered," even though she was only three when Irish terrorists accidentally killed her parents by planting a bomb meant for the Black and Tans, British counter-terrorist soldiers. Attracta did not learn until she was 11 that the Anglo-Irish Protestant, Mr. Devereux, and his Catholic servant, Geraldine Carey, had killed her parents—a puzzling revelation because these Irish nationalists befriended the child in order to seek redemption for their terrible mistake.

Attracta grieves so much over this outrageous incident that she suffers the loss of her position as a schoolteacher in the community. Her overactive imagination causes her to internalize the gruesome horror of rape and suicide, reenacting again and again in "the scenes from the tragedy" (593), the terrors of staring into a box at the "dead eyes" of your husband, grotesque horrors of mouse "droppings on [a] body." Trevor's interests here transcend the political situation, most importantly pointing to Attracta's imaginative response to life and her capacity to empathize, especially in response to suffering. Attracta questions all of human life. She wanders the strand, withdrawing from society for the moment. She fails to respond when two fishermen speak to her; nonetheless, she realizes that

withdrawal and isolation are "not very agreeable" responses to suffering (594).

Instead of withdrawing, Attracta finally assumes responsibility for what happened to Penelope by changing her own life dramatically, worrying that she "has been saying the wrong things to the children in her care," feeling "she should have told them about herself" (592). After a great deal of soul-searching she reveals herself beyond what seems proper to her students, her community, and the school. She reenacts her personal response to Penelope Vade's tragedy and ruminates out loud about the tragic loss of her own parents. Fully envisioning Penelope's suicide in greater and greater detail, the schoolteacher loses her sense of self, assuming the first-person perspective while explaining to her class, "I drag my body across the floors of two rooms. . . . I eat the aspirins until the bottle's empty" (604). She finally proclaims in her own voice, "I only hope . . . [Penelope] knows that strangers mourn her."

Attracta meant "to tell [her students] . . . never to despair" and "to prepare them for a future that looked grim" (604), but her compulsion to talk reveals too much. She not only agonizes over the murder of a particular husband, the rape and suicide of a particular despairing wife, and her own grief over her own parents' deaths but also links these tragedies and all the tragedy of Ireland's past and human history. Her students, like the members of her community who ask her to retire early, cannnot fathom the urgency of her point that, as human beings, we must develop the capacity to mourn for strangers and that no human being is truly a stranger to human suffering of any kind.

Meaningful, reciprocal lines of communication never develop, however, between the schoolteacher and her students. After her startling revelations, the children ask to recess, and when they return the teacher continues the day's routine as if nothing had happened because she realizes she has bored her students. The social order does not encourage self-revelation, intimate talk, or "excessive" sympathy for the suffering of others.

This story expresses Trevor's compassionate engagement with human suffering and serves as a reminder that language can be used to establish arbitrary boundaries *between* rather than engagement *with* others. Language designates insiders and outsiders, Protestants/Catholics, British/Irish—boundaries in a constant state of flux, depending on power lines in a violent world. Geographical boundaries promote only an ephemeral illusion of social order. We all frequent the globe. Attracta's classroom globe is not "out of date" because it does not designate boundaries. Rather, the lack of boundaries infers a reality we would prefer to

ignore—the reality that none of us can truly isolate him- or herself from world suffering.

"The Blue Dress": Talk and Intersubjectivity

Memories of public and private, past and present traumas again "coalesce" as Trevor presents in "The Blue Dress" an investigative reporter, Terris, gone mad, apparently because he responds to traumatic world events too intensely, not to mention his heightened responses to recent personal tragedies revealed by childhood memories and more urgent daydreams about his divorce, the death of a beloved mother-in-law, a failed affair. So confused by conflations and condensations of his own history and world history, this mad journalist declares he has "never in all [his] time here looked out of" the actual window of his asylum room (712). He finds it "easier to remember, to conjure up this scene or that," rather than face an external world of unbridled evil, rather than comply with the psychiatrist urging him to tell the story of his mental breakdown, "to write it down" (714).

Terris demonstrates a capacity for sympathetic identification completely foreign to the apathetic bystanders he sees everywhere on the job. Disturbed by his recent and distant past, he recalls childhood memories of worrying about other people's sorrow and even then tries to root out the truth, such as the betrayal of Miss MacNamara, the music teacher apparently seduced by a married man and then abandoned by him when he returned to his wife. Terris apparently has always been curious about misdeeds everyone else ignores. His life as an investigative reporter forces him to confront "horror . . . nonsensical" (721) daily, but he was predisposed from childhood on to seek the grim truths of existence, to master the "crossword puzzle" of life. He probes the nightmares of world events but cannot face the terrible indifference of his betrothed, Dorothea Lysarth, and her family to the murder of a child. Terris's beautiful young lover indifferently relates her childhood memories of willfully tugging on the blue dress of her friend Agnes Kemp, thus causing the unsuspecting girl to tumble to her death from the top of a forbidden tree. Having just endured a terrible divorce does not help him resolve his conflict when he finds and then loses his dream girl.

On the one hand, Terris seems limited because he is so idealistic that he operates within simplistic frameworks defining good and evil. Dorothea must be seen either as an angelic "creature" dressed in white, Terris's first impression, or a murderer/trickster, a conflation of the usual type he

23

encounters on the job and with his ex-wife, Charlotte. On the other hand, the gloomy imaginative construct of his bride as murderer "clawing at the blue dress" (721) of Agnes Kemp, seems believable given the appalling indifference of the family to the event. This suspicion regarding his ideal helpmate drives him to madness, because now he must face the fact that he himself is not the soothsayer, the brilliant investigative reporter. He was completely wrong in idealizing his bride-to-be.

Terris's problem seems to be that he sees as equally egregious everything that happens in the world and everything that happens to him personally. He conflates the "pornographer [who] pretends he's selling Christmas cards," the "Russians [who] promise tanks," his earliest memories of his drunken grandfather's corruption, his more recent experiences uncovering the corruption of community dignitaries he interviews everywhere, and the indifferent Major Trubstall, who lies in order to defend his men against a charge of rape. His memories of Brussels and a corrupt "English politician [who] breakfasts with his mistress" merge with his memories of his own casual affair in Rotterdam with "a nameless woman" (712), who asks in Dutch, "Feest wezen vieren . . . Gedronken [Was this sexual tryst due to drunkenness]?" Should the reader relate this affair to Terris's pious outrage over Charlotte's affairs, his grandfather's drunkenness, and his own tendency to drink away the world's misery?

Trevor seems to insist that we as readers should contemplate the significance of Terris's habit of mind. As in so very many Trevor stories, the clue to the story's plot is given at the start but not recognized until the story completely unfolds and the reader returns to modify his or her initial impression of the situation. In this case the reader puzzles over whether or not to trust Terris's judgments.

Terris is indeed a truth seeker who sees falsity in current world leaders, past friends, recent acquaintances, and his own family. But he is also very human and therefore accepts no responsibility for his divorce, which he blames on Charlotte's being "unfaithful with anyone she had a fancy for" (713). When he meets his lover-to-be, Dorothea (also his last, best hope for redemptive love), she declares his divorce a "very rudimentary mistake" (713), an all-too-poignant remark.

Terris thinks Charlotte's weaknesses are best described by his mother-in-law, who calls her daughter "a handful" (713) and "a tricky kind of customer" (719). And yet we are not given enough information to judge his ex-wife, and the judgment of his mother-in-law, this "old, grey woman" (713), seems somewhat suspect, given the insensitivity suggested here as a mother speaks disparagingly of her own daughter. Finally, we cannot

really judge Terris's past relationships or decide whether or not Charlotte is completely to blame for the divorce.

Trevor develops as complicated a case as possible, demonstrating both the worst and best sides of his protagonists. Terris's failures have to do with his all-too-human tendency to repress past failures; he says he does not "want to think about" Charlotte's infidelities (713). He represses memories of "a failed marriage" and an "unhappy childhood" by "imagining" himself with Dorothea "in a clean, empty house that appeared to be [their] home." Past trauma then, "like smoke evaporating," is easily overcome by a hyperactive imagination, by living in a dream.

As in a dream, Dorothea declares her love at their second meeting; he proposes marriage within a matter of days. Terris's need to assuage the pain and guilt of divorce may be responsible for his idealistic view of Dorothea, who is indeed a "beautiful creature" (713), a "creation" of his own fantasy. Yet on the job he writes disdainfully about the fantasy of others, such as Major Trubstall's sham: "Fantasy rules." He feels self-satisfied because he is certain, "knowing it was the truth" (714). We can perhaps be less certain in terms of Terris's fantasies.

Because this first-person story is limited to Terris's perspective as he recalls his past and because modern fiction so often undermines characters who withdraw into a world of fantasy, most readers would question Terris's credibility sometime during the tale's unraveling. Both Terris's defensive stance regarding his divorce and his experiences as an investigative reporter render him vulnerable to seeing life as infinitely better or infinitely worse than it is. The crux, however, is whether or not we should accept Terris's condemnation of Dorothea as a murderer. He trusts what he sees "vividly in [his] mind's eye" and is convinced he knows the "truth" (713) about Charlotte. But does he know the truth about Dorothea's nightmarish deed? Is it possible that, like this woman who reads Jane Austen and "[speaks] as though these fictional characters were real" (714), Terris may not be able to distinguish reality from fantasy?

Many readers may also question whether or not Terris's perceptions are reliable, because throughout the story he is shown imbibing some alcoholic beverage. His first suggestion to Dorothea is "*Let's* have a drink" (713; my italics). During the train ride from Bath to London he sits "in the bar drinking one after another of those miniature bottles of whisky that trains go in for" (714). When he meets Dorothea's family, his dream girl pretends to be serving Terris sherry but instead serves him whiskey, because, as the narrator puts it, "she knew I probably needed it" (716). Later, while talking with Dorothea's father, Terris apparently drains his glass of port, and the

elderly gentleman *twice* gestures for him to have more by pushing "the decanter towards [him]" (717). At the end of the story, Terris affirms, "I am right" (722), while asylum attendants prepare him for shock treatments further obliterating his memories of "Charlotte [passing him] a drink" (722).

Even though Trevor raises these doubts about his protagonist, some of Trevor's most important truthsayers are seen by others as "drunks"—"The Mark-2 Wife," for instance, and Mrs. Fitch, who rightly pigeonholes Raymond Bamber. "The Blue Dress" actually offers considerable evidence that, in the case of the Lysarths, Terris's judgments are sound. Indeed, the Lysarths are one of Trevor's most dramatic cases of indifferent and dishonest bystanders. Right from the start Terris guesses that Dorothea is a liar: she lies to her family in order not to admit that "she'd been picked up by a middle-aged journalist" (713). Her character becomes more and more suspect as the story develops, starting with her confession that her family regards her as "compulsively naughty" (713). When Terris rides the train home after initially meeting her, she takes on an ominous aspect when he notes that "her face jumped about in my imagination, unnerving me. Again and again her white, even teeth smiled at me" (714).

Terris then must subliminally suspect Dorothea's guilt when he meets her family and learns more about the "mishap" of her childhood; the investigative reporter in him relegates her to the category of murderer. If he never forgave his parents for hiding the fact that his grandfather was a drunk and a crook, how can he forgive Dorothea for what he perceives as murder?

The Lysarths, including Dorothea, all too easily commit Agnes's death to the past, better forgotten. The family's apathy, their aristocratic superficiality, mechanical politeness, and appalling indifference to the destruction of a child is clear. The memories of the terrible deed, so easily forgotten by the Lysarths, are resurrected by Terris until they haunt him to the point of madness. Trevor draws attention to Terris's sense of himself as singularly superior to all others, all the liars of a corrupt world. And this hypersensitive, emotional, and imaginative truthseeker does indeed seem superior to the Lysarths, this "tightly bound family" (716) of blue-eyed look-alikes who live the "lie" of Dorothea's virtue. That Dorothea's brothers are twins reinforces the effect. They strangely stand "protectively, by their sister" (716). The twins "had their mother's oval face, the pale blue eyes their parents shared, their father's languid tallness" (716). The good doctor/archaeologist/father at first greets Terris "vaguely" (715) with a smile—all of a kind.

The inevitability of Terris's fate seems the point. His paralysis results from his disappointment at not finding the perfect woman, his intense imaginative response to public and personal tragedy, and his despair over his own vulnerability, his self-doubt. When Terris claims at the end of the story that he is "right" (722), he is referring to Dorothea's guilt, not his own failures in life. The story gains in poignancy when the reader realizes—after questioning Terris's judgments off and on throughout the story—that this painful judgment regarding his dream girl is precisely "right."

The Sins of the Fathers
and the Destruction
of the Alienated Child

Trevor's Stories and the Oedipus Complex

Alienation from the community due to a painful adolescence is a factor in a great many of Trevor's stories. Parent-child relationships in these stories are precariously maintained as if survival itself were at stake—which indeed sometimes is the case. Aggressive fathers and narcissistic husbands overpopulate Trevor's best stories about conflicts between the generations and about parents who discourage the independent development of their sons and daughters—not, of course, that mothers and wives are innocent. In the stories discussed here, mothers and wives in fact may be accomplices in an incompatible parent's effort to force a child to obey.

Oppressive fathers in Trevor's stories may be cruel because they struggle to survive economic hardships. Most of them nonetheless develop a sense of self-worth, but it is self-worth using materialistic yardsticks. Trevor attends to both lower and upper ends of the social scale when representing antagonists who dominate their children. The father/antagonist all too often uses the child to extend his or her will in time through the acquisition of things, which are then transmitted to the next generation, usually to the one child most resembling the progenitor. The child's self-worth is validated by following in the parent's footsteps and by earning money. The father worries over economic demands affecting the self and the self's double (the child), neglecting less favored children. Some fathers demand that *all* of their children conform to their wishes, thus reaffirming again and again their own self-worth.

Fear drives fathers who ambivalently seek and feel threatened by their own offspring—fear of economic failure, fear that others will discover past sins, fear that in old age they will be abandoned by their children, and, at the most basic level, fear of the naturally occurring progression of the generations, the natural replacement of the father by the son, the mother by the daughter. Trevor is attuned to the problems that develop when men are discouraged from developing tenderness and when men dominate women economically.[5] To understand these issues, we must consider father-child conflicts and Oedipal neuroses with an emphasis that differs from recent feminist philosophy, which focuses too much on Freud's inadequate view of female sexuality.

Freud's primary point in formulating Oedipal theories has to do with narcissism, the drive to control others, and the tendency toward exclusive love, seeking only others who reinforce the ego. In Trevor's stories about parenting, courtship, and marriage, narcissistic Irish and English men combat their ambivalent desires for and hatred of the mother by retreating into their own Oedipally inspired "family" of other men/selves.[6] Freudian revisionists tend to stress the difficulties of relinquishing the mother, especially for daughters who more easily identify with the same-sex parent. When considering Trevor's work, however, it is important to focus on the dominant father/husband antagonists, whose empowerment by masculine gender codes encourages them to feel superior to women and to isolate themselves from the weaker members of the community (women and girls) by perpetual drinking, storytelling, and gossiping at the local pub—as in "The Raising of Elvira Tremlett," "A Choice of Butchers," and "Teresa's Wedding."[7]

A sort of exception to the rule that women are excluded from the masculine domain is the story "Downstairs at Fitzgerald's," a tale about a father who *does* take his daughter to a man's-world pub but still communicates his bias about the superiority of a masculine pub "downstairs" when comparing the domain of men to that of women—the latter more suitably dining in the "upstairs," more feminine restaurant, where "both men and women sat at tables covered with pink tablecloths" (663). Later he takes his daughter to the races and advises her not to bet on the horse Amazon Girl because there is "never a hope" she might win (675).

Men withdraw from their wives, sisters, and mothers because the mother represents comfort only if perceived as self. The mother threatens her children and her husband when she exacts obedience or asks that her independent needs be recognized—that is, she is threatening when perceived by sons and husbands as a "foreign" other, a fleshly woman also needing comfort. The woman as autonomous other in fact challenges the masculine need for mastery over the self's sexual drives, not to mention mastery over existence/death and the physical body generally.

Imitation of the father's behavior ordinarily allows the son to feel he can master the threatening feminine principle. Trevor's fathers, however, rarely appear to their sons as "rescuers"—that is, they rarely appear, as Jessica Benjamin describes the usual case, as fathers who "intervene to spring the child from the dyadic trap, the oneness with the mother."[8] Instead, Trevor depicts formidable fathers who wield their power over both their sensitive sons (who are most compatible with their mothers) and their daughters.

Of course the bond with the mother is a danger for gentle sons according to the traditional Freudian view. Thus sons must bond with the rescuer/father, a terrible problem for Trevor's sensitive, adolescent male characters who suffer from cruel, overbearing, and lusty father/rivals, such as Father Devlin in "The Raising of Elvira Tremlett," the butcher/father/master in "A Choice of Butchers," and even the community father, Lynch, in "An Evening with John Joe Dempsey." Lynch is overbearing in his role of community soothsayer destined to preserve the "purity" of community sons vulnerable to the charms of the temptress. This purportedly celibate "father" is a curious anomaly given the shameless behavior of most husbands and fathers in John Joe Dempsey's community.

Despite the pressure from religious codes to respect the sanctity of marriage, insensitive sons may conform to the more (phallocentrically) acceptable promiscuous behavior of the father rather than heed the mother's admonitions promoting monogamy. Various lovers substitute for the mother before marriage. After marriage the wife satisfies the man's physical needs as well as his egoistic needs because his apparent monogamy and his virtuous wife confirm his own purity in a God-fearing community, even though husbands covertly develop sexual relationships with other women.

Sometimes daughters substitute for the wife/mother of the father. Daughters suffer from interdependent Oedipal attachments when the father encourages the incestuous feelings of the daughter, a situation further complicated because daughters are conditioned to acquire mothering behaviors. The would-be bride in "The Ballroom of Romance" precisely serves as mother to her own father. In more subtle cases the daughter conforms passively to the father's demands, sacrificing any thought of her own well-being, which seems to be the case in "Kathleen's Field."

The destruction of a child because of ignorant insensitivity, parental egoism/aggression, infidelity, or neglect is an issue in Trevor's stories and figures prominently in Irish myth—for example, Cuchulain's accidental murder of his own son. In the literature, myth, and folklore of various cultures the parent uses the child to affirm a safe, secular identity and generates so much narcissistic energy that the child withdraws, sometimes to the point of madness.

"The Raising of Elvira Tremlett": Wearing the Father's Stamp

This first-person narrative portrays an adolescent boy rejected by his parents because he was conceived in an adulterous union between his mother and a paternal uncle who continues to share the family residence. Sensitive and imaginative, this boy is confused because he sees in the eyes of his father, uncle, and mother "shame," which he interprets as indifference or even antagonism toward himself. These parent figures project their own guilt onto the youngest son and externalize their pain in order to be rid of it. The boy knows that he makes the adults in his family "uneasy" (625), but at first he doesn't truly understand why. Worsening the boy's sense of alienation, the family focuses exclusively on the family business, the Devlin Bros. garage. The boy feels he cannot "fit easily into the [family] business" (625) like his siblings, who conform to their parents' demand that they wear the family stamp designating them all as workers in a domain ruled by the father.

The issue here is precisely child "raising." The ambiguity produced by alluding to the raising of spirits in this context seems appropriate given the deadly force these parents wield when indoctrinating their children into the family business and encouraging conformity to materialistic community standards. The disheartened, less-favored child is likely to be more individualistic, thus more threatening to the parents. Father and Mother Devlin in fact fail to provide the love necessary to preserve the sanity of their sensitive, youngest son, who is thus rejected also by his friends, teachers at his school, and various church representatives. Apparently the gossip about the bewildered youngest son's illicit conception has alienated him from everyone except an imagined friend, Elvira.

The story opens with the boy's thoughts regarding his mother's preference for English goods and his father's preference for cars built by British factories. A certain pretentiousness of this Irish family is here suggested. Although country people "of the province of Munster" (624), the mother and father promote what is British, what seems therefore progressive. The industrial world associated with England intrudes on rural Ireland. The mother works "a machine that stuck labels on to tins" in a meat factory; the father and uncle convert a bicycle shop into a garage.

The commercial enterprise of the family business is treated with some enthusiasm by every member of the family except for the youngest son. The mother had approved the new sign, "Devlin Bros.," at the time of the conversion from shop to garage; she admired the "gleam" of the sign and was glad then that the business was being updated to accommodate the automobile. The nameless child narrating the story, however, can only remember that the sign "drooped," the letters were peeling off, and "a rivet had fallen out" (622). The boy's view is fragmented, his life insecure, because his family ignores him.

The father in particular defines his children's futures in relation to the family business or their ability to be economically secure. The two eldest brothers are "destined for the garage" just as the father and Uncle Jack had "automatically" inherited the family bicycle repair shop. Effie is destined to do the father's bookkeeping because he considers her homely—certainly not pretty enough to get a husband. He encourages sibling rivalry by favoring his daughter Kitty over Effie and the two elder sons over the youngest. Kitty receives the most "fondling" and praise: the father declares that she will "do well," by which he means she will "marry money" (624).

All of the children get some of the father's attention and some praise except for the nameless, youngest son, whom the father taunts by calling out for "His Nibs" and asking, "Haven't you a word in you, boy?" (627). The fact is that the father hasn't a word for his youngest son, who is also ignored by the mother, the uncle, and the other siblings. When the father explains to a customer the future destiny he plans for each child (except his youngest), the customer asks about "your man here," meaning the boy the father sees as a misfit. The father then vaguely announces that "the Lord would look after [him]" (625).

All of the children in this family are comfortable with the family business, the garage, except the youngest son, who "fitted nowhere" (625) and who recognizes that the source of his woes is the Devlin Bros. garage, a "pit" (624), "a kind of Hell" (626). He thinks of his uncle "at work, sparks flying from the welding apparatus." He associates both the uncle and the father with "the smell of the garage . . . an oily smell that mingled with the fumes of [his] uncle's pipe and [his] father's cigarettes." These two parent figures are "marked with grime" (624).

From the nameless boy's perspective, the garage is an alien, masculine domain, with "its awful earth floor made black with sump oil, its huge indelicate vices, the chill of cast iron, the grunting of [his] father and uncle." This terrible place seems an outward expression of the secret "indelicate vices," which the reader later identifies as the uncle's promiscuity and the incestual act resulting in the boy's birth. This defiant act of adultery apparently represents the mother's revenge against the father for his neglect of her—his spending more time at the pub than at home. But the conflict seems to have been resolved, and the business of running a garage and a home continues as usual.

The garage signifies to the youngest son the demand to follow in his father's footsteps—a demand the boy cannot meet not only because he represents his mother's and uncle's "shame" (626) but also because of his delicate, feminine nature. This boy simply isn't *interested* in the only models of masculine endeavor he is given; he feels revulsion for the uncle's and father's "fingernails rimmed with black, like fingers in mourning" (624). He cannot talk to his elder brothers. Suspecting that his two elder sons skip school, the patriarch does treat them somewhat harshly, but this treatment acknowledges their toughness, their manliness. The sons imitate what the father/uncle pair used to do when they skipped school to smoke Woodbines and conform to their father's expectations. They will inherit the family business.

The rejected son becomes more and more aware of his predicament as the story develops. He apparently withdraws, talking to no one, not even at the dinner table. The misfit instinctively knows that his "silence . . . must have begun" (626) with the family garage. The youngest son's silence (owing in part to his lack of enthusiasm for the family business) eventually alienates him completely from his family and his community. The father boisterously teases his children, which confirms his dominance and contributes to the boy's reticence. The brothers who behave "obstreperously" and the "cross" mother who rules the house all seem to understand one another, all communicate aggressively. All those around the silent boy "chatter" at some time in the story—the father and uncle report "difficulties . . . in getting spare parts"; the mother, town gossip; the sisters, "news from the convent"; the brothers, "the money [Jack] lost on greyhounds and horses" (626).

By participating fully in family discussions, each member of the family affirms that they belong. The nameless boy sees them all "the same" as his parents and uncle, perhaps sensing only a slight difference in the uncle's behavior when he "looks at the ground" and does penance for fathering the outcast son by "performing chores" at the church (624). A striking contrast to the other members of his family, the neglected son suffers from feeling absolutely different—a difference most evident when he is silent.

This alienated boy's behavior does not change very much when he goes to a Christian Brothers' school; he is still "silent in a classroom" (626). Conditioning to conform to societal demands begins with the parents and continues in school, usually run by the Roman Catholic Church in Ireland. The boy's teacher, Brother Flynn, undermines his discouraged fledgling when he reports, "Slow as a dying snail, that boy is" (624).

The school fails to help the boy and so does the Church. No one explains to him that the "shame" he feels is inappropriate. Acutely aware of the fact that his family and his community feel uneasy in his presence, he wanders into the town's Protestant church seeking solace, but the sexton, "an old, hunched man in black clothes" (627), further alienates the boy by threatening him, warning him that "it isn't your Church" (627). Modern religion has here fallen to a destructive exclusiveness. The sexton fails to be a kind and accepting masculine role model.

Because the sexton threatens him, the boy does not return to "wander among the pews" of the Protestant church, wherein he had discovered the memorial tablet for his imaginary friend, Elvira Tremlett, months before he was finally noticed. British and Protestant, she had died at the young age of 18. He imagines her as "quiet" like himself and totally unlike the aggressive father and the aggressive mother who both "shout angrily" (626). He compensates for the shame and isolation he feels by "resurrecting" Elvira in his mind. She becomes a "friend," who is delicate and feminine, totally compatible with himself. He gives "her her long hair and her smile and her elaborate earrings, and . . . her clothes, wondering whether [he] had got them right" (629). He has ironically been affected by his mother's attitude that British goods are superior to Irish and thus hopes to find a British friend better than the members of his own Irish family. He allows himself to be haunted by this British familiar, who only later becomes an antagonist.

As the boy conjures up Elvira, aspects of himself that have been silenced by his family are clarified, especially his delicate, feminine nature, emotional depth, brilliant imagination, and sensitivity to others. Furthermore, his relationship to Elvira suggests a stifled sexuality because he serves as the scapegoat for his mother's and uncle's sexual transgressions. His repressed sexuality finds expression only in fantasized seductions:

> In the stony field the sunshine made her earrings glitter. It danced over a brooch she had not had when first I imagined her, a brooch with a scarlet jewel, in the shape of a dragon. Mist caught in her hair, wind ruffled the skirts of her old-fashioned dress. . . .

In the bedroom which I shared with Brian and Liam I came, in time, to take her dragon's brooch from her throat and to take her earrings from her pale ears and to lift her dress from her body. (630)

Revealing a terrible loneliness, the boy channels his sexual energy into dreams of Elvira, who gives him "voice," inspiring him to articulate what he can't say to his family, encouraging self-awareness, and finally allowing him to understand the truth that, as he puts it, "I was curious and my family weren't." He doesn't really understand why his uncle made love with his mother or why his father gets drunk at Keogh's, but Elvira helps him to "guess" that Uncle Jack, his father, "went after women as well as greyhounds in Cork" (630). It is Elvira who reassures him that "the three of them have made you what you are" (630). The guilt is theirs. He himself should feel no shame.

And yet the guilt-ridden boy cannot really fathom himself or his family predicament. If he could truly believe in his own innocence, he might overcome his bafflement over his family's past. In fact, his concern for getting Elvira's past "perfectly correct" (629) relates to his uncertainty about correctly understanding his own past—a bafflement more bearable by imagining a friend willing to share that uncertainty and helping him to gain a sense of control.

Unfortunately, the comforting voice of Elvira actually confirms a loss of control. He speaks out loud to Elvira at the dinner table and astonishes those who had accepted his silence "for years and years" (632). Having failed to recognize his silence as a symptom, the family acknowledges his madness only when he finally speaks and threatens their economic security: "Who would marry Kitty now?" they ask. They worry that gossip about the boy's insanity will hurt business. At a less conscious level, they worry because his madness "speaks" for their neglect.

As the family grows more alarmed, Elvira takes on more and more threatening forms that cause the boy nightmares. One form is Susan Peters in the novel *Random Harvest*—Peters being a character representing a product of someone else's imagination and not "a figment" of his own. The title infers something about the circumstances of his conception. He dreams of an "old woman," a sort of mother-monster punishing the impure son, "one eye half-closed in blindness, the fingers . . . misshapen . . . a gleam of fury in her face" (633). He cannot accept his own emerging sexuality as a positive, natural threshold to adulthood because he is confused by his three "parents." Their rejection seems to him punishment for his own sexual "transgressions."

Elvira then changes from friend to foe, thus satisfying the boy's masochistic needs for self-punishment. The creation of an alien voice within the self marks the concluding stages of madness.[9] Only the schizophrenic hears a voice within the self, a voice at first comforting but finally representing alien personality traits "embedded in the body as pieces of shrapnel," to quote R. D. Laing in another context.[10] The boy is institutionalized, and he imagines another consoling figure like the early Elvira—a weekly visitor who reports his story as gossip to entertain visitors to his town, who "listen in pleasurable astonishment to the story of nightmares" (634). The appalling indifference of the family and the community toward the boy's plight is clear when the story of the actual local boy who went mad becomes gossip probably elaborated on as if fiction. In Trevor's stories gossip is often the story-within-a-story transmitted without compassion. Trevor's stories, however, precisely demand that readers compassionately involve themselves in these lives so tellingly rendered in order to more benevolently trace the movement of their own lives.

"A Choice of Butchers": A Sort of Butchery

In this story another son rejects his father as a model of masculinity, refuses the father's occupation, and feels rejected himself. This is one of the most insightful of Trevor's stories about a child's quest for a secure identity and a son's relationship to an incompatible father. Trevor here again indicts the society that fails to encourage sensitive masculine models.

The seven-year-old boy in this story is totally at odds with his father, who is a butcher, and finds a better "choice" in his father's new assistant, Dukelow, a masculine model of tenderness very different from the aggressive father. Introduced at the start, Dukelow comforts the boy, who is weeping in bed because he has seen his 59-year-old father kiss and "roughly [hug]" the 25-year-old maid, Bridget. The boy had been waiting on the stairs for his usual goodnight kiss—administered regularly by Dukelow, not the father or the mother—when he was shocked by his father's behavior in the stairwell below. This is a bad scene, but it worsens at the end of the story when the reader learns that just as the boy had accepted Dukelow as a better father because he was more sensitive like himself, the mother had accepted Dukelow as a better husband because he was more sensitive like herself. In other words, the boy's mother has been carrying on an affair with Dukelow. Like a mystery, this story builds to a revelation that the central event is not the father's seduction of Bridget as the son assumes but rather Dukelow and the mother's affair, about which the son never does learn, engrossed as he is in struggling to dissociate himself from an incompatible father.

This is one of the many Trevor stories culminating in a revelation requiring that the story be reread to grasp the complexities of the situation. When we discover that the boy's comforter is also his mother's lover, the whole story suddenly falls into place and our perception of the situation dramatically changes. All the "clues" the boy takes to signify his father's transgressions must be reconsidered in relation to the mother's "transgressions." On our first reading we share the boy's perceptions—indeed, we wonder with him "why this series of events was taking place" (298). We then in fact share intimately the boy's feelings of confusion and limited sophistication. Trevor poignantly conveys the boy's innocent suffering from his father's misdeeds.

When the father discovers his wife's betrayal at the end of the story, the son is totally bewildered because his beloved Dukelow must leave. Although the mother has also been unfaithful, the son's distress over his father's betrayal of his mother seems justified. As we become better acquainted with the father's insensitivity, which is what we notice most of all on first reading, the boy seems right in preferring Dukelow as a father figure. And yet the vulnerable son is entirely wrong in his conclusions about what has caused tension in his family.

Throughout the story the boy focuses on his father's lust for the maid and cannot imagine his mother, with whom he identifies, as a sexual being. Moreover, the young son interprets his father's pursuit of the maid as boding his father's rejection of both his mother and himself. His feeling of rejection is worsened by the fact that he rejects his father's trade. He cannot conform to his father's wish that his youngest son become a butcher devoted to "cutting up dead animals" (295). His revulsion for both his father's behavior and occupation creates a need for approval and love, which Dukelow satisfies.

The narrator-son has come to think that the new assistant to his father loves him "as much as [his parents] did" (287), and in this we sense that the boy's perceptions are right. The facility with which the boy accepts the assistant as a parent reveals the pain of being "neglected" (290). Dukelow attempts to compensate by serving as confidant and by entertaining his lover's son. The situation is complicated by the fact that the mother also has been neglected by her husband and feels incompatible with him. The mother allows Dukelow to put her son to bed because she is, as the boy has learned to think of her, "a tired person" (287). Mr. Dukelow also notices what her husband ignores: not only the boy's neglect but also the fact that the mother's "face bore a fatigued look" (288).

Dukelow's sensitivity to and interest in the mother, then, is clear, as is the fact that before Mr. Dukelow's arrival the mother had been lonely, like the "figure of the Holy Mother on a table, all by itself" (286) in the hall. The mother seems lonely again when Dukelow first appears to ask for work as an assistant butcher. The mother tries to retain the timid man for tea while the husband wants to take him to Keogh's, the archetypal Irish pub that recurs throughout the Irish tales. The boy's mother senses that the humble applicant is hungry, even though he claims to have recently eaten. She notices the "fear in his face" (287).

The boy's compatibility with the new assistant and with his mother's "quietness" (290) affords comfort, but at some level it must damage his sense of self-worth, because sons are usually pressured to be like their father. This aggressive father's habit of "shouting" (294) is a narcissistic assertion of self almost as powerful as his wish that his son follow in his footsteps. His desire for his son's conformity is intensified because the elder sons, now married, have refused the butcher's trade. His youngest son is his last chance to pass on the business. Like his elder brothers, this would-be butcher cannot identify with "butchery." Nor can he identify with his father's boisterous "ringmaster" (288) style, which is evident, for example, when the father addresses his son as "mister-me-buck" (292) and "Buck-o" (293). The first nickname claims the son as his own ("me"/"my"), and both nicknames convey a possessiveness that threatens the son's gentle nature.

The two father figures in this story are in fact opposites: the natural father is "a giant" (289), loud, virile enough to attract younger women, often drunk, and clumsy, having lost three fingers because he is inept at his trade; the substitute father, on the other hand, is "a small man" (288), gentle, quiet, feminine—not, in the butcher's view, man enough to be interested in Bridget (294)—and, finally, "civilized," practicing the trade with "style." He is "delicate" and assumes the motherly role of bedtime storyteller who can "[sense] everything, as though there was an extra dimension to him" (292). The blustering father, conversely, cannot even sense his son's humiliation when he belittles him, much less his son's distress over the attention given to Bridget at the breakfast table.

The father's insensitivity is most evident in a lengthy breakfast scene the morning after the boy sees his father kissing Bridget. That night, after being comforted by Dukelow, the boy had fallen asleep, as if to escape the nightmare of that day, but the nightmare returns when he awakens the next morning: "the first thing [he] thought was that the day was the last day of the summer holidays. Then [he] remembered [his] father kissing Bridget" (291). Guilty moments of the past always return to haunt the conscience, but in Trevor's stories they haunt the innocent as well as the guilty. And sometimes the character who seems most guilty to the reader (in this case the insensitive father) feels no guilt at all.

On first processing this pivotal scene we focus simply on the father's insensitivity, not only to his son but also to his wife. At first we trust the narrator-son's interpretation of his family's behavior. He clearly identifies the leer for what it is when "Bridget knelt down to open the iron door of the oven." And the son may even sense the sexual innuendoes when the father addresses Bridget, seeming to ignore the mother: "There's nothing like cutting chops . . . to give you an appetite for breakfast, Bridget" (292). The boy feels "jealous on [his] mother's behalf"; his sense of self depends on the feminine qualities the mother and son share.

Moreover, the son closely observes the father's gross insensitivity to his wife's feelings when he complains about her "lumpy" potato cakes, then praises Bridget for being able to "claim the best" (293) in men (himself). The son wonders if his father is "trying to hurt" (293) his mother, and the reader accepts the boy's perspective. The father seems so engaged with his own bravado—with asserting his own virility at his wife's expense—that his son (and the reader) notices little else.

When the father learns his daughter is pregnant, his braggadocio over the prospect of becoming "a grandfather" (294) seems to confirm his own sexual prowess; his daughter's fertility confirms his own virility. The son meanwhile feels disgust over his father's behavior, perceiving his father as odd man out: "we were all quiet except himself [the father]" (295).

But after we have learned of Dukelow and the mother's affair, the complexity of this breakfast scene demands more than the boy's simplistic reading of his family's behavior. The boy/narrator seems doubly vulnerable and doubly limited when we realize how much he is misreading things. For example, the boy sees his father "eyeing Mr. Dukelow's hands as if he was thinking they wouldn't be much use harvesting potatoes" (293), but we now know that the father is more likely imagining Dukelow's guilty hands on his wife's body. Knowing about the wife's infidelity leads us to ask new questions, such as when and how did the father learn about it? How to explain the puzzle of the cuckold's buoyant mood? We must then focus less on the boy's distress over the father's attentions to Bridget and more on the turn of events—the essential change in the father's mood, which becomes paradoxically "better" (297) when he learns of his wife's infidelity—a mood change that previously had seemed to be simply a well-satisfied lusty spirit.

The story does not really provide enough evidence for us to assess the situation accurately, but we wonder if the father's good mood signifies compensation for his wife's adultery owing to relief from his own guilt. The son notices that his father "addressed all of us except [his] mother" (292). On second reading we notice that, while speaking to everyone else, the father keeps his eye focused on his wife: "he was glancing down the length of the table" (293) at her throughout the scene. After taunting Dukelow for his alleged lack of interest in Bridget, the father is "still staring at [the] mother's head." And after the news that his daughter is pregnant, "there was a silence while [the] father looked at [the] mother" (294).

The son attributes the "heavy atmosphere" to the kiss that the father and Bridget have shared, but it may be that they shared more than a kiss. Given this new context, the sexual liaison of master and maid now seems less important than the revelation about the master's wife's affair—a revelation that must have occurred that same night. Bridget is after all the only one who would be motivated and in a position to reveal the mother's affair with Dukelow. In fact, it may have been guilt that had inspired Bridget on a previous occasion to declare to the son her "fondness for [his] mother" (296), thus masking her fondness for his father. The mother believes her when Bridget reveals her secret plans to marry "the porter at the Munster and Leinster Bank," a secret revealed with the warning: "don't tell" the master of the house or the postman "or anyone like that" (296). If the son's insights are partially valid and Bridget "didn't mind it when [her master] kissed her" (291), then this "secret" of Bridget's may be designed to hide guilt.

During the breakfast scene, then, the father comes to the table with blood on his hands but adopts the obnoxious pose of pious cuckold. Even so, our sympathies remain unchanged. We will probably not agree with Dukelow's generous reassurances to the son that his father is "a decent man" (291). We have participated too much in Dukelow's and the mother's suffering, previously evident when Dukelow explains the mother's "fatigued look" to her son by saying that she "probably didn't sleep well." Dukelow moreover places himself among the many "people who [do not] sleep well" (288).

The undercurrent of tension at the breakfast table becomes a crisis when the family returns to the kitchen for the noon dinner. The father announces, "Isn't that terrible . . . Henry Dukelow's shifting on" (296), then leaves for Keogh's with his assistant to "have a talk about what [Dukelow] will do" (297). He ignores his wife's objections and returns "later that day . . . in a better mood than ever" (297), because he has entered not only a state of drunken insensitivity but also the world of the self-righteous.

Most important, the father no longer suffers guilt about taking advantage of the maid. He can now openly apologize to Bridget "about that thing" (298), a gesture quite incongruous with his previous behavior. We cannot admire the husband's role-playing when he shames his wife and rails against Dukelow, calling him "a chancer . . . [s]ent up from Satan" (298). Issues of class and economics further darken the father's position.

Bridget prefers the master of the house over her boyfriend because he's "got more money" (291), another of the son's insights complicates his "innocent" perspective. However naive, the boy has been corrupted enough to understand that others conform to the power lines of money and class, although he values others according to less materialistic standards. He values the friendship of Dukelow, who had at his previous job been a "manservant," ironically a servant with a name inferring nobility ("Duke"). The boy learns to love his new friend because this nurturing parent-substitute is sensitive and honest, unlike his father who sells "bad meat" when he thinks he can get away with it (291).

In the boy's view, then, Dukelow "outclasses" (291) his father precisely because he serves others humbly and offers his lover's son affection in the form of attention and intimacy, even confiding that he appreciated "the kindness of [his] mother that first time" (289) when he timidly stood in the doorway to answer the ad for an assistant. Dukelow shares his feelings and even "a kiss" (290)—a kiss the boy sees as superior to the kiss his father had given Bridget. Dukelow had been the best of fathers for the short six months he lived with the family, generously spending time with the boy, playing marbles, constructing airplanes, and telling stories.

The son's sense of alienation from his own father is epitomized in the boy's observation that his father's "way of touching [the son] with his stumps instead of with the fingers that remained with him" is like the father's gesture when "pushing from him a plate from which he'd eaten a meal" (297). The boy's misunderstanding about his family is countered by a few truly remarkable insights. His outrage at being underestimated ("they were assuming I had no mind" [298]), on the other hand, seems only partially justified. He is wrong that his father looks at Dukelow's hands at the breakfast table thinking about his farming skills; he is right when he compares his father's hands unfavorably with Dukelow's "thin clear hands," which he imagines "on the white sheets" (298) of his mother's bed. He is wrong when he imagines that Bridget thinks Dukelow is "nicer"

(299) than her boyfriend, since she judges "niceness" according to wallet size. He is right when Dukelow leaves and he presumes to know "what expression would be there if my mother cared to permit its presence" (299). The agony of the adult situation emerges when the miserable and bewildered boy concludes, "No one but my father could not love Mr. Dukelow" (299). Little does the boy realize what it means to wish Dukelow would "kiss [his mother] as [his] father had kissed Bridget" (299). The boy wrongly believes Dukelow is leaving because of his father's jealousy—not in matters of love, but in matters related to the assistant's superior skills of the trade. His judgments regarding the relative value of other people's "choices," however, are absolutely correct.

William Trevor is an author who admits, "I don't have any answers, just questions."[11] This story, like so many of Trevor's others, raises a number of questions that the author does not answer: we are left puzzling over whether or not this mother's son—if he knew the truth—could still see his mother in terms of the purity he assumes for her when Dukelow leaves. She *is* the one who placed "a little crucifix" (291) on the wall by his bed. She must have also arranged his room so that he could "see the face of Our Lady [a sacred picture] from where [he] lay" (291) in bed. Dukelow reinforces the boy's sense of the mother's purity when he tells him to pray to Saint Agnes, a third-century martyr who died a virgin rather than marry a lusty nobleman she didn't love. The boy's trust in his mother's "purity" is what prevents him from understanding what has happened.

But of course the boy's moral sense probably has not been developed to the extent that he could overcome conventional codes condemning the adulterous affair no matter what the circumstances. We are left worrying about how this son will develop given that he can find no model of "decency" except that of an adulterer? This story is one of several in the Trevor canon depicting a young boy unable to formulate a place for himself in a society that fails to offer acceptable masculine models—models like Dukelow, whose sensitivity and compassion are not valued because they are seen as too feminine.

"An Evening with John Joe Dempsey": The Community Fathers the Child

In "An Evening with John Joe Dempsey" a fatherless boy suffers the pain of adolescence and other trials, not unlike the sons dominated by stern, insensitive patriarchs. This story most emphatically indicts sexually wayward father figures and, paradoxically, pious, apparently celibate male models who remain bachelors unable to conceptualize women except as prostitutes or, at the other extreme, symbols of purity. Since John Joe cannot find anyone to help him understand normal sexuality, he feels betrayed by the men in his community and alienated from what is considered "normal" social behavior.

The wisdom Trevor conveys is impressive in these stories about adolescent sons suffering the whims of aggressive fathers and struggling toward mature sexual identities. Sons alienated from their fathers or lacking fathers naturally seek other models. In "The Raising of Elvira Tremlett" the narrator might have found such a model in his teacher and the Protestant minister, but he received no encouragement from either of those. In "A Choice of Butchers" the boy did find a substitute in his father's assistant. In the case of the fatherless "John Joe Dempsey" the boy cultivates the company of Quigley, who is "an elderly" "crazed dwarf," "the town's idiot" (243–52), and a voyeur. Unfortunately, John Joe cannot find any other male model in his community worth emulating. This deficiency causes this adolescent boy to suffer from Lynch's fatherly advice.

Apparently seeking a father figure for some time, John Joe judges the men in his community according to their honesty and measures their integrity according to their sexual behavior. These men lie, particularly about sexual matters. For example, those who loiter outside Kelly's Hotel lie to their wives about their associations with "dancing girls" (249). In the boy's view Mr. Lynch, the pub crawler who tries to father the boy, is "not an honest man" (249) and perhaps the worst liar of all because he represses and denies his own sexuality, seen as an evil force by John Joe's community. Lynch in fact presents himself as a moral example, but John Joe suspects that he too has "sinful," sexual thoughts. John Joe's only friend, Quigley, even though a deformed Peeping Tom, is at least honest, the boy reasons.

Sent by his mother to the grocery store/pub to purchase bacon, John Joe is "snagged" by Lynch, a lonely bachelor seeking company. Lynch encourages John Joe to drink his first beer in celebration of his fifteenth birthday and entices him with a fatherly lecture on the evils of "dirty women" (237). Lynch wants to inform the boy "man-to-man" about his "manhood" (244), to warn him about avoiding "tarts" (235), and to advise him about living "a healthy life" (239), since the boy lost his construction-worker father at the age of two.

Lynch's lecture to John Joe insinuates that masturbation causes "pimples"; the mentor declares that "the body is God given. There's no need to abuse it" (239). In the course of this birthday celebration turned sermon, both John Joe's and Lynch's inadequate attitudes toward sexuality are revealed. Raised without fathers, both are alienated from their community. What Lynch tells John Joe does not help him in his quest for community acceptance but instead further alienates the confused adolescent.

Unfortunately, there is a disparity between the content and the message of what Lynch claims to be a "moral story"—that is, the story of his own "virginity" and his supposedly first sexual temptation. Lynch tells John Joe about the "Piccadilly tarts" he encountered as a soldier in London during the war. Unfortunately, this storyteller relishes explaining that "the tarts were everywhere" with "their breasts cocked out" (236), this latter description a comic mixed metaphor, revealing gender confusion. Lynch spares no detail as he describes the "tarts," "big and little [breasts?] . . . enticing you up to them. Wetting their lips . . . with the ends of their tongues" (235). John Joe knows that Lynch has told this story before, since he has heard the boys at the Christian Brothers' school "sniggering over [it]" (236). Lynch's self-righteous pretense is undercut by the vivid descriptions here and by his relish at the telling. This "relish" turns sadistic when Lynch mentions a gang rape in Belgium where he "saw a Belgian woman held down on the floor while four men satisfied themselves on her" (236). Why this spectator did not rescue the poor woman rather than simply watch is hard to tell.

Although Lynch claims his purpose is to warn the boy against "temptations" (236), his tales of sin actually stimulate sexual daydreams. John Joe listens while drifting off, conflating Lynch's lecture and the pious moralizing suffered at school. But the former are far more difficult for the adolescent boy to endure without responding by activating his body rather than his mind.

Lynch's story about how Baker, a fellow soldier, arranged with a prostitute for group sex is most clearly incompatible with Lynch's declared purpose. Lynch invites John Joe to imagine the effect on the men of Baker's "talk of the glory girls taking off their togs," "the motion of their haunches," and "the private areas of the women's bodies" (237). Lynch is forced to reveal the point of the story prematurely—"Amn't I saying to you those girls are no good to any man?" (237)—because John Joe wants to hear more about "the soldiers' pleasuring" (237). Lynch also finds himself having to scold John Joe for showing "disappointment" when he learns that his initiator into manhood abstained from participating in the entertainment at hand because he had "a vision" of "the Holy Mother."

45

John Joe may rightly perceive that Lynch's mother's demand for celibacy, her enforcement of the religious community will, prevented Lynch from marrying. Indeed, Lynch celebrates mothers as symbols of purity: "There's honour due to a mother" (242), he says. The community father marvels that the instant he saw the "vision of the Virgin" (237), which saved him from sin, his mother had dreamed that his "legs were on fire" (238). Lynch says he "didn't marry, out of shame for the memory of listening to Baker making that bargain" with the prostitute—not marrying being an overreaction to this "sin," to say the least. John Joe rightly sees the mother as someone Lynch wanted "to get away from" (238).

And yet John Joe's reservations about the mother's influence are contradicted by the fact that he is sexually attracted to mother types: "rotund [women] approached the proportions John Joe most admired," like the pub matron, Mrs. Keogh, who "wore spectacles and had grey hair" (244). The boy does not understand his normal sexual feelings and worries that he might become like Lynch and Quigley, both oddball bachelors. He worries because "like Mr. Lynch," he also spends Sundays with his mother (24). That his sexual fantasies involve various mature women in town further alienates him from normal boyhood.

Trevor describes John Joe as an "oddity" who is "pale of visage, as his father had been" (237). His teacher, Brother Leahy, and his classmates apparently ostracize him becuase of his tendency to daydream and his association with Quigley, who encourages his sexual fantasies—most particularly his strange fantasies about older women. This Peeping Tom relates in detail the lovemaking he has witnessed, which seems to include everyone in the community and always is related as lewd and not loving.

When Lynch warns John Joe, as does his mother and Brother Leahy, against his association with Quigley because it may disqualify him from getting work at the sawmill, Lynch paints a worst-case scenario: others may see John Joe as being like Quigley, "two of a kind" (243). The point, however, is that Lynch and Quigley are alike: they both offer perverted views of sexuality. Lynch implies that women, but not men, are "dirty." If not "tarts," women in Lynch's view are responsible for maintaining the purity of the race. Quigley celebrates sexual gratification in the form of voyeurism. Neither of these bachelors has taken the first step toward community—that is, marriage.

Since this story is told from a perspective of many years later, it is clear that the "world [John Joe] did not know" mentioned at the start of the story is the world of loving sexuality, a world he will never discover—a world defining men in more positive roles than that of the pervert, the child beater maintaining the purity of the sons, or the lusty gang. Since John Joe finds no loving, faithful male as a community role model, he assumes a cynical posture at the end of the story. Lying in his bed "all alone," he concludes, "It would have made no difference . . . if his father had lived. His father would have been like the others" (251).

"Matilda's England": Madness Shared by Two

The adolescent characters—John Joe, the woebegone butcher's son, and the would-be lover of Elvira Tremlett—are all baffled by their sexuality and confused about the sexual behavior of others in the community. When the developing adolescent protagonist is a young girl, as in "Matilda's England," sexual curiosity and parental models again are issues, sexuality less so. It is interesting, however, that father figures are nurturing in Trevor's most important story about a daughter's struggle to achieve autonomy and a sense of self-worth.

Matilda has loving parents, but she models herself according to her misperceptions of an elderly woman outside the family, Mrs. Ashburton, the aristocrat who employs Matilda's father to work the farm on her estate. The irony is that when Matilda loses her father and her brother during World War II, she does not focus on her loving, however distressed, mother. Instead she seeks the friendship of Mrs. Ashburton, a benign figure who is a destructive influence only because circumstances cause Matilda to distort the elderly woman's basic character. Matilda's distortion of reality owes not to any malicious feelings for others but to the terrible pain she suffers from the loss of her father and brother.

Matilda is "adopted," then, by this community mother, Mrs. Ashburton, who grieves over a miscarriage suffered years ago, over the more recent tragedy of her husband's shellshock during World War I and his subsequent death at home, and over the decline of Challacombe Manor. Mrs. Ashburton sees Matilda as the child she miscarried, the child she then could not conceive. The old woman's loneliness and her wish for a daughter provide the basis for their friendship. In turn, Matilda responds by encouraging this relationship, not because she consciously admires the old woman but because she seeks to understand her world and later the horrors of war.

A Freudian seeking to understand this girl's attraction to the elderly aristocrat might delve into Matilda's childhood. Oedipal feelings and a powerful need to identify with her mother, the object of her father's love, is clear at the start. The normal possessiveness all children feel for their parents emerges when Matilda recalls her "father breaking a fountain-pen" as "the first thing [she remembers] in all [her] life" (497)—a hyperbolic claim that can only be explained by her association of this angry act with a loving one: her father's anger did not last, but rather, as Matilda imagines it, "after a minute or two he began to laugh. He kissed my mother, pulling her down to the knee he'd broken the pen over" (498).

The exaggerated importance Matilda gives to this incident when she identifies a broken pen as one of life's crucial memories is best understood when related to the child's jealousy when the father kisses the beloved mother—jealousy of course being an infinitely natural response when the tie to the mother is threatened. Matilda's behavior later as a young woman, then, is regressive and owes to her grief from losing her mother to her father, then being abandoned by her nurturing father, who had comforted his five-year-old daughter, "cuddling" her to him, "caressing" (499) her tenderly, when she had a nightmare. On this occasion the father had told his daughter that "big girls of five don't cry," and this small suggestion is another factor that hampers Matilda's development. When her father dies she is "unable to cry any more" (511). With the news of her brother's death, she feels she "would never cry again" (523). As she matures this incapacity to cry forms the basis for Matilda's incapacity to love and feel sympathy for others despite her father's example, not to mention the example of her affectionate mother also depicted as kissing her daughter before putting her gently to bed.

When Mrs. Ashburton freely shares her grief as well as her tea-time treats, Matilda imbibes more than an afternoon's tonic. She does not offer sympathy, however, as she imbibes Mrs. Ashburton's terrible sense of loss from an unfortunate pregnancy, from the tragedies of two world wars, and from a widow's sorrow over losing her husband. Because of these losses Mrs. Ashburton might have withdrawn from everyone, a frequent enough response of the bereaved and exactly what Matilda does in the course of the story. The plot may in fact be traced by the sequence of friends and family members Matilda crosses off her list: her friend Belle, her sister, her mother, and finally her purportedly loving husband. The plot, then, traces Matilda's "progression" toward adulthood and madness as a regressive movement. What would otherwise be the story of a blossoming young woman is perverted by war.

Embittered by the loss of her father and brother, Matilda becomes obsessed with restoring Challacombe Manor to its previous grandeur and with assuming Mrs. Ashburton's identity. But Matilda re-creates Mrs. Ashburton in her own image. She relates to the manor and to place instead of relating to people, unlike the outgoing Mrs. Ashburton. Matilda neglects members of her own family who survived the world war and rejects her new father-in-law when her mother remarries. She marries the son of the new owners of the manor and eventually alienates herself from her family, friends, and community. Her new husband is forced to suffer her mental decline. Mrs. Ashburton seems to have passed the madness of her shellshocked husband onto Matilda, "almost like someone having a disease," as Trevor explained to me in an interview. Matilda is finally attracted to Mrs. Ashburton because the old woman makes no demands, unlike her own mother, who hopes that Matilda will accept her new stepfather.

Whereas Matilda responds to grief by alienating herself from her family, Mrs. Ashburton responds to grief by seeking community. She exemplifies the best characteristics of femininity and is the most positive example of a community mother (cf. Lynch's poor modeling of masculinity, his neurotic performance as a community father). Mrs. Ashburton's "eccentricity" (496) might well have biased the community against her and embittered the lonely old woman; she might well have isolated herself within the walls of her estate. But this has not happened. Instead the old and somewhat destitute Mrs. Ashburton drives "about the lanes in a governess cart drawn by a donkey." Matilda's insights, precocious for a nine-year-old, are sound when she explains that Mrs. Ashburton "drove about the lanes . . . in order to meet us [the neighborhood children] cycling back from school" (498). She allows her donkey to graze the land of nearby estates, assuming that others are as generous as herself. Her favorite color, green, is the color of spring, regeneration, the resurrection, and of course, Ireland—associated with conviviality, good humor in the face of suffering, and storytelling. The Irish are master storytellers well aware that intimate communication reinforces lines of affection.

Mrs. Ashburton plays host to the children even though she is "frail" (496) and vulnerable. She explains that her possessions—her "bald fur coat," hat-pins, dresses, shoes, governess cart, and donkey—are "valueless" (496). This lady of the manor in her decline crosses generational lines and seeks the company of children.

Not only does this aristocrat cross generational lines, but she crosses those of class as well. She represents fallen nobility. The manor had once been active with servants, gardeners, and guests: "a showpiece" (499). Matilda's family lives in the home-farm on the Ashburton estate. Over the years, the Ashburtons were forced to sell off the land, and eventually Matilda's father purchased the farmhouse when Lloyd's Bank foreclosed the estate's mortgage. In sum, the bank allows Mrs. Ashburton to remain lady of the manor, but she does not hesitate to seek the company of her former, working-class employees. The children she cultivates consider her odd: Matilda describes the "throaty, crazy-sounding way" the old woman whispers the young girl's name (496). But there is a wonderful sanity in the way this 81-year-old seeks others. She has no relationship whatsoever to such other "crazy" characters in the Trevor canon as Quigley, the "crazed dwarf" so alienated from his community in John Joe's story, unless we consider the fact that the diseased, deformed, and elderly are all outcasts of a modern world conditioned to judge "goodness" according to physical beauty, wealth, or youth.

This lady of the manor represents society's and humanity's graces driving the lanes, sharing sweets, cigarettes, and conversation—not to mention encouraging the children to resurrect the manor's tennis court as a way of resurrecting her memories of her husband, who so "loved it" (501). Motivated by her affection for others, Mrs. Ashburton brings people together, eventually planning a community gathering that allows her to share more extensively her cigarettes and her memories of her husband.

Matilda, on the other hand, develops into a mature woman who hates being actively engaged with others. As a child she had been disturbed rather than pleased when Mrs. Ashburton repeated Matilda's name because she considered it "dear" (496). Matilda is the "wild flower" the old woman seeks on the outskirts of life. Mrs. Ashburton demonstrates a capacity to love beyond Matilda's.

It is not that Matilda lacks the potential to be loving; in fact, early in the story she demonstrates an outgoing warmth of attitude. For example, she recognizes the value of Mrs. Ashburton's tennis party, which she compares to her sister Betty's love for Colin. Both of these events she sees as "very beautiful" (508). Her father's delight in seeing people "he hadn't seen for years" (506) also suggests a capacity for love Matilda might have inherited. But she loses whatever glimmer of this potential within her psyche when her father and brother die.

The potential for emotional warmth suggested at the start when Matilda notices that Mrs. Ashburton's smile "made her thin, elderly face seem beautiful" (497) is fleeting. Matilda soon imitates her older brother's skepticism. More precisely, her brother Dick at first doubts Mrs. Ashburton's motives when she works to spark their interest in restoring the manor's tennis court. Considering the old woman's "frail, almost beautiful way" of smiling suspiciously, Matilda finally wonders "if Dick wasn't right about Mrs. Ashburton's cunning" (502).

Matilda's suspicions reveal her own inadequacies rather than Mrs. Ashburton's. It is true that Mrs. Ashburton's enticements of "fruitcake" and cigarettes are meant to motivate the children to repair the tennis court, but Mrs. Ashburton had been seeking the children's company for some years. Ultimately, Dick changes his idea that he and his siblings are being used; even this skeptic finally helps in readying the court for the tennis party. Matilda, however, stubbornly retains Dick's skepticism, just as she eventually retains the negative aspects of the old woman's grief.

Mrs. Ashburton manages to gather together the entire community. The merriment of her tennis party mixes generations: Dick wears "old Mr. Bowe's" (505) tennis flannels. The party knows no class: everyone in the community is invited. At the party "Mr. Race [says Mrs. Ashburton] shook hands like a duchess" (506); the question of nobility, as in the case of "Dukelow," has to do with the capacity for love, congeniality, and kindness, not with wealth. Mrs. Ashburton's tennis party is wonderfully effective in bringing the community together, however fleeting such occasions are. Betty and Colin's tryst during the party serves as synecdoche for the party's significance generally.

To some extent Matilda rightly resists losing her identity by becoming the daughter Mrs. Ashburton could not conceive. Yet even though it is true that Matilda's identity is threatened by Mrs. Ashburtons's need for a substitute daughter, we should consider that the capacity to extend one's love beyond one's own family is what builds community. Some deficiency to love emerges in the course of this girl's development. She witnesses Mrs. Ashburton's exemplary capacity for love, her sister's love for Colin Gregg, her mother and father's "happy" (499) marriage. Matilda clearly understands that her parents "were very good friends" (498). An emotionally cold aspect of her character—evident when, early in her relationship with Mrs. Ashburton, she is repelled by the old woman's kisses—begins to dominate when she loses her father. Mrs. Ashburton does contribute to Matilda's pathology during their many visits prior to the tennis party when Matilda listened to the elderly widow trying to master her grief, repeating to Matilda "in particular" what her shellshocked husband had told her "about the men who'd died" (499). But the old woman does not intentionally damage the young girl. A complicated set of circumstances, not least of which involves the war, results in this parent-child relationship that cripples the daughter-substitute.

During their visits Matilda had believed Mrs. Ashburton was talking "in particular" to her young visitor, but more likely the old woman was either talking to herself to relieve her pain or talking to the unborn daughter she lost: "she smiled and just talked, always returning to the men who had been killed" (500). Both Mrs. Ashburton and her husband manage their trauma by talking. Mrs. Ashburton repeats "word for word the things her husband had told her, things that had maybe been the cause of his affected mind." She even manages to replicate "the terror that had been in [his voice]" (500). Mrs. Ashburton, then, passes her husband's shellshock on to Matilda, an impressionable and imaginative child, but one whose judgments are limited by her lack of experience, by the circumstances of her family, by her class, and by a certain vulnerability owing to her overactive imagination.

The memories of the tennis party are coincidentally ruined by news that World War II is imminent. When Matilda finds Mrs. Ashburton sitting alone in the dark of her manor after the party, the young girl judges the elder woman's "face [as] almost sinister" (507) but kisses the "face . . . like crinkled paper" anyway. This is a rare moment for Matilda, a spontaneous and unusual show of affection, as if the party enlarged her sympathies for others as surely as the war diminished this capacity of so many. And yet what Matilda allots is disproportionate to what she receives. She proffers only one kiss after being showered with Mrs. Ashburton's kisses throughout the day of the tennis party, throughout her young life. Matilda cannot quite respond fully in kind to this motherly figure.

Unfortunately, Matilda cannot understand Mrs. Ashburton's character enough to assume the role of daughter by more precisely emulating the would-be nurturing matriarch. The individual imagination provides its own interpretation of what it sees; reality is therefore fragmented by clashing perspectives. This is surely the case after the tennis party when Matilda and Belle wonder why Mrs. Ashburton is crying. Matilda chastizes Belle for her "soppiness" when her friend tries to "imagine being eighty-one . . . knowing you'd have to die soon" (508). Belle imagines that Mrs. Ashburton is crying over her own imminent death; Matilda imagines that she is crying "over the past" (509). Given Mrs. Ashburton's history of seeking others, her guilt over the ill-will she feels for the Germans, and her ability to bring the community together—all evidence of self-transcendence—she most certainly must be crying because the respite of peace is "all over . . . yet again" (507), and not simply her own party, her own life.

The individual does not die "yet again," but humanity suffers war and loss again and again—loss not only because of death but because of madness, or the fact that people and relationships change. Matilda imagines her father being bayoneted, the farm workers "missing in the trenches," and

Betty's boyfriend shot. But then she considers the worst loss of all: when a loved one is forced to assume an alien identity. Matilda is no less horrified by her own imaginings of death than by her imaginings of her brother's assuming the role of aggressor: Dick bayoneting "another soldier" (509).

Not much better than the actual killing of someone else is the mother's or wife's death wish for "another soldier" rather than her own son or husband. Mrs. Ashburton confesses to Matilda that she applied "the law of averages" to the score sheet of the dead and dying, not caring when "another man from the estate or from the neighborhood had been reported dead [because] she'd felt that there was a better chance that her husband wouldn't die" (500). She then explains how "ashamed" she later felt, aware of her own "cruelty," which she considers "horrible." She chastizes herself as one of "the women who were left at home and became cruel in their fear and their selfishness" (500). Interestingly enough, at the end of Part 1, "The Tennis Court," Matilda, even before she actually experiences the loss of her father, adopts "the law of averages" and prays only for his survival, also aware of her own "cruelty," which Mrs. Ashburton had said "was natural in wartime" (509). An important difference between the old woman and the young girl, however, is crucial. Matilda is "beginning to hate the Germans," she is but "not feeling ashamed of it, like Mrs. Ashburton was" (509).

In Part 2, "The Summer House," Matilda tries to accept her father's death, the end of a life, and returns to the tennis court, imaginatively reenacting how her father marked "the end of the day" of the party by surprising everyone with beer and cider. This party marked the beginning of World War II and "the end of [her family] being as [they] had been in [their] farm-house." This "ending" she also relates to Mrs. Ashburton, to "another end: when the farm had ceased to be the home-farm of Challacombe Manor" and Mrs. Ashburton lost her estate.

Indeed, the imagination conflates and reconstitutes reality. This is clearest when Matilda recalls the husband Mrs. Ashburton lost, but she cannot "see him in [her] mind's eye" at first. Then she reconstructs an image of him as a "silent man," unlike the compulsive talker Mrs. Ashburton had mentioned. Finally, the "image" of Mrs. Ashburton's lost husband in Matilda's mind "would disappear," replaced by the image of her own lost father (512). In fact, Matilda's imagination distorts reality as well as Mrs. Ashburton's motives and values. Unlike Mrs. Ashburton, who had longed for a child, Matilda wants no children after her marriage. Matilda has somehow missed Mrs. Ashburton's capacity to become engaged with others. When Dick, Betty, and Mrs. Ashburton had considered who to invite to the tennis party, they "cast a wide net" (506). Matilda's development is toward alienation from others, although she does place the old woman on the side of benevolence when she imagines, "Noah and Moses and Jesus Christ and old Mrs. Ashburton" (513) in Paradise.

Feeling betrayed by her mother when she remarries, Matilda withdraws into a world of prayer. But religion is inadequate to explain the atrocities of war. Matilda's confusion is shared by all who mourn and all who question whether a benevolent "God existed and was in charge" (513). Matilda rejects Rev. Throataway's ideas about God as a presence and invents her own theology. Her God-the-Father exists in Paradise as a figure maintaining her memories of her father. This provides consolation: "It was as if being close to him was being close to God also" (513). As she works on "keeping [her] father vivid in [her] mind" (517), she loses sight of her mother. At the end of the story and the end of her marriage, Matilda decides that "God, if he existed . . . was something to be frightened of" (545).

In Part 2 Matilda accidentally discovers her mother with her lover just as she had once accidentally discovered the lovemaking of Betty and Colin. In a stroke of genius, Trevor encourages the reader to share Matilda's romantic expectations regarding her sister's affair with Colin. She imagines that her sister's tryst explained the dirty ashtrays and farmhouse rugs in the summer house. Indeed, fully expecting to be comforted by peeping at Colin and Betty, she is rather shocked by the scene of her mother and a strange man. Her shock is understated and displaced: "I had never in my life seen my mother smoking a cigarette before" (519).

Matilda hopes to find comfort by peeping at lovers, but she cannot relate her mother's affair to her sister's "beautiful" love. Her intolerance of the new rival can be explained not only by her need for the dead father but also by her need for the long-lost mother. Moreover, jealousy prevents her from accepting her mother's lover, even though he offers her marriage and is affectionate toward his stepdaughter. When he toasts Matilda on her twenty-first birthday as his "best," she corrects him, because "it was that that I didn't care for in him. I wasn't his best, my mother was." It is the narcissistic child that wants exclusive love, to be the parent's "best."

As Matilda turns from the summer house to religion for solace, ironically she suffers more. Her Protestant Christianity paradoxically causes her to withdraw from her loved ones and to find "consolation [by imagining] Paradise . . . with [her] own God in it." This makes her feel "closer . . . to [her] father." This inner world "gradually became as important as the reality around [her]" (513).

Religious feeling isolates Matilda from her family, friends, and community—a terrible irony given the Christian emphasis on brotherly love. Christianity does not enlarge her understanding of her family but provides a reason for Dick's death, which Matilda believes was caused by her mother's sin of adultery. It is more comforting to believe that God punishes those who deserve to suffer than to believe we live in an absurd universe where events develop randomly, following no moral law except as humanity, not God, defines or fails to define it. Matilda therefore feels no moral responsibility to comfort her mother. Rather, she rails against her when Dick dies—even blaming the poor woman for her own son's death, which, in Matilda's view, is the logical punishment for "kissing a man when your husband has been killed." Matilda *does* suffer, especially since she tends to "catch" other people's "gloom" (517). Nevertheless, her cruel treatment of her mother again suggests a regression to childish, narcissistic, and sadistic behavior, which is never outgrown.

Part 3, "The Drawing-room," begins with Matilda's twenty-first birthday party and ends with her finally confessing to her husband, "I despise you. ... I have never felt affection for you" (547). For a brief moment she even imagines herself as his murderer, conniving a means to do him in by coaxing him onto the roof to replace a tile—a ruse before shoving him off to his death.

At this point we should consider another character more distanced from these tragic events. In Part 3, Miss Pritchard, a primary school teacher, briefly commands center stage. This teacher had earlier warned Matilda's mother that the impressionable and imaginative young woman was deranged because "she dwells on her father's death," not to mention dwelling on Mrs. Ashburton and her manor. Moreover, it is Miss Pritchard who declares what Matilda also understands: "There are casualties in wars . . . thousands of miles from where the fighting is" (546). She seems to speak for the author when she defines Matilda and Mrs. Ashburton's relationship as folie à deux.

Trevor speaks more than once through a sympathetic schoolteacher (cf. "Attracta"). Indeed, Miss Pritchard should have the last word—not Matilda's husband, who blames Mrs. Ashburton for Matilda's decline: "Some kind of bloody monster she was," he declares. The final irony, of course, is that the one who seems most victimized by Matilda's madness—that is, her husband—assumes an angry, wrongheaded, and judgmental stance—a stance as "deranged" (545) as that of his wife. No other work in modern literature so poignantly clarifies the defensive postures of suffering humanity, while at the same time, locating the most painful wounds as those inflicted by the parents on the child.

Stories about Courtship: Bachelors/Spinsters, Fathers/Daughters

While codes governing courtship and marriage are changing in some parts of the world, in most places feminine and masculine gender identities are governed by two antagonistic codes of behavior—purity for women, promiscuity for men. Certainly Trevor's stories about courtship—such as "The Ballroom of Romance," "Teresa's Wedding," and "The Property of Colette Nervi"—reflect these codes. In these stories young women driven by a fear of spinsterhood marry undesirable suitors in communities governed by men. Economic concerns override considerations of love or happiness in marriage. "Kathleen's Field" tells the story of a farmer's daughter so submissive to her father she does not even recognize she is being condemned to a lifetime of servitude and spinsterhood. "The Wedding in the Garden" traces the development into manhood of an initiate whose "progress" is partly responsible for the "regress" of at least two women in his community. The deprivation of servants and the deprivation of women go hand in hand. Such deprivation deems certain women as appropriate targets for male lust and certain others as marriageable.[12]

Although the setting for stories in this vein is frequently Ireland, the universality of prizing sons and conditioning deprived daughters to be submissive to fathers is most important. Trevor's sensitivity to the suffering of women is evident in the many stories that culminate either in a wedding motivated by economic concerns or permanent spinsterhood. Destructive gender codes as represented in Trevor's stories discourage fidelity, discourage sensitive men who nurture, and encourage frigidity and submissiveness in women.

Trevor's stories focused on gender should be seen not only in relation to the nineteenth-century British novel of manners and morals, courtship and marriage, but also to the eighteenth-century Augustan tradition. Writers in this latter tradition directed satiric barbs toward men but not with the same relish that they excoriated the folly of women (e.g., Pope and Swift).

Part 1

When Trevor deals with gender he directs his ire toward the folly of men—not exclusively but emphatically. He portrays women—even the most neurotic (as in "Raymond Bamber and Mrs. Fitch")—with an inordinate amount of compassion and tenderness. Carolyn Heilbrun explains female neurosis in relation to sexual repression as follows: "A woman must enjoy the full cycle of experience, or she would become riddled with complexes like a rotting fruit."[13] Terrible barriers between men and women in the nineteenth century caused wives to envision sexual freedom as the freedom to say no to their husbands. I am not suggesting in any way that promiscuity on the part of women should be encouraged, but as Dorothy Dinnerstein, among others, has shown, conditioned responses to feminine stereotypes result in "the special muting of woman's erotic impulsivity,"[14] which is a tragic development underlying the cause of the "midlife crisis" serving the older man so well when he wishes to abandon his wife for a younger woman (cf. "The Mark-2 Wife").

Men and women indeed suffer when faced with only two viable models of womanhood: whore or Holy Mother. The consequences of this ancient predicament are self-hatred in the case of women, distaste for the body in the case of men as well as women. Gender codes in a patriarchal society privilege men and objectify women. Few can overcome such social conditioning that so profoundly governs relationships between men and women.

In Ireland gender codes are further complicated by colonialism. In her work on Joyce, Suzette Henke points out that "unconsciously emulating their English masters, the Irish assert a specious manhood through blustering claims to patriarchal privilege, making infantile demands that frustrate and feminize those already demeaned by colonial subjugation."[15] Irish women—but also women everywhere—bear the brunt of blustering husbands and fathers. Subjugation because of gender, then, is the most important factor in the stories to be addressed here.

"The Ballroom of Romance": A Cacophony of Voices—Masculine, Feminine, Silenced

The best example of Trevor's sensitive rendering of women is "The Ballroom of Romance,"[16] although given the preponderance of overbearing and narcissistic fathers in the Trevor canon, the father in this story is an anomaly. Even though Bridie's father *does* care about his daughter, he must be understood in the context of a society endorsing fathers, husbands,

58

brothers, and womanizers who are insensitive to the suffering of girls trying to salvage their floundering self-respect in a world that targets them as
sex objects or ignores them; of submissive wives; of middle-aged women
desperately trying to maintain their physical appearance; and of elderly
women marginalized because they are alone—treated like children because
physically fragile and suffering from an inferiority complex not unlike that
of adolescents. Understanding the subtleties of "The Ballroom of
Romance" and the stories depicting elderly women is crucial to understanding Trevor's many stories about courtship, sexuality, and gender.

The mother dies before we enter the lives of Bridie, the ballroom spinster, and her crippled father, who is not obviously narcissistic or domineering. Nonetheless, the gender codes governing Bridie's exaggerated,
self-sacrificing nature are indirectly but poignantly revealed in the way she
interacts with other members of this Irish community—the conforming
spinsters and brides as well as the rebelling mothers; the womanizers of
the dancehall in hot pursuit; the "father" representing the voice of the
Church; and the businessmen, exemplified in Mr. Dwyer, the dancehall
owner.

Bridie's father is apparently admired by his community and loved by his
devoted daughter; despite his concern about Bridie's subservience, however, his handicap clearly requires that she spend most of her time meeting
his every need. This physically crippled father—through no fault of his
own—requires so much "mothering" that he "smothers" his emotionally
crippled daughter, a plot line that inverts the more common scenario of a
son entangled in his mother's apron strings.

Of course, gender codes in every society dramatically determine
whether a daughter or son develops autonomy by separating from both
parents. As Jessica Benjamin and other gender critics have argued, the
son's individuation from the mother is more readily accomplished than the
daughter's individuation from either parent. The son's idealization of and
identification with the father is untainted by submission because cultural
constructions of maleness incorporate concepts of power, thus encouraging
independence from and actual authority over the mother. On the other
hand, the daughter "idealizes deprivation" (Benjamin, 85) and submission
to the father.

The daughter cannot identify with the father and thereby establish an
identity independent of the mother. Indeed, the mother is not a figure
encouraging individuation for either child. To teach sons to be like the
mother stereotypically conceived—affectionate, nurturing, sensitive, and
tender—is to castrate them. Mothers may therefore inculcate in their sons

an unfeeling stoicism, competitive independence, and "natural" aversion for nurturing to ensure their access to the power lines of a phallocentric world. Mothers likewise indoctrinate their daughters to be submissive and attractive to men. Furthermore, daughters are conditioned to develop what Benjamin identifies as "an adoration of heroic men, who sacrifice love for freedom" (88)—heroic men like those found in American wild west novels, Bridie's father's preferred entertainment.

Bridie is indeed radically limited, nervously worried whenever she "abandons" her father, which is only twice each week: on Sunday to attend Mass and on Saturday to attend "a wayside dancehall" (185) where she hopes to "[drum] up" a husband, perhaps Dano Ryan, the drummer in the band. Bridie struggles to snag a husband without regard for her own needs or her own suffering.

In the first paragraph an understated, matter-of-fact narrator casually highlights Bridie's *father's* woes from "having had a leg amputated after gangrene had set in" (185). The farm pony's death is mentioned before the mother's—the latter death related in one sentence and with the same intensity as the former's. The narrator flatly outlines in a shopping-list tone the routine comings and goings of the central characters as well as the usual visitors to the family farm[17]—that is, three "in-comers" to Bridie's world: Canon O'Connell, the milk lorryman, and the grocer Mr. Driscoll. Bridie is a limited "out-goer."

The discourse of routine at the start of this story masks Bridie's suffering—her fear of growing old without a husband, her despair over her mother's death, her isolation. The absence of eulogy, a more appropriate response to the death of a parent, clarifies the neglect of Bridie by everyone in her community except the undesirable bachelors whose motives are suspect.

Bakhtin explains the subtlety at issue here when he discusses the reflexive nature of language and its tendency to distort, idealize, or mask the tragedies of life.[18] The prominence of routine in Trevor's stories has already been mentioned; the discourse of routine in this story most emphatically "weatherizes," as Bakhtin imagines it, adjacent texts defining Bridie's struggle.

A pattern of subtexts conveys Bridie's entrapment by societal norms. The discourse of routine functions as an underlying refrain in many of Trevor's stories. Here this discourse marks the malaise of Bridie's life and the inevitability of her fate. On the first page alone we learn what was done "Sundays," "Mondays," "two years later," "not long after," "by the week," "daily," "during the week," "weekly," "once each month," "on a Friday afternoon" (185), "by now," "often," "at night," and "in the evenings" (185). Trevor demonstrates that Bridie functions "in time" (186, 199), with little freedom to develop the self.

Bridie is defined by her routine activities—domestic chores, the hard farm labor, the mothering of her father, and regular cycling to the nearest town (11 miles from the farm) to shop. She buys "for herself, material for a dress, knitting wool, stockings, a newspaper, and paper-backed Wild West novels for her father" (185). The masculine communal voice relegates women to domestic tasks such as knitting and men to pioneering the wild west—adventures demanding that men be courageous "out-goers" and rescuers of helpless females, who foolishly presume they can survive a life beyond domesticity. There is an unhappy gap between the realms of women and men in this Irish community. When reading wild west novels, women less readily than men identify with masculine heroes and less easily feel vicarious enjoyment when aggressive men assert their will in gun battles and their freedom in the exploration of new frontiers, arenas closed to women.

Elaine Showalter quotes Louise Bogan to clarify the limitations of female domesticity in a similar context:

> Women have no wilderness in them.
> They are provident instead.
> Content in the tight hot cell of their hearts
> To eat dusty bread.[19]

Bridie's dry domesticity, passivity, and entrapment, then, are subtly conveyed by reference to the wild west and a literary genre sentimentalizing the heroic feats of men. The father's reading of such novels is only one clue that we should be looking, as Annette Kolodny puts it, with "an acute attentiveness to the ways in which power relations, usually those in which males wield various forms of influence over females, are inscribed in the texts (both literary and critical) that we have inherited."[20]

Trevor in fact manipulates many different voices so that the dialogue of others tells the *real* story of Bridie's plight with a tragic tone. The point is the absence of feminine power in the Irish community, the silencing of women. When Bridie converses with "some of the [town] girls she'd been to school with, girls who had married," she notes enviously that "most of them had families." But a rebelling feminine "they" tells Bridie, "You're lucky to be peaceful in the hills . . . instead of stuck in a hole like this" (185). The narrator then relates Bridie's feelings of "surprise" that the girls

61

"envied her life" because this aging spinster longs to conform to gender codes that place more value on the *fact* of being married than on the importance of marriage based on love.

It is an ironic, authorial voice that counters Bridie's wish to marry at any cost by defining married Irish women as "tired . . . from pregnancies and their efforts to organize and control their large families" (185). The authoritarian voice of the Church urges women to have "large families" and to be happy despite the difficulties of "controlling" children when child-rearing is accomplished by mothers alone. The women characters in this story either assume mindlessly the proper female role or rebel by complaining about being "stuck" as mother-women exclusively—a role that is tiring. Nonetheless, Bridie and the other spinsters doggedly conform and romanticize the wife/mother role.

Bridie is "usually" thinking about how best to serve her father, "mending clothes or washing eggs" (189). She agonizes over the possibility of becoming "a figure of fun in the Ballroom" (192)—that is, a spinster like Madge Dowling, the hopeless case still chasing middle-aged bachelors. Bridie is radically determined by societal norms, first perpetuated by her father and later by the various men she imagines as rescuing her from spinsterhood. She deludes herself about the romantic potential of these bachelors: Dano Ryan, Eyes Horgan, Bowser Egan. Also, metonymy works to hilarious effect as "the guy with the long arms" appears and reappears (188, 190, 192, 196), further darkening the romantic horizons of the spinsters.

Bowser most clearly conveys the masculine view of marriage: "he'd want a fire to sit at and a woman to cook food for him"—a woman "great at kissing" (199). On the other hand, Bridie's fantasies about marriage do not include a sexual element. Benjamin argues that "daughters [reject] sexuality as a component of woman's autonomy" (85). Nonetheless, the authorial voice describes Bridie physically and suggests a certain "masculine" vitality—an anomaly given Bridie's conformity to asexual feminine roles but a promising factor.

Bridie's repressed energy has the potential to counter her malaise. The narrator says that Bridie is "tall and strong," qualities more commonly attributed to men; "the skin of her fingers and her palms [are] stained and harsh to touch. The labor they'd experienced had found its way into them, as though juices had come out of vegetation and pigment out of soil: since childhood she'd torn away the rough scotch grass that grew each spring among her father's mangolds." Her "hands daily [root] in the ground. . . . Wind had toughened the flesh on her face" (186). Rooted here in nature,

Bridie tragically cannot fulfill the "natural" functions of wife and mother except by assuming the role of both wife and mother to her own father.[21]

The same mindless dialogues grind up Bridie's day: the ballroom owner, Justin Dwyer, has been promising "for twenty years" he would visit Bridie's father (187). We are told that Bridie "never minded" "cycling" to either the ballroom or Mass. But the fact that "she'd grown quite used to all that" (187) assumes the reality of a potent time past when she minded it "all" very much.

Furthermore, the dialogue of others tells the *real* story with a tragic tonality that must be reconstructed. Again at the start, after mention of Bridie's mother's death, we see Canon O'Connell's response, not Bridie's. He tells her not to "worry about it all." The narrator tells us that the good Canon here refers to "the difficulty of transporting her father to mass" because her mother is no longer there to help (184). The public rhetoric of this authority figure provides soothing evasions that ignore Bridie's suffering over the death of her mother. Surely "it all" encompasses more than getting her father to church.

Bridie suffers the loss of her mother. She worries about growing old, about becoming a spinster, about being isolated on a farm with a crippled father, about properly performing the domestic chores inside and the hard labor outside, and about fulfilling the duties of errand girl, daughter, wife, and mother to her father. Bridie's father sympathetically articulates the problem: "It's a terrible thing for you, girl" (185). It is easier for her female friends to see the problem. Cat Bolger asks, "Are you on your own, Bridie?" Dano Ryan orders, "Tell your father I was asking for him" (196) when she wishes he'd be asking for her instead. Patty Byrne asks, "Are you O.K., Bridie?" A nameless youth asks, "Is there sense in it, Bridie?" (189).

This nameless youth is also isolated, supporting his uncle until he can earn enough money to emigrate. The emigration of men owing to a poor rural economy in fact has limited Bridie's choices. Men are free to move "to Dublin or Britain, leaving behind them those who became the middle-aged bachelors of the hills" (19)—leaving behind the women. Emigration is defined as escape from the mother country. Abandoning one's country seems as inevitable as abandoning one's parent, but abandoning one's parent is the first and necessary step toward autonomy. Women are limited in terms of emigration because of economics and in terms of independence because gender codes demand the dependence of wives, mothers, and daughters on husbands, fathers, and brothers—a painful dependence requiring no small measure of self-sacrifice.

Bridie suffers but behaves "as though nothing had happened" (196). Her suffering is more evident when we consider not only how Wayne Booth perceives it but also how perspective is refined and clarified by Bakhtin. Authorial, narrative, character, communal male, and communal female voices vie with one another in Trevor's stories to form an underlying grid of relationships poignantly impinging on women characters. In this case aggressive forces oppress Bridie's personal freedom. She is habituated to behavior more appropriate for mother and wife than for a young maid seeking a husband.

Thus Bridie rides her mother's bicycle, the "old Rudge" digging deeper ruts in the same old track that forces her subservience to her father, who still calls his 36-year-old daughter "girl," even though it is *he* who depends on *her*. Bridie's father declares that he would "be dead without *the* girl [my daughter?] to assist [him]" (186). We should notice that the father's comment implies the reverse of the usual case: parents ordinarily sustain the life of the child, not vice versa.

Unaware of her oppression, Bridie looks forward to being controlled by a husband. She daydreams about "when she was just sixteen" (191) and had anticipated that Patrick Grady "would *lead* her into sunshine, to the town and the Church of Our Lady Queen of Heaven, to marriage and smiling faces" (191; my italics). Appropriately, given the inspiration of "The Ballroom of Romance," Bridie romanticizes the social and religious codes demanding that men lead, women follow. When contemplating marriage, Bridie does not fantasize a husband who assumes the role of helpmate as expected but a husband who takes part in an oddly formulated threesome. The father-in-law and son form a pair: "two men working together" outside in the fields. Bridie thus attends "to things in the farmhouse" (193). Her ideas of courtship and marriage are based on communal fantasies, not on reality (cripples don't work fields), and the inadequacy of these communal fantasies is implied as the story progresses.

Community codes condition women to be self-sacrificing, but Bridie sees her father, not herself, as a martyr, believing that he "had more right to weep, having lost a leg" (196), a sort of castration. Even though the father's helpless "hobbling" deserves some sympathy, still the authorial voice solicits the largest measure of sympathy for Bridie, whose passivity and de-centered relation to the community is common enough.

All of the women at "The Ballroom of Romance" assume their proper "places on upright wooden chairs" and "[wait] to be asked to dance" (188). These women are furthermore "too embarrassed to do anything about" the men who dance too close. Bridie is so conditioned by societal and religious codes regulating proper female behavior that she does not really belong anywhere and cannot escape her possessive father, who also suffers because he is unable to fulfill masculine norms of independence and freedom of movement.

Neither the father nor the daughter can openly express their suffering. Bridie feels it "improper" to weep "in the presence of her father" (196), which also suggests that gender identity is inappropriately conditioned behavior—and that Bridie's response to such conditioning is confused. Societal codes in the Irish community and elsewhere require that men stoically repress tears, women weep or threaten to weep in order to control men. Bridie sublimates her own needs, and her "tears" are seen as "a luxury" (196). Trevor amazingly presents weeping in a positive light. When men cry in this story, however, their tears are associated with an ailment, with disease. Dano develops "a watering of the eyes that must have been some kind of cold" (187). Bridie, of course, tries to *mother* Dano by suggesting he take "Optrex" (195), which she uses to bathe her father's eyes when he has similar trouble.

Unfortunately, Bridie is not aware enough to identify what she subconsciously wants—recognition as a subject. Margot Norris discusses Joyce's "The Dead" in a similar context and posits a reason for a wife's wish to be controlled by her husband: "Being treasured as a valued and cherished object—that is, relations more proper to the parent-child relation—is easier to achieve than recognition and significance as a subject."22

Trevor's story about Bridie's plight finally identifies failures of male-female and parent-child relationships owing to the pressures of gender codes in a materialistic society idealizing the conventions of romance and mandating the subservience of women. The point emerges most clearly when readers relate the romantic delusions of Bridie's daydreams to those of aspiring brides everywhere.

At the root of male-female conflicts in the modern world is the failure of "romance" to result in meaningful relationships. "The Ballroom of Romance" has no humanity. The misanthropic capitalist, Dwyer, hates "the middle-aged bachelors who . . . came down from the hills like mountain goats, released from their mammies and from the smell of animals and soil" (192). Indeed, Dwyer reduces love, the "evening rendezvous," to "business." His wife counts the "evenings takings" (187, 198) and raises turkeys rather than children.

"Teresa's Wedding": Reluctant Grooms

Feminine and masculine perspectives on marriage are diametrically opposed as bachelors and spinsters at "Teresa's Wedding" reveal them. In Trevor's stories women want to marry to avoid spinsterhood and to make themselves economically secure. Bachelors, on the other hand, do not want to marry and generally avoid providing economic security for women. Men also resist the concomitant assumption that their sexuality will be restricted, fidelity being demanded once married but not before.

The guest list for Teresa's wedding includes a fair share of young women suffering from spinsterphobia and elderly spinsters who haunt the memories of the would-be brides. Kitty Roche, one of Teresa's bridesmaids, fears she'll never marry because she is asthmatic and compares herself to "Miss Lewis, the Protestant woman on the Cork road, who'd never got married because of tuberculosis," and also to "old Hannah Flood, who had a bad hip" (396). The narrator declares that poor Kitty's problem is not "that no one would want to be saddled with a diseased wife" but rather her "recurrent skin complaint on her face and neck and hands" (376), a contradiction in logic.

Women are "naturally" associated with disease in many different cultures. Teresa's problem, of course, unlike some of the spinsters in the community, is not health. And attractiveness she does not lack. Her short-term reason for marrying Artie is that she is "a month and a half pregnant" (396) and needs a father for her unborn child. In the long term she needs economic support. Her sister Agnes is similarly motivated. She also selects her husband for the wrong reason, marrying out of necessity—she "had settled for George Tobin because George Tobin was employed in Cork and could take her away from the town" (400)—not marrying out of love.

Fear of spinsterhood motivates women like Teresa to get pregnant and women like Agnes to settle for something less than love. Fear of sexuality, on the other hand, causes women like Teresa's sister Loretta to destroy her marriage by preventing its consummation. Loretta feels humiliated because her marriage has failed; she now lives "with her parents, like an unmarried daughter again" (397). In most cases, nonetheless, the fear of spinsterhood is stronger than the fear of sexuality.

The fear of sexuality in Trevor's tales is subtly expressed. In this story the dialogue between Teresa, her bridesmaids, and her sisters warrants attention. Teresa's bridesmaids and her sisters wish her well in a worrying tone. Kitty does not congratulate the bride but says twice, "I hope you'll be happy," followed by an anxious qualifying wish, "I hope you'll be *all right*" (my italics). The other bridesmaid, Philomena, also qualifies her well-wishes: "We'll think of you. . . . We'll pray for you" (396)—a comment more appropriate to offer a bereaved widow weeping at the side of her husband's corpse than for a bride.[23]

That Loretta was abandoned by her husband adds to the uncertainty of the well-wishers here, but the primary point of the uncertainty reveals the fact that many women abhor sexuality, which they associate with animality and painful child-bearing. When Teresa tells her mother she is pregnant, "her mother [felt] sick in her stomach." Loretta first thought of becoming a nun when she was informed of this "bad" news. Loretta conveys the feminine communal attitude toward sexuality when she declares that "she didn't want to think about any of it, about what had happened to Teresa, and what would happen to her again" on her wedding night. Loretta indeed had "fainted when it had happened to herself, when [her husband had] come at her like a farm animal. She'd fought it like a mad thing" (398).

The enthusiastic comments of the young men regarding sexuality counter Loretta's despair over how women perceive sexuality when women suffer a narcissistic lover. In fact, masculine enthusiasms for one-sided sexuality are a potent factor in determining the attitudes of the women in Trevor's stories. Men are enthusiastic toward sexuality because men throughout the ages are represented in a dominant position—whether the partner is sexually fulfilled is of no matter. Women try to avoid providing men "a great bloody ride" (398), as Screw Doyle puts it to the groom when bragging about deflowering the bride, but here the potential of sexuality for promoting understanding between men and women is assailed. When the "best" man claims that "sure there was no harm done, Artie" (399), the rift is clear between the responses of men and women to sexuality—a significant threshold if one considers Freud and Erikson's respect for marriage, an honored institution that determines lifetime helpmates and sustains the energies of parents and community health.

Of course, the phallocentric community's unwritten assumption is that male sexuality should be given full rein in terms of promiscuous entanglements—despite Church doctrine. How is it that the only restraint demanded of men after marriage is to adjust to a monogamous life? Ironically, Eddie Boland encourages Artie's lust on the wedding night by saying, "Bedad, there'll be no holding you tonight," while Artie starts to worry that Teresa's baby is not his. Knowing that his friend seduced his bride makes it difficult for Artie to "pretend" love (400). Obviously, the double standard is breaking down, but men and women still function according to *separate* gender codes.

Both the bride's and groom's fathers, Mr. Atty and Mr. Cornish, celebrate "in their particular way the union of their children" (396). That they are distancing themselves from the women, however, does not bode well for the spirit of "union." The long-term result of masculine attitudes toward sex at odds with feminine attitudes dooms the marriage. The groom and his friends, the two fathers, and Father Hogan undermine the wedding ceremony, either consciously as in the case of the groom's and bride's fathers or unconsciously as in the case of the overly enthusiastic priest. The father of the bride—who "shared a feeling of unease, caused by being in the lounge-bar of Swanton's, with women present" (396)—attends the wedding reluctantly, hoping to spend the remainder of the day" with the men who enjoy "Power's whiskey" and "talking about greyhounds, keeping close to the bar" (395–96). The priest attends to the mothers of the bride and groom he coerced into marriage.

Given the disparity between the attitudes of various men and women toward courtship, sexuality, and marriage, Father Hogan's doublespeak seems appropriate: almost nothing he says is clearly understood by the women. Mrs. Tracy misconstrues his meaning when he exuberantly declares, "Aren't they as fine a couple as ever stepped out of this town?" (397). This cliché is taken literally to mean, "Are they leaving town?" because so many young couples escape to Cork and beyond. Father Hogan's mindless declaration, "It's a great day for a mother" (397), is ambivalent. Does he refer to the bride or the mother of the bride or the mother of the groom? Does he approve of Teresa's pregnancy? When he asks, "Isn't it great God gave them life?" (397), he could be praising God for creating them or praising them for the adultery that resulted in the baby.

This confusion in the priest's attempts to communicate reflects the confusion in the community over how to conform to Church doctrine regarding the sacrament of marriage. The only supposedly positive masculine models in this story are the priest and George Tobin, Agnes's husband. The latter, however, appears as an outsider who does not conform to the sexual codes that separate men from women and the gender codes discouraging men from nurturing. He is "a teetotaller and had no interest in either horses or greyhounds" like the other community fathers. This nonconformist remains outside the pub, "sitting patiently in the Ford Prefect, reading a comic to his children" (397), rather than joining the other drinking men. Agnes's marriage, the community believes, has "turned out well"

(397). George is a feminine man. But doesn't Trevor here imply that a man who seems subservient to his wife and who nurtures his children is mentally defective at best or alienated?

At the end Teresa sadly asserts that her own marriage will succeed because "they had no illusions" (402)—a terribly suspect notion. The men and women in Teresa's community live in different worlds. Gender codes produce illusions. The bride offers a final litany of the women her age who failed to achieve wedded bliss: Loretta, who suffers from sexual "shock"; Agnes, who is "[going] sour . . . [because] she married to escape from a town"; Philomena, who accepts "an elderly vet" whose "car smelt of cattle disinfectant" (396); and Kitty Roche, who sought "encouragement" from "anyone at all" (402).

James Joyce complains about attitudes in the Irish community toward marriage and sexuality by pointing to "the atrocities of the average husband," noting that the Catholic Church does not recognize our "full biological humanity" and declaring marriage "a simoniacal exchange."[24] But whether Puritan, Protestant, Evangelical, Jewish, or Catholic, sexuality is problematic. Literature everywhere suggests that men and women differ dramatically in their view of sexuality. Trevor is one of many modernists inferring that this difference can be destructive.

"The Property of Colette Nervi": Courtship and Theft

In "The Property of Colette Nervi" the "crippled and misshapen"[25] Dolores, like Bridie, also settles for an undesirable, middle-aged bachelor 20 years her senior in order to avoid spinsterhood. Community economics here encourage a coerced marriage when Dolores welcomes this bachelor—a neighbor twice her age and also a thief—as a husband.

The story begins by focusing on a business establishment, "a single shop at the crossroads" within walking distance of Drumgawnie Rath, a "ring of standing stones that predated history." The shop's owner, the widowed Mrs. Mullally, watches over her spinster daughter, Dolores, and somehow ekes out a living. The Mullally shop is not a center of the community but rather an incidental shop that tourists only notice if they are uncertain of the way to Drumgawnie Rath. The sightseers seem to be Mrs. Mullaly's only customers.

Being at a crossroads suggests uncertainty. Dolores's unknown future and her loneliness is evident as she observes with interest the arrival of two tourists in love—a French couple who park their car and don "gumboots" needed to make their way through weeds and water to see the landmark. Demonstrative in their affection for each other, they embrace—the man "leaning his body against" the woman, Colette Nervi. This victim of Cupid's arrow loses her purse because, distracted by the embrace, she leaves it on the roof of their car. Dolores barely observes and pays little attention to "what appeared to be a shadow . . . an object" left behind "carelessly" (87).

When Colette and her lover return from their walking tour of the area, Dolores again scrutinizes them. Alarmed over the loss of her purse, Colette and her lover search everywhere for the bag, but to no avail. Dolores cannot help them because she "had been too intent on the embrace to have observed" (93) what had happened to the purse—which is that her husband-to-be, "Old Garvey," had taken it after the couple embarked on their archaeological trek.

Dolores's life consists of watching tourists come and go, imagining their lives after they leave, and reading her father's wild west novels. It seems that her only opportunities to escape her isolated existence are related to the past and her father, who used to take his daughter to see the ancient stones and to town to peddle vegetables. Dolores feels little consolation for her father's death as she remembers when the Crowleys, their neighbors, occasionally "took her and her mother to mass" (89), and "once a year" her mother takes her to the nearby town of Rossaphin to shop and have "a meal in Love's Café" (89). The father, then, is associated with freedom of movement, whereas the daughter alone is restricted to home and shop.

Dolores's confinement in her mother's shop is also due to her confinement in an imperfect body, a disastrous circumstance for a young woman wanting to attract a husband. Despite her "affliction" (89)—her "leg, shrivelled to the bone as a result of infantile paralysis" (88)—she still pauses "for a moment by the looking-glass on her dressing table to smear fresh lipstick on her lips and to run a comb through her long black hair" (91). Apparently, however, the only "compliment" she had ever received was from her father, who compared her "brown and serious" eyes to those of his beloved dog. Suffering from "the ugliness of [her leg]" (89) in a world that demands women meet impossible standards of attractiveness and youth, Dolores reads wild west novels to identify with masculine power—an activity offering some compensation for losing her father and for feeling condemned to spinsterhood because of her deformed body.

When Henry Garvey visits the Mullallys' shop Dolores chats about "the Wild West stories she read" (96). Henry at first ignores her, but his miserly uncle convinces his nephew "that a substantial sum of money was owing to the Garvey family" because tourists had paid "no toll" for crossing their property on the way to Drumgawnie Rath (96). Thus Henry justifies stealing Colette Nervi's purse to acquire Mrs. Mullally's property by marrying Dolores.

This story, then, develops courtship and theft as point-counterpoint motifs. Henry, a man in his forties, drinks and gambles, even offering odds on "the year of his uncle's decease" (95). He also judges his chances with Dolores as a cynic might when he "scrutinise[s]" the young woman in her twenties: "He lifted his eyes to her face . . . her long dark hair . . . her shoulders . . . her hands" (97). Their courtship is framed not by love but by economics and chance circumstances that allow the theft of Colette Nervi's property. The groom gives the bride the necklace he stole. Dolores essentially allows herself to be sold because she longs for "the world of love and passion" represented in her father's novels about a sentimentalized and one-sided sexual world. As Bridie also sees it. Dolores longs to go to the Electric Dancehall, where she can dream that "she danced beneath fairyland lights" (98).

This romantic dreamer amazingly finds herself feeling "on a level with [Henry]" (99) during one of his frequent visits when he discusses business—whether or not he should sell "the old fellow's [his uncle's]" heifers (99). But few women are ever "on a level with" a man in Trevor's stories. Dolores knows enough not to offer advice; instead she shrugs, implying that "Henry Garvey was his own master, that he alone had the privilege of reaching a decision about his late uncle's heifers" (100) or, as he calls them, "lassies" not worth "the trouble" of keeping.

Dolores allows Henry to marry into the shop just like her father because "he would bring with him the rent for the grazing of his fields," and "he could take her father's place" (100). She imagines herself with Henry, her "crutch secure on the pavement" (100) as she limps "beside him towards the cinema at Ballyreddy." Economic security is the issue. A crutch is never secure.

Henry's declaration—of course not motivated by love—that "there's nothing I like better than talking . . . to you" (101) is a "compliment" paid "without looking at [Dolores]." He does not talk "with" her. She is silent except when retelling plots from her father's novels. For the most part "she did not reply" (100). The courtship involves little communication, no sharing. Those who attend the wedding are "all the shop's customers" (103), not family or friends.

Moreover, Henry's discussions focus on fixed races or Tim Durcan's efforts to teach the groom-to-be how to drive: "a man driving a car needed to be sensitive with the clutch and the accelerator" (103). There is little in the story to suggest that Henry will be sensitive on his wedding night. Dolores's dreams before the wedding clarify every woman's nightmare—that her future husband will "ride away like one of the cowboys of the Wild West" (104). Dolores wonders if Henry, "being a bachelor for so long" (104), might prefer a room of his own. She would "share her mother's room" just as all women share the same fate. Like Bridie, Dolores cannot really conceive of herself as equal partner to a prospective husband.

"Kathleen's Field": The Son's Inheritance

"Kathleen's Field" is the most sinister story in this vein—a vivid and painful portrait of feminine vulnerability and parental narcissism. Hagerty, the father in this story, unknowingly drives his daughter to despair as surely as he drives three bullocks to market in a futile attempt to muster enough money to purchase a lush field adjacent to his farm. Establishing his son's financial security is the father's goal. He worries that his eldest son's inheritance of the farm and land will be inadequate to attract a good wife. He worries about being abandoned by the three younger of his 10 children, the elder seven having already emigrated because of the poor rural economy. Con is his only remaining son, Biddy and Kathleen the last of his daughters.

Thus Hagerty justifies his scheme to ensure that his remaining son and two daughters remain within his grasp; his son especially must be restrained "from being tempted by Kilburn or Chicago" (223). He manipulates "his youngest daughter," the 16-year-old Kathleen, whom he rationalizes as "his favorite" (232), until she agrees to work for the pretentious owners of Shaughnessy's Provisions and Bar. Her wages are applied against the father's debt so that Con "would be left secure" and the mentally defective Biddy "would be provided for" (233). This father unwittingly sells his daughter Kathleen into slavery. Mrs. Shaughnessy clarifies the arrangement when she tells her husband that Hagerty "has a girl for us" (234), as if claiming her "property." The father reassures the lady of the pub that her efforts to train his daughter will not be wasted: she will not "go off to get married" (233).

When her father explains that her "wages . . . would be held back and set against the debt" as a "convenience" (238), Kathleen notices her father's relief: "the fatigue in his face had given way to an excited pleasure" (238).

She responds by agreeing with his plan. His suffering is over, hers just started.

This is yet another case of the daughter nurturing her father: the daughter here is focused on the father's pain—on his needs rather than her own. It does not seem to matter to the father that the son's welfare is won as the daughter's welfare is sacrificed. The loan for the land and the "loan" of a daughter are both reduced to a matter of doing business (235). Whereas purchasing the field expands the borders of her father's farm, the daughter's "field" of existence is radically circumscribed. This conforming daughter suffers unbearable working conditions and an overbearing taskmaster, Mrs. Shaughnessy, who deems Kathleen "raw," resolves "to train every inch of her" (233), and complains about her "country accent" (243). Worse, the child-molesting husband abuses the inexperienced young girl. This devious molester "liked the style" of having a servant (234) because it afforded him the opportunity to sexually harass Kathleen.

Mrs. Shaughnessy expresses to Kathleen's father her worry that after spending a year training his daughter she'd "go off and get married" (233). A cruel irony obtains when Hagerty assures his investor that "Kathleen wouldn't go running off, no fear of that" (234)—exactly the fear that inspired his scheme in the first place to prevent her from leaving *him*.

The first view of Kathleen on the job focuses on her alarm (236) and the fact that Mrs. Shaughnessy renames her new servant "Kitty," the name of the servant Kathleen has replaced. Mrs. Shaughnessy thus strips Kathleen of her identity and avoids the bother of herself adjusting to change. That this overbearing woman wants to call her new servant according to the name of a past one testifies to her regressive traits. Mrs. Shaughnessy complains that her last "girl" was "queer" because she ate raw onions (234), but the reader suspects this was the young woman's ploy to escape the clutches of Mr. Shaughnessy, who "liked to have a maid about the house" (234) to molest.

Mrs. Shaughnessy trains Kathleen to set the table, cut kindling, dust "all the places where grime would gather," and rake the yard. Kitty's uniforms do not fit Kathleen well, making her uncomfortable. She is restricted to using the outhouse. And Mrs. Shaughnessy refers to her abusive husband as Kathleen's "master" (244). Kathleen works six days, going home only on Sundays. During one visit she explains to her parents that she doesn't want to return, but her mother expresses her fears that the farm will consequently fail, the family will end up "no better than tinkers" (245). The good daughter returns to the Shaughnessy establishment despite Mr. Shaughnessy's bold advances: "his hands passing over her clothes" (248). His attentions only deepen an old track—her memories of rejection because boys her own age never tried to kiss her. Mr. Crawley, the butcher, often asks her if she's "going dancing," but "no one displayed any interest in her whatsoever" (250). The shame that Kathleen feels over what becomes in her mind a "surreptitious relationship" (249) with Mr. Shaughnessy is worsened by the shame of not being courted, of a future most certainly that of the spinster maid abused by "a grey-haired man" (Mr. Shaughnessy? her father?) because "a bargain was a bargain" (251), as her mother puts it in the last line of the story.

"The Wedding in the Garden": An Initiation into Womanhood

Those who labor in fields or work as servants of the great house in Trevor's stories would seem at odds with those who celebrate weddings in gardens. As in "Kathleen's Field," however, the son's inheritance is a central issue in "Wedding in the Garden," and it is a vulnerable young woman who suffers because of this concern. Moreover, we also again explore the terrible rift between men and women owing to differing attitudes toward sexuality and marriage.

Gender differences in "The Wedding in the Garden" are complicated by class differences. Gender and class codes determine not only *whether* one marries but also *who* one marries. Although Mrs. Congreve "married beneath her" and indeed the Protestant British aristocracy would normally shun Mr. Congreve, the middle-class proprietor of the Royal Hotel, still her son, Christopher, must seek a higher level. The plot, then, centers on an appalling event from the perspective of the Congreves, who focus strictly on economic concerns: Christopher seduces their servant girl, Dervla. These parents worry that because of this indiscretion the "stylish" family pretense will not be maintained.

This story most suitably ends this discussion of gender and marriage because it subtly raises issues related to the covert nature of the double sex standard: the code that encourages the promiscuous behavior of men worried about their manhood and the frigidity of "ladies" worried about their virginity—with servant girls somewhat exempted.

The authority of the Church and the aristocracy are represented by the "clerical sombreness" of Mr. Congreve's "clothes" and the "ladylike" nature of Mrs. Congreve mentioned right at the start. Social hierarchies are then undercut when this paragraph ends with a superb double entendre.

The voice of the young heir's lust merges for an instant with a voice expressing lower-class values, which have been determined by the pretentious upper class. More precisely, Dervla's lower-class father defines aristocratic virtue: "The Congreves have great *breeding* in them."[26] The "breeding" that takes place between Dervla and Christopher would certainly not meet with her father's approval. The elevated discourse of the upper class sometimes imitated by the working class encourages the reader's disdain for such considerations as not just "good" but "great breeding."

The proprietors of the Royal Hotel are concerned with improprieties of class that would undermine their stature in the community. They "naturally" condemn Christopher's affair with the maid. Such socioeconomic concerns as class—Mrs. Congreve's "stylishness" and that of her children "imbued with this through the accident of their birth"—are, in Trevor's view, superficial differences. Nonetheless, the Congreves demand that Christopher marry an affluent Protestant minister's daughter. Dervla is condemned to the life of a servant/spinster devastated by lost love.

Class codes coincide with gender codes as this story develops. In a typical phallocentric and classist society, women and servants are often invisible. Christopher does not apparently notice the new servant, Dervla, for "a year or so" (264), perhaps not until he reaches puberty. She appears at first as "a solitary figure in a black coat"; Christopher "didn't [even] know her name or what her face was like" (264). Servants are faceless. She is simply "the girl." His sense of Dervla is so vague that he "couldn't remember the first time he'd been aware of her." Likewise, his sisters "paid her no attention," even though she was "a child as they were" (264). Finally, Christopher, while wandering about town, "had never noticed Thomas MacDonagh Street," Dervla's neighborhood. When he does finally notice the young and physically attractive servant, he "[follows] with his eyes . . . the movement of Dervla's hips beneath her black dress" (269). This sort of attention is of course suspect.

Dervla's invisibility is most subtly conveyed when Trevor represents Christopher's return from boarding school. Greeted by "a great fuss," "excited" sisters, and his father, apparently anxious to hear his son's "tale of the long journey from Dublin," Christopher recalls his experiences at boarding school to an eager audience, which at first seems to include only the family. The presence of the servants is only evident halfway through the paragraph when abruptly one line of direct dialogue intrudes: "Like the game of tennis it would be," the yardman Artie here responding to Dervla's inquiry about "what cricket was" (268). This snatch of dialogue, the second half of the exchange, then transfers the reader's attention from Christopher's story of boarding-school exploits to Dervla's "excited" interest, and the second half of the paragraph relates Dervla's vicarious living of Christopher's experiences.

This "turn" in a single paragraph effectively conveys the invisibility of the servant class, yet at the same time it infers Dervla's interest in the event, although the Congreves ignore her. Her inspired imaginings reprocess Christopher's story of "the big grey house . . . and bells always ringing, and morning assemblies, and the march through cloisters to the chapel" (268). The breathlessness inferred by the sequence of "and . . . and . . . and" approaches a sense of awe, which is also felt by Christopher's sisters, who stand on the sidelines and are also generally ignored.

Women and servants *are*, on the other hand, noticed if they behave as if they do not know their proper place, if they do not observe "the formalities," as Mr. Congreve puts it. Mary, the elderly and "rheumaticky" maid Dervla replaces, refuses Mr. Congreve's offer for her to rest on her long way to her attic bedroom: "'It was unseemly,' Dervla had heard old Mary saying in the kitchen" (268–69), that servants should sit on the furniture. Voice becomes complicated in this passage as we are told by a narrator what Dervla heard old Mary and Mr. Congreve say. Sequence provides a clue as to whose voice we hear: Mr. Congreve complains that "it took [Mary] half a day . . . to mount the stairs to her bedroom at the top of the hotel, and the other half to descend it." This criticism darkens the atmosphere of the next sentence, the cheery claim (probably the servants' misconception) that Mr. Congreve "was fond of" Mary.

Similarly, this paragraph ends with another suspect conclusion that "Mr. Congreve was devil-may-care about matters like that." This sentence continues with a series of elitist and chauvinist considerations surely meant to represent Mr. Congreve's ambitious perspective on proprieties governing the servants—"but what would a visitor say if he came out of his bedroom and found a uniformed maid in an armchair? What would Byrne from Horton's say, or Boylan the insurance man?" (269). The "visitors" who would be disturbed by a servant overstepping her bounds are presumed to be men. The next paragraph represents Mr. Congreve's concern over "the formalities" (269). Surely his attention to Mary's infirmities are insincere, not only because she is a servant but also because she is a woman.

Mr. Congreve charms Dervla with the same pretense of interest as he does all the servants when he seems to care about the infirmities of the old maid, Mary. The master of the house tries to converse with the younger maid by "asking how her father was." Dervla is "somehow—in front of him . . . embarrassed" and later suffers "a nightmare . . . that [Mr. Congreve] was in *the* house on Thomas MacDonagh Street and that her mother was on her knees, scrubbing the stone floor of the scullery" (271; my italics). Reluctant to claim her home as "my house," she realizes the disparity between her family and Christopher's.

Disparities owing to class are clear when we consider the differences between Dervla's and Christopher's families. Disparities owing to gender are clear as Christopher relates to Dervla and also to his sisters. Sons are given preferential treatment over daughters early in their development and emphatically so when they approach manhood. In this case Christopher avoids his sisters because he wants "to be alone at that time of his growing up"; "his sisters [are] too chattery" (264–65). Indeed, Christopher's puberty is defined in terms of romanticized notions of a boy's initiation into manhood, his need to be "alone" (264)—that is, not in the company of girls—and to explore the world beyond the home. His "wanderings about the town" (264) end with the shops where as a child he bought sweets but now buys *Our Boys, Film Fun,* and *Wide World* (265).

Whereas Christopher enjoys "lingering by the shops that sold fruit and confectionery" (265) and Christopher's sisters enjoy playing games in the garden, Dervla seems to work at least a 12-hour day, "arriving before breakfast, cycling home again in the late evening" (264). The difference here depends on class differences more than those of gender, but of course aristocratic attitudes toward the working class often involve drawing boundaries according to what is "natural." "Nature" likewise limits women economically and physically. Christopher knows it is not "natural in any way at all" (270) for him to sit with Dervla on a rug in the sun or "to wheel the bicycle of the dining-room maid" (270). Trevor appropriately allows much more space to define Dervla's awareness of class difference than to define Christopher's, whose awareness of such differences eventually causes him to abandon the maid.

Dervla in fact is "fascinated" (262) by the status, "stylishness," and wealth of her employers, whose worth is measured according to their possessions. Christopher's "grand" initialed "green trunk" captures her imagination each time he returns home from boarding school. She imagines the Congreves in "their motor-car, an old Renault" (263), surely in a state of grace when they "[make] the journey to the Protestant church" (263) and "the bell ceased to chime" (264) upon their arrival.

Despite the Congreves' conformity to theological dogma on regular church attendance here, other transgressions seem less weighty. Trevor relates Dervla's seduction by Christopher in a very few lines, affording this event very little space in comparison with other passages—say, those focused on status symbols, which are developed at some length. The seduction, the first tender tryst, encompasses six sentences strategically positioned to follow Dervla's father's litany of her marriage prospects—Buzzy Carroll, who worked in Catigan's hardware; Flynn; Chappie; Butty; Streak; and the nameless "porter . . . [whose] toes joined together in such a peculiar way that he showed them to people" (271). Trevor's concision suggests the ease with which Christopher initiates the affair by declaring, "I'm fond of you, Dervla," and then leading "her upstairs to Room 14, a tiny bedroom" (272). There follows a brief discussion of how the seduction developed into a routine. In the seventh sentence of this sequence we learn that "after that first afternoon they met often to embrace in Room 14." In the eighth sentence Christopher declares, "They would marry [and] live in the hotel, just like his parents" (272).

The promise of this loving relationship is also all-to-briefly developed in the bat of an eye when "the warmth of their bodies [becomes] a single warmth." Christopher's "love" for Dervla changes his attitude toward his community, which he had previously seen as "a higgledy-piggledy conglomeration of dwellings, an ugly place." After the affair he sees his community as "Dervla's town, and . . . his own; together they belonged there" (273). That basic human need for a sense of belonging is central to the story. Christopher envisions his future: "in middle age [he walks] through [the town's] narrow streets . . . returning to the hotel and going at once to embrace the wife he loved with a passion that had not changed" (273)—again, a fleeting embrace.

Trevor here does celebrate the potential of love to nurture the lovers' sense of belonging—to each other and to their community. Love does stave off the ravages of time, does overcome the adolescent's sense of alienation. The promise of Dervla and Christopher's love, however, cannot last. Dervla's father first intrudes. Trevor frames the seduction passage by the paternal voice urging his daughter to accept suitors of her own class. The frame is completed by her father's insistence, "Not a bad fella at all. . . . Young Carroll." And Dervla wonders "what on earth [her father would] say if he knew about Room 14" (273).

The need to belong reappears when Mother Congreve develops five reasons to convince Dervla to relinquish Christopher. She admonishes Dervla to consider "propriety" given certain social hierarchies ("there are differences between you and Christopher that cannot be overlooked. . . . Christopher is not of your class, Dervla. He is not of your religion" [274]). She shames Dervla by appealing to her sense of honesty and duty (she blames the poor maid for "betraying" their trust). She clarifies the relationship of the powerful ruling class to the servant class in terms of economics (she threatens that Dervla will lose her job, Christopher his inheritance). She tries to instill a feeling of obligation in Dervla ("We have trained you, you know. We have done a lot" [276])—obligation that should yield to authority. Most cleverly, she targets the adolescent's need to belong when she asks, "Don't you feel you belong in the Royal, Dervla? . . . You will not be asked to leave" (275–76).

The Church further undermines Dervla's determination to defend her love. Dervla considers that "it was a sin" (277) and relucantly writes to Christopher, conforming to his mother's wish that the maid be the one to break off the affair. After he receives Dervla's letter written in "tidy, convent handwriting" and declaring the affair over, Christopher's "bewilderment turned to anger" (277), a conditioned masculine response to loss. Before he can confront Dervla, his father confronts him, chastizing him for "messing about with maids" (277) and then exhibiting the typical masculine perspective on sexual violations of women: "it's a bit of a storm in a tea-cup" (278). Only after having a clear sense of his parents' attitudes does Christopher confront Dervla with, "Is it priests?" and "Did my mother speak to you?" Dervla answers in the affirmative—"Your mother only said a few things" (278)—but Christopher is unresponsive to her reply. The moment of opportunity to seize love and retrieve his ethical sense is lost. He does not question Dervla enough and all too quickly becomes "reconciled to the loss of their relationship [because] between the lines of her letter there had been a finality" (278). The "finality," however, is based on class lines.

When the no-longer-maiden maid finally confesses to "the priests" about "the sinning that had been so pleasurable in Room 14" (279), the priest, like Christopher's father, sees the servant's affair as a "misdemeanour" (279). Dervla herself comes to realize that her lover "would *naturally* wish to forget it now: For him, Room 14 must have come to seem like an adventure in indiscretion, as *naturally* his parents had seen it" (280; my italics).

Dervla remains in the Royal Hotel and is forced to observe the development of Christopher's interest in the archdeacon's beautiful daughter. The maid listens to stories told by the more suitable maiden, who converses during dinner about her past. Dervla feels abandoned while "expertly disposing of chop bones or bits of left-behind fat" (280). She herself was as easily disposed of and has become "leftovers." Her realization "that this was the girl who was going to take her place, in [Christopher's] life" is more poignant on Christopher's wedding day, when "a new maid with spectacles" (281) appears, probably to replace Dervla just as Dervla replaced Mary.

The reality of what was lost fades because the routine of "Dervla [clearing] away the dishes" (280) no longer calls attention to young love. The servant is again invisible. Dervla's previous prayers—ironically, to "the Virgin's liquid eyes"—that Christopher's "little finger might accidentally touch her hand" (271) are soon eclipsed by confessions. By the time of his wedding, in fact, the ritual of confession and the ritual of the wedding toast have lost meaning. Pretense causes the "excess of emotion in the garden, an excess of smiles and tears and happiness and love" expressed by "glasses . . . held up endlessly, toast after toast" (282).

Indeed, the marriage celebration is really "a business arrangement," like the archdeacon's agreement "as convention demanded" to pay for the reception to be held at the hotel. Christopher realizes that Dervla "was not beautiful" even though "once, not knowing much about it, he had imagined she was." When he acknowledges that there "was something less palpable [than physical beauty] that distinguished her" (283), we are left to ponder exactly what the groom has in mind. What is it that finally distinguishes the uniformed maid? It was precisely Dervla's "palpability" or physical attractiveness that first caused Christopher to notice his "servant."

The priests finally "get" Dervla; the archdeacon's daughter "gets" Christopher. And yet a sense of less permeates this outcome. The bride's unnaturally beautiful "skin like the porcelain of a doll's skin" causes us to question her humanity. Routine, ritual, convention, the civility of shared memories, and "speeches . . . made in the sunshine" (281) round out our days. The cliché-ridden voices of various community members resound throughout the garden as guests share fond memories of the past to affirm that they truly "belong" in this elegant present.

Whereas Dervla's father had admired his wife for having "the strength of an ox," thereby surviving childbirth and producing Dervla at the age of 42, Christopher's bride is virginal, her hand "as delicate as the petal of a flower" (283). The point of the story, nevertheless, is that few women possess the strength to emerge from an affair without scars—sometimes wounds that eclipse any possibility for wedded bliss. Dervla's vulnerability is clear when Christopher realizes, "She would indeed not ever marry" (283), and then turns away.

The vulnerability of women emerges most emphatically at the end of the story when we are surprised to discover that Christopher's sexual adventures may not have been limited to his purported love for Dervla. The best man, Tom Gouvernet, declares that "Christopher had been "a right Lothario" with a "shocking reputation at school" (284), then encourages the bride to remember her groom's best man when she gets "tired" (284) of her new husband. The mood here changes; actually it is not much different from the mood of the best man in "Teresa's Wedding" (no harm done by his "great bloody ride"). This jubilant mood is ominous: the groom more likely will tire of the bride.

Finally, the disparity between Dervla's and Christopher's perceptions of their "romance" and the conventions of "Ancient Romance," as Bakhtin explains it, may sharpen the reader's conception of the circumstances in this story. In ancient romance the boy and girl are expected to be "exceptionally chaste." At the end of this story the best man casts doubt on Christopher's chastity when he seduced Dervla—also on his pretense of romantic feeling. Dervla, on the other hand, retains her innocence because she maintains her fidelity to her lover, like the classic case of the romantic heroine.

In ancient romance the lovers are beset with "obstacles that retard and delay their union," as Bakhtin explains it. The deft lover here wins Dervla's immediate submission. The hero and heroine do not know their lineage in ancient romance: "The first meeting of hero and heroine and the sudden flare up of their passion for each other is the starting point for plot movement; the end point for plot movement is their successful union in marriage." Their "love remains absolutely unchanged. . . their chastity is preserved." In this story Dervla and Christopher, conversely, are all too aware of their lineage. Their first meeting is a nonevent. The plot develops around the dramatic change of events when Dervla is confronted by Christopher's mother.

In ancient romance the heroine withstands trials and tests while maintaining her fidelity, which proves her triumph over her humble origins. Dervla is tested but never rises above her class. The "maid" is not transformed into "lady," and in fact she is fallen, no longer a "maiden." The hero of ancient romance does not give in to materialistic temptations as Christopher does when conforming to parental authority in order to preserve "his inheritance," which Trevor ironically defines early in the novel in terms of a "greenish. . . threadbare" carpet (267).

Christopher realizes that he must endure a lifetime of pretense and suffer the constant gaze of his faithful servant: "while he and his parents could successfully bury a part of the past, Dervla could not. It had never occurred to him that because she was the girl she was she did not appreciate that some experiences were best forgotten. . . . [Such] subtleties had

81

naturally eluded the dining room maid" (283–84). Christopher wishes he had told his bride about Dervla and realizes he cannot because the Archdeacon's daughter would certainly dismiss her servant. Poignant irony obtains in the groom's scruples here as the reader conflates "a promise made to a dining-room maid [that] must be honoured" (284) with the promise to marry Dervla that was not honored.

Marriages are not likely to succeed if based on secrets and determined by business "arrangements"—the Congreves' conniving a case in point. Although gender codes are central to the stories addressed here, the force of "business as usual" also has been a constant undercurrent.

Commerce, Communication, and the Business Class: The Comic Tales

Trevor's stories about the world of commerce encourage laughter inspired by human recognition and the kind of humble self-defense/self-love needed for a strong sense of community. Whether focused on likable bunglers or despicable and materialistic egoists who damage others, these stories make the reader laugh with a blush, wistfully wishing, "If only *I* could tell one like that," knowing that the ability to be such a teller may depend on having been such a fool.

Laughable and pathetically self-absorbed, Trevor's comic protagonists carry the self's flag for survival's sake, often treading the battleground of middle age. Comedy at its best, these stories develop single-minded protagonists struggling in a ludicrous workaday world of pretense, lockstep self-interest, and conformity.[27]

The four representative comic masterpieces of human insight to be considered here are like many others in which Trevor studies various businesses and businesspeople or professionals (institutional do-gooders) working in industry, education, or human services (social workers, psychologists). In these stories business "arrangements" tend to replace human relationships. Commerce impairs communication. Companionship, meaningful intimacy, and fidelity are outmoded. Someone in power (often money power) indifferently violates a human heart, or a lovestruck protagonist hilariously runs amok because of financial limitations or worldly ambitions. And we laugh. As Mark Mortimer's notes,

> Trevor is above all a great humourist, gifted with the healthy laughter of the great comic writers—Cervantes, Shakespeare, Molière, Joyce—and balancing sadness and sordidness with fantasy and fun. He is also a deeply compassionate author who can, over and over again, engage his reader's sympathy with the motley throng he portrays. If, as Shaw once said, the best kind of humour "draws a tear along with it," then [Trevor] rates high.[28]

Focusing on economics as a travel agent, salesclerk, shopkeeper, pornographer, advertising artist, or welfare do-gooder might see it, these stories force readers to peel off the bandages hiding the wounds of a socially competitive, culturally deprived economic life. A writer sympathetic to the suffering and struggle of those in the lower echelons of society, Trevor, according to Doris Betts, "is steadily against the smug and self-righteous."[29] Yet we should also recognize "the high value [Trevor's] fictions persistently grant to everyday humanity," as Valentine Cunningham notes.[30] That the everyday humanity of the business world has been satanically represented by such diverse world figures as Marx, Lenin, Stalin, Hitler, and Mao Tse-tung should encourage us to value the humanity of Trevor's comedy, the comic at the heart's core—comedy that must be appreciated, even if barbed. And Trevor's comic tales, despite their author's compassion, are indeed barbed.

Two of Trevor's best stories about courtship in the business world are "Lovers of Their Time," a romance about a travel agent's affair with a drugstore clerk, and "The Forty-seventh Saturday," a romance that runs its course as though regulated like a business. "Mulvihill's Memorial," on the other hand, is far from a romance, conveying as it does a rather sad sense of alienation along with self-conscious, sexually defensive hilarity. This story associates the advertising world with the business of pornography. And, finally, in "Broken Homes" the commercialization of caretaking, for children and the elderly, receives attention as a particular wise old woman suffers from those who approach suffering in the spirit of "big business."

Trevor's experience working in an advertising agency allowed him to study at close hand the effect of contemporary advertising on human relationships. In many of these comic stories, advertisements transmogrify sexuality from a means of expressing tenderness to a commodity subtly promoted on the open market. Women measure their "success" in the material world according to their ability to fit the stereotypes of beauty that commercials promote, thus attracting the "successful" man. Men measure their "success" in the material world according to their ability to possess and control women—to get the girl.[31]

Advertising appeals not only to those seeking sexual gratification but also to those wanting to control their destiny—in essence to master their existence by cultivating a false sense of power, thereby exercising control over any number of authority figures who can force us into helpless situations: priests, teachers, headmasters, landlords, psychologists, social workers, employers, community fathers, government officials, and, in the Anglo-Irish context, even terrorists. Narcissistic needs deter those in the fast lane of material success from offering affection to those beyond an immediate circle of family and friends. Differences related to gender, class, religion, and nationality become bulwarks around exclusive communities, rural or urban.

Lovers Out of Sync

"Lovers of Their Time" is a "love" story that somehow seems to focus more on economics than on love. This story starts with a commercial exchange: on an errand for his wife, the travel agent, Norman Britt, buys "toothpaste and emery boards" for her, ironically *from* his lover-to-be, Marie, a clerk at Green's the Chemist. Norman eroticizes this "moment when [Marie] handed him his change"; he later recalls it "deliciously" (609) and chooses to replay the event in his daydreams. Considerate husbands run errands for their wives, the reader may note. What to do with Norman's adultery and seduction of the young virgin, Marie?

Establishing the first glimmers of a tryst in a drugstore at the start dislocates the reader's attention: commercial setting detracts from the usual interest in character. The plot in fact seems structured around "places"—the first meeting at the drugstore and subsequent meetings at the travel agency, the Drummer Boy pub, the Paddington train station, and the Great Western Royal Hotel, where the loving couple finally consummate their affair in a public bathroom. Focusing on place rather than character encourages readers to be less sympathetic toward the husband/lover, the wife, and the mistress.

Indeed accompanied by the Drummer Boy, the middle-aged Norman marks time nursing tenderly memories of his affair with Marie, "looking back [to] . . . that particular decade," the 1960s and the New Year's Day it all began. As he reminisces, Norman aggrandizes the importance of a personal event by relating it to great historical moments: "Could it have happened . . . at any other time except the 1960s?" (613), Norman asks himself, convinced that the answer is self-evident. Then infidelity and betrayal seemed the natural thing to do.

Trevor's answer to this question, however, might be different from Norman's because, although comically mottled with bric-a-bracs of contemporary life and various regalia of advertising, the story finally addresses the transience of existence and the mystery of personal identity, which all too often depend on relationships to others (parents, lover, wife) rather than on oneself. A certain understated desperation drives Norman to offer Marie a tinseled hope for a meaningful relationship. This understated desperation allows us to feel sorry for the protagonist while at the same time it intensifies the story's humor—for the same reason that shell-shocked soldiers laugh when telling of close calls.

At the start of the story a third-person narrator introduces the protagonist, Norman, who soberly ruminates about a past affair with a younger woman as might the great poets—first rendering the affair monumental by relating it to public time, a bank holiday. Norman claims importance for memories of his personal life because he celebrated his affair with Marie "long before that day became a holiday in England." He then relates the affair to an ancient archetype—celebrating the new year. New Year's Day is an appropriate starting point for such an event because it is the time we throw out the old (Norman's wife, Hilda) and bring in the new (Marie). Thus the Changing of the Wives unmasks the child.

Unfortunately, the child in this case lacks an authentic self. Outlined right at the start, occupation is the primary determiner of identity and authenticity for the threesome. Norman knows Marie's name first according to the "badge" on her pharmacy "shopcoat." Norman seems to know his own name because "it said so on a small plastic name-plate in front of his position in the travel agency where he worked" (606). The sexually aggressive wife, Hilda, "worked at home, assembling jewelry for a firm that paid her on a production basis" (606).

An economy based on production invades the home in Hilda's case and ultimately invades the hearts of Norman, Hilda, and Marie, members of a love triangle struggling in an assembly-line world. Being in a long line of customers or part of "a sizable collection of [Marie's] 'Fellas'" (606) weakens one's identity. When Norman first leaves Marie at the drugstore counter, she is already "serving another customer" (607).

Throughout Trevor's comic tales focused on the business world, self-worth is most importantly measured according to appearances—specifically, those paradigms determined by idealized types promoted on television and the radio, in film, romance novels, and advertising—Norman's "David Niven moustache" (606) and his "[Sinatra] eyes" (610).

The voice of the census worker further determines one's identity: statistical information such as place of residence and age (for Mr. and Mrs. Britt, Putney, both age 40; for Marie, Reading, age 28). Norman's height is given, however imprecisely ("tall"), as well as his build ("thin"). Hilda's build ("thin also") and appearance ("grey . . . pale") is vaguely outlined in one sentence.

The space given to describe this husband and wife is disproportionate to the more detailed and "poetic" physical description of Marie—one conveying Norman's first impression of this shopgirl, who seems "tartish," a tender morsel with "lips like sausage," a garish simile—especially so given the bland treatment of the other characters.

Appearances, then, prove deceptive: Hilda appears to be "dried up" (609, 616) but behaves like a nymphomaniac; Marie appears at first to be "a tart" (621) but is virginal, "prim and proper" (616); Norman's boss, Blackstaff, reveals that his "stout middle-aged," asexual wife is actually passionate. This wife cannot be judged superficially because "appearance[s] . . . apparently belied much" (617).

Furthermore, descriptions of Marie's appearance define Norman's character more than Marie's, encouraging the reader to examine his response to her. His egoism is the point when he decides that "the occasion [of buying her a drink] could easily lead to a hug" (606), not to mention his misjudgment when he decides she is "tartish." From Norman's perspective, Marie is "a little outside reality . . . there to desire, to glow erotically . . . to light cigarettes for in a dream" (606). But he does not see that her reality is clouded because he reconstructs her *exactly* to suit his dreams, which in turn have been determined by the media: she is a type of "girl as voluptuous as any of James Bond" (621).

Norman wants to be associated with "an eyeful" (608), who in fact loses her identity when he imagines showing her off to Ron Stocks and Mr. Blackstaff in the pub. Then she is no longer "Marie" but "the girl from Green's the Chemist" (607), a female showpiece or, as Hilda refers to her, "this piece [Norman] fancies" (619). Marie is not important for her own sake but only as an appendage to Norman's ego. Relating to others according to projections of our own needs is like knowing people according to occupation, superficial appearances, and vital statistics. So is trying to communicate through "business jargon," which destroys the immediacy of relationships, to say the least. Norman knows that the "unfussy voice he'd used [with Marie] was a business one" (607).

Comic innuendoes fray the edges of Norman's sentimental romanticism as the language of covert love gets mixed up with the discourse of business and, appropriately, the need to establish timelines. Racing ahead, Norman wants to control time and wangles a meeting with Marie because he is most interested in what will happen after "their bit of business" is over. He remarks, "If you need any help"; she replies, "Just the bookings" (what else?; 607).

Lagging behind, Marie seems to ignore time, neglecting to keep her appointment with Norman at Travel-Wide. By chance meeting Marie on the street and undaunted by being stood up by her, Norman encourages her to come "some other time." The starstruck lover calculates the number of times in his office it will take to seduce her (first she'll book the flight, then pick up tickets).

Unsuspecting, Marie inverts the seller-customer relationship when she argues, perhaps coyly, that *he* "wouldn't have the time," declaring that *she* would be an imposition on *him*. He suggests their "business" will only take 10 minutes—certainly enough time for a one-night stand. In the context of this business arrangement, Marie says twice that she is "taking advantage" (607) of Norman, inverting the stereotype that men take advantage of women sexually. Later she again asserts herself when she argues that she "should pay" (608), resisting the old-fashioned stereotype that men pay for women.

The sexual suggestiveness of the dialogue continues. Norman promises to help Marie book her vacation, which is of course a pretense on the way to the seduction—a pretense made stark by double entendre. She offers to "slip out" at 4 P.M. to meet him. He promises to "keep an eye out for [her]" (607), revealing a touch of voyeurism. She declares, "We want to fix it up" (607), meaning the vacation, but the reader realizes that blind dates are usually "fixed up" and men on the prowl are "up." Later, having lunch at the Drummer Boy, the would-be lover plans to "buy [Marie] another gin and peppermint to get her going" (611)—discourse more appropriate to the auto mechanic than to the lover. The fact that Norman engineers every move he makes to seduce Marie undermines the seriousness of his sentimental romanticism.

Much of the third-person narrative in the first half of the story relates Norman's perspective, although the reader learns Marie's inner thoughts now and then—for instance, her awareness that "he was making a pass" (610). Just before the seduction, however, reality sharpens the narrative edge, which is complicated by subtle authorial tracks. Trevor develops irony with carefully placed euphemisms—"Romance ruled their brief *sojourns* [trips to the bathroom?]"; with hyperbole—"love *sanctified* . . . the passion of their physical intimacy" (617); and with direct authorial intrusions such as "or so they believed" (617). It is the author who declares that Norman's "love affair . . . was touched with the same preposterousness" as "a jolly trash-can, overflowed with noise and colour" on "Carnaby Street" (616). Is it possible to experience "a passing *idyll*, in the bathroom of a hotel" (617)? Can the privacy needed for intimate love be found in a public bathroom?

Norman declares that his affair with Marie is "different" from "Hilda's bedroom appetites" (616), but the story offers no evidence to support his claim. There are no tender descriptions of their embrace. Trevor chooses not to detail "the passion of [Norman and Marie's] physical intimacy" (617) but instead develops at this crucial point a sort of mini-subplot. Let's call it the journey of the towel, which travels from Marie's handbag to the bathroom, where it is used by the lovers and returned in a dampened state to Marie's handbag, finally to be transported home.

Moreover, lyrics mentioned in the next paragraph further waylay our Peeping Tom instincts. The line "Why she had to go I don't know" prefigures the course of the affair as it brings to mind the Beatles, "all those lonely people" and "the lonely hearts club band." Yet the narrator's lens fails to catch even a glimpse of the main event and instead refocuses on the Drummer Boy and Mr. Blackstaff's "coarseness" when he turns his intimacies with his wife into a joke by sharing the "details about [her] . . . more intimate preferences" (617) just when the reader expects the narrator to provide such details in the case of Norman and Marie.

Numerous other techniques serve as a reality check. The love banter, for instance, lacks originality:

> Marie: "I lie awake and think of you."
> Norman: "You've made me live."
> Marie: "Oh, Norman, you're so good to me." (612, 616)

Even in his dreams, originality is beyond Norman's characterization. He imagines Marie saying, "I could tell you were a deep one" (609).

Various contradictions of the rules of reason most dramatically undermine Norman's romanticized sentiments. Illogical throughout, Norman decides that his wife's sexual aggression is caused by her sterility. Is it logical that because he cannot seem to satisfy his wife sexually he should seek sex elsewhere? And only when Marie agrees to sex is "his early impression" of her "tartish disposition . . . dispelled" (616). Finally, Norman wishes for one night with Marie and sees it as "the privilege of being man and wife," which requires a lifetime commitment.

Another sort of illogical contradiction, anthropomorphism, infers the illicit affair's mechanical dimensions. During a penultimate moment when Norman finds the vacant hotel bathroom, "two monstrous brass taps . . . *seemed to know* already that he and Marie would come to the bathroom.

89

They seemed almost *to wink"* (613). After the deflowering of Marie, *"it became a regular thing"* (616). And as time goes by the lovers rationalize their affair by concluding that "only love could have found in them a willingness to engage in the *deception of a hotel"* (617).

Since comic lines invariably call attention to Norman's romanticized delusions of grandeur, the reader wonders why Trevor develops the horrific side of Hilda's character toward the end of the story, perhaps even to imply that Norman *justifiably* contemplates murder, or as the husband euphemistically puts it, "causing Hilda's death" (617). Hilda's dismal talent for sexual expression—stroking "his face with her fingers, [thinking] . . . it would excite him" (619)—does not surpass Norman's most sensuous move when "he ran his forefinger between the bones on the back of [Marie's] hand, so gently that it made her want to shiver" (611), hardly a move out of Masters and Johnson. Indeed, three unappealing versions of Hilda precede the horrific one: Hilda the automaton working the production line at home; Hilda the aloof, bored, sterile, but sexually demanding wife; and Hilda the aging wife with "pasty limbs," a sad reminder of middle age and death—"who'd get worse as she grew older . . . scrawnier; her hair, already coarse, would get dry and grey" (611).

Trevor gradually musters sympathy for Norman, most emphatically by developing the horrific view of Hilda when the husband confesses the truth about his affair. Hilda's lecherous stories about affairs and even "a foursome" (619) dramatically upstage Norman's feeble confession. Although Norman dehumanizes sexuality when he ponders what Hilda would do if "deprived of bedroom mating" (612), his wife's diction is worse, even obscene ("You're no tomcat, you know old boy . . . no sexual mechanic"). She reveals a shocking and gross insensitivity by asking, "How long's this charming *stuff* been going on?," by offering some womanly wisdom ("All chaps fancy *things* in shops"), and by demanding sex because Norman's story about Marie excites her (618). Norman's sad tendency to be cowed by Hilda is evident in an unfortunate turn of phrase: "It seemed at first that [Hilda] was keeping her end up" (619).

Norman, then, is by no means unsympathetic, as is the case with most of Trevor's comic portraits. To answer my question about this sometimes considerate husband who acknowledges that "he wasn't being fair to his wife because 'she did her best'" (611), Trevor's outline of Norman's shortcomings finally point to vulnerabilities we all experience to some degree. Norman is infinitely human, desirous of what we all desire: true love, the basis for a secure sense of identity and purpose in life; reenactment of a happy, youthful past (Norman reenacts his courtship with Hilda by courting a younger woman); control over time and an uncertain future (Norman lives "a fantasy that had miraculously become real" [621]); and power over the fear of death.

The Business of a Forty-seventh Saturday

Economic exchange again casts a shadow on love in "The Forty-seventh Saturday." And like Trevor's other comic tales, the story begins with a purchase that reveals something about a major character, in this case the miserly side of Mr. McCarthy, who stops at a wine shop to buy a bottle of cheap wine, then quibbles over the price, refusing to pay "threepence" for "the carrier bag" (201). Since he splurges on a taxi as transport to his regular Saturday tryst with a younger woman, Mavie, the reader knows his niggardly behavior is not due to poverty.

McCarthy's young, working-class mistress, however, does seem on the edge of poverty. She is exploited by this older businessman, "who *remained* at fifty-two" (203; my italics) and never manages to develop beyond the pleasure principle. He in fact lies about being unhappily married when in fact he is a bachelor—a status he maintains in order to avoid commitment and expense. Despite her selfish lover, Mavie miraculously maintains a relatively well-adjusted life. She tries not to mind being "alone" (200) the rest of the week; her loneliness is made clear in the second sentence of the story (200). She does not mind driving a "motor-bike" with an unused "sidecar" because she has no one to use it on a regular basis. She feels grateful she shares a basement apartment with another working woman gone on weekends. She represses her awareness of the loveless and one-sided nature of her regular Saturday affair, and she represses the difference in economic status between herself and her lover.

It is important to notice that Mavie's relationship with McCarthy offers her more than sexual satisfaction. Having McCarthy as her lover also allows her to feel elevated in terms of class. Her vulnerability is complicated by her working-class background and McCarthy's relatively elevated, middle-class stature. McCarthy's thoughtless condescension to working-class expectations (drinking cheap wine when with his mistress) counters Mavie's efforts to attain the stature of the business class, although her efforts in this regard seem motivated by an honest desire to please McCarthy and not by ambition.

Mavie poses as a sophisticated imbiber of dry sherry (a British brand), but McCarthy does not want her to "get ideas above her station" (203). Her Scotch-Irish lover arrives bearing gifts—most importantly himself, secondarily the wine he plans to drink himself, noting that it would "cheer us up," as he puts it. It is Mavie and not McCarthy, however, who soon feels "low and sad" (204), because her fatherly lover measures his days by his weekly affair but has forgotten her twenty-seventh birthday. Before his arrival the dashing prince imagines his princess posturing, with "the thumb and forefinger of her right hand grasping a glass which contained sherry" (201). And she does strike "a pose in the basement kitchen" (201), just as her lover had anticipated. Before Mavie offers the first kiss (ironically initiating the pose he really wants), he is "drinking his way through the wine" (202).

Mavie wears "a plastic apron [that] covered a navy-blue, rather old-fashioned suit" (201)—a suit appropriate to McCarthy's middle-class stature and age but still a hand-me-down from Mavie's sister. Her friends ask her if her lover wants her to wear "pith helmets, chukka boots" (201), but Mavie explains that her lover prefers her to wear nothing—a preference appropriate given his miserly propensity.

The discourse of business in this story dramatically qualifies McCarthy's capacity for love, which he expresses with "horseplay" (203) and lies. Diction sets the tone. McCarthy's drinking habits are explained in terms of "his *policy* on these visits" (202; my italics). McCarthy reflects "on his continuing *good fortune*" (203) while anticipating Mavie's generosity. To McCarthy this tryst is just another "Saturday appointment, a business appointment" (207); he always leaves in fact within "the hour" (206) and without "dawdling," on the pretense of a 4 P.M. appointment. Mavie reinforces her battered ego by claiming to be "enterprising" (204). When she asks McCarthy if he loves her, he responds inappropriately as if involved in a business dispute that requires taking sides: "I'm all for you" (204), he says several times. McCarthy is distressed when Mavie then shares her "depression" (204) but only because "he had not fully exacted his pleasurable *due*" (204; my italics).

Even in Mavie's dreams the world of commerce displaces love; she imagines McCarthy spending more time with her and telling his wife that "he had been called away on vital business" (204)—exactly the lie that excuses him from his naive lover. McCarthy's endearments ("my young heart") convince Mavie all too easily. The reader sees the older man as defective, especially when he fails to praise his lover for cooking "more elaborately," preparing what she thought was more appropriate to his station. In response, this anal-retentive feels a disturbance "in the bowels" (202). McCarthy treats Mavie not only according to her lower-class status but also like a child, "sitting her on his knees" (203), kissing "her on the head, his usual form of farewell" (207). He tells her to brush her teeth before meeting his sexual demands.

The most outrageous evidence of McCarthy's narcissistic and miserly character is evident when he performs a dance for Mavie—the gesture of an exhibitionist. He again offers *himself* as a bargain—better than buying her "roses and presents of jewelry and lamé gowns" (205). This incident ironically highlights the importance of what Mavie does—unconditionally, honestly giving of the self. McCarthy's guilt for his behavior asserts itself when he asks Mavie to whip him with "the braces off his trousers" (205). Mavie refuses to play the role of the sadist in a sadomasochistic farce because in reality the sadist she would play suffers more than the masochist who seeks punishment.

What stands for an expression of love here is perverse. To make matters worse, McCarthy's focus on sexuality—"nuzzling her neck"—saves him from having to communicate intimately: "he was not speaking" (203) and "prevents Mavie from explaining" that it was her birthday and that her childhood memories of previous birthdays were not happy. McCarthy only knows Mavie in a physical way, and her physicality is also superficially studied. Again a Trevor love scene lacks detail and ignores anatomy. McCarthy begins by "stroking [Mavie's] navy-blue clothes" (203); later "his hands [seek] the outline of her ribs" (204). He focuses on the human frame and ignores the substance—rib titilation being unpromising foreplay.

After Mavie's "peckish" lover departs to "go to the pictures" and not because of an appointment, Marie imagines McCarthy's wife as "the woman [who] shrilled abuse, upbraiding her husband for . . . some small deceit" (207). The story ends with poignant irony again condemning the lie.

Commerce and Love

The adverse effect of commerce on love is most evident when considering the recent proliferation of pornography, an important concern in the Trevor canon. "The Blue Dress" starts with a brief mention of the pornographer who "pretends he's selling Christmas cards" (712), and "Mulvihill's Memorial" intently examines this destructive byproduct of the commercial world.

Pornography alienates men from reciprocal love. Like advertising, pornography objectifies women and exploits them for profit—an age-old tradition but one never so efficiently and methodically instituted as today. Simply put, pornography and advertising undermine the human capacity for understanding beyond self-interest, undermine the human capacity for love.

Trevor's most important story about pornography evokes the world of advertising haunted by the ghost of Mulvihill, a victim of a fatal heart attack and former undercover pornographer working as a label designer for Yngis and Yngis and sneaking shots of his boss's sexual exploits with the firm's secretary. The serious philosophical implications of yin and yang are evoked simultaneously with comic inferences related to the firm's name. Trevor suggests that essentially the mind-set of the ad man Mulvihill is precisely that of the pornographer, not to mention the porn devotee. We first see Mulvihill in his office on a Friday evening enacting his end-of-the-week ritual of secretly watching the "sexual antics" of a porn flick taken from his stash that includes some of the homemade variety. This is his weekly habit before joining his colleagues for a drink at the local pub, the Trumpet Major.

The particular porn flick represented at the start of this story is apparently viewed through Mulvihill's eyes: two men remove the clothing of two women—a "dress, petticoat, stockings . . . a grey skirt and jersey"—that is, what one would expect ordinary, middle-class, working women to wear. The clothing and general appearance of the two male performers are left unmentioned, rightly so since the women catch the attention of the hetereosexual voyeur—in this case Mulvihill, who participates imaginatively in "complex sexual union" (677).

The clothing and general apearance of Mulvihill are meticulously detailed to suggest the character of a man very different from what might be imagined given the reader's first view of this label designer's peep show. Pornographers are most often associated with drug dealers, drug addicts, prostitutes, and poolhall sleaze, but Trevor emphatically presents Mulvihill as an average "man with glasses, middle-aged, of medium height, neither fat nor thin" (676)—that is, average in terms of age, height, and physique. He is a middle-class, conservative type, a certain kind of man, who might have stepped right out of an ad. "Given to wearing Harris tweed jackets looking not unlike an advertisement for the Four Square tobacco he smoked" (677), he is only incidentally a pornographer.

And yet the world of advertising is finally likened to the world of pornography in this story. Both advertisers and pornographers exploit sexuality by encouraging false needs that cannot be satisfied; both condition potential buyers to seek instant gratification of profound needs for tenderness, intimacy, and love—needs that can be satisfied only by reciprocal, enduring affection, not narcissistic, promiscuous love.

The fantasy of fake happiness promoted in the commercial world, the idyllic settings where "girls [stand] aloof by castle walls," cannot survive occasional touches of comic realism. The castle walls come tumbling down while "children [laugh] . . . full of beans that did them good" (678). Advertising propaganda promises miracles as it conjures up magical worlds of glimmering labels, wrappers, containers, stickers, packets, posters, billboards, and photographs—a world of television and movie campaigns, trade names, slogans, bright colors, and beautiful people forever joyful. The ads displayed on the office walls of Ygnis and Ygnis are "rich in sexual innuendo" (690) and represent a "glamour" that "glitters" but offers no human solace.

Trevor's methods throughout these stories cultivate fragmentation. Mulvihill's character is developed piecemeal so that the reader constantly sees the contradiction between the respectable facade of label designer and the secret practice of watching and making porn flicks. Throughout the story the reader struggles to piece together the puzzle parts of Mulvihill's existence according to various conflicting versions of his character, as imagined by his sister, his office partner, and his boss, Ox-Banham. We maintain our initial portrait of Mulvihill, the Friday-night porn-flick artist and viewer, throughout the story, however—a view that contradicts idealized versions constructed by Mulvihill's colleagues and sister after his sudden death.

When Wilkinski finds porn flicks in the deceased's desk, on the other hand, Mulvihill's office partner resists the shocking reality and ponders his previous view of Mulvihill as a camera-happy naturalist photographing "ducks in springtime" (683). In the minds of his associates, Mulvihill, the respectable label designer, does not fit the stereotype of the pornographer. Hence, Wilkinski cannot process this new aspect of Mulvihill without altering it somewhat to fit the old image. Then a new Mulvihill emerges in Wilkinski's imagination. The kindly Wilkinski imagines that Mulvihill was "in terror of losing his job" and consequently attempted "to escape from his treadmill by becoming a pornographer instead" (684)—a rationalization denying the possibility of motivation based on pure lust.

Unfortunately, Wilkinski's deductions that Mulvihill was worried "about the safety of his job" and stayed late on Fridays "to finish off his week's work" (681) were merely a cover to explain to Mulvihill's sister and others his extended workday at the week's end when he entertained himself with *Virgins' Delight* or *Naughty Nell*. That Wilkinski colors his version of Mulvihill with a rosy hue bespeaks the generosity of the surviving office partner and further undercuts Mulvihill's character.

Mulvihill's self-indulgence would have shocked his sister, who lived with him and "looked after him as a child" (685). She knows only his innocence. From her perspective he is a respectable man of predictable and responsible behavior. She looks forward to the gossip he shares when he returns from work on a regular basis at a regular time each day. She sees him as a hobbiest interested in photography, carpentry, and other "do-it-yourself stuff" (681). The respectability Mulville's sister accepts is radically contradicted when the reader acknowledges the underlying sense of "stuff." We should recall here the start of the story when Mulvihill recognizes that "it would be terrible if [his sister] discovered the stuff" (675)—that is, not carpenter's blueprints but pornography.

Authority figures of a sort, sisters alert the sinner with an emphatic call to moral attention, but the most telling perspective on Mulvihill is that of the supreme authority figure at Yngis and Yngis, his boss, Ox-Banham. When Wilkinski presents Ox-Banham with the stash of pornography, this leader of men ironically sees Mulvihill as "nasty . . . in spite of his pipe and his Harris tweed jackets" (684). The irony here rests on the fact that Ox-Banham's character is no better than Mulvihill's: "Like Mulvihill, Ox-Banham was known to work late on Fridays" (678). That is, at precisely the same time on Friday evenings that Mulvihill watches pornography, Ox-Banham satisfies his sexual urges with Rowena Smithson, his secretary and the daughter of an important client, Bloody Smithson. Both Mulvihill and Ox-Banham, then, regularly indulge their lusts around the same time on Friday. Both Mulvihill and Ox-Banham routinely use others to satisfy their most basic needs. Mulvihill uses his sister as a mother substitute who provides creature comforts other than sexual ones. Ox-Banham uses Rowena as a mistress. Rowena in turn uses Ox-Banham as a means of getting a promotion to the copy department. Love is not considered in any of these relationships.

Love requires spontaneity in human relationships, but Mulvihill and his associates mechanically follow fixed routines. Every Friday, Mulvihill watches pornography, smokes his pipe, and then joins the office staff at the Trumpet Major. The revelers celebrating the end of the work week do not deviate from their routine even in terms of what they drink: everyone has "the same as usual" (679). Everyone behaves predictably.

Mulvihill's habits are so regular that others express amazement when he deviates from them. Mulvihill's sister "was surprised" when her brother failed to appear at "his usual time on Fridays." Wilkinski "was surprised" when Mulvihill did not arrive on time Monday morning as he "normally" did (680). In the case of the sister Mulvihill's deviations from his routine eventually result in her paralysis. The night Mulvihill dies his sister waits until the wee hours of the morning to telephone the police, even though she feels "fear" by 11 P.M. when he does not appear as usual.

Most of the time, however, disruptions of the regular routine seem momentary, insignificant glitches barely noticed by those indoctrinated into the system. With ease and indifference the office staff, "refreshed after their weekend," returns to business as usual after the death of Mulvihill. This is typical of the apathy, the automatic indifference and superficial reactions to horrendous events so often represented in Trevor's stories.

Habit takes over, and the new context demanded by Mulvihill's death is ignored. Wilkinski learns the bad news from the tea woman, Edith, who pours "a cup for the deceased" as if nothing had happened. She participates in a cliché-ridden exchange (she "couldn't believe it . . . he'd been Friday, right as rain. . . . it just goes to show") and then moves "on to spread the news." The gap between what she feels (the enthusiasm of a gossipmonger) and more appropriate responses (grief or sympathy) is suggested by a case of inverted syntax forcing the reader for a moment to visualize Edith rather than Mulvihill laughing: "she said, laughing and joking he'd been Friday" (681). Moreover, Wilkinski's grief is also short-lived: his thoughts echo the tea woman's fake sentiments ("it just goes to show"). He manages only "to reflect for several minutes" on Mulvihill's death, and he is joined by a handful of others in this brief moment of pause. But "elsewhere in the building life continued normally that morning" (681) and "the next few weeks" (682).

The most callous reponse to Mulvihill's death is Ox-Banham's; he even considers using the sudden death of his employee as a "talking point" to win over "the confectionery men"—the clients whom he might astonish by telling the story of "the chap who'd designed the wrapper for the GO bar [and who'd] had a heart attack in the lift" (682). Ox-Banham restrains his impulse to exploit this grim event only because he doesn't want to "cast a gloom" on the deal (682).

In this world of advertisements, cinematography, and pornography, moments of genuine human emotion are fleeting and insubstantial. Modern-day memorials do not last. Mulvihill is remembered by the stash of pornography found in his desk and for his design of a wrapper for a candy bar called Go, not for any admirable deeds preserved in the memories of loved ones. Label designs outlast the designer. Mulvihill's films of Wilkinski's daughter's wedding outlast the marriage.

Traces of the past betray characters struggling with present exigencies. Although "no trace of the death remained" in the lift (680), this amateur pornographer's films leave traces that define him more emphatically than his taste in clothes, customary behavior, and relationships with others during his lifetime. His co-workers all too easily label him a pornographer—an identity totally at odds with what he seemed to be previously. When Ox-Banham accidentally shows to his secretary's father a porn flick Mulvihill secretly made of Ox-Banham and the man's daughter "banging away" (690) on the office floor, he loses an important account and worries that others will follow: "the men of the chocolate account . . . the toiletries people . . . the men of Macclesfield Metals" (689)—nameless clients identified by the products needing promotion.

In this story people are more easily identified and categorized than the films Mulvihill leaves as his memorial. *Easy Lady* and *Let's Go, Lover* get mixed up with "Mr. Trotter's Retirement Occasion" and the "domestic" (684) reels about Mulvihill's sister and her dog. Ox-Banham finally destroys the family films along with those revealing his and Rowena's promiscuity. Trevor ends the story with Wilkinski's lie that the films "had been destroyed in error" (690)—an appropriate finalé given the false images projected by the world of advertising and pornography, false fronts invariably cultivated by those whose values are embedded in the world of things.

Broken Hearts/Homes

In "Broken Homes," one of his most comic and sad stories, Trevor masterfully writes from a third-person point of view while conveying the "insidedness" of Mrs. Malby, an elderly widow who lost her sons during World War II—both "killed in the same month" (477). The world of commerce marginalizes the poor, women (spinsters), and the elderly (widows living alone), subtly undermining their sense of self-worth. In her eighties, Mrs. Malby now lives above a "greengrocer's shop" and suffers a terrible "dread of having to leave Agnes Street" because someone "diagnoses her as senile" (478).

Most of this elderly woman's ties to the outside world are commercial ones. Besides a niece that visits twice a year, other visitors in various "service" industries attend to the old woman's needs: deliverers of "meals on wheels," a social worker, Reverend Bush, and "men [who] read the meters." The Jewish couple running the grocery store watch Mrs. Malby's "coming and going" with no effort to hide the fact that they soon expect her death. All of those who participate in the old woman's life are to a greater or lesser degree involved in business or behave according to the competing dictates of a commercial world.

Mrs. Malby's alienation and insecurity is most evident when a nameless teacher from Tite Comprehensive school approaches her with a proposition: he is promoting a welfare project—arranging for "good kids from broken homes" to work in the community, in this case, to paint her kitchen. The anonymity of big government and business intrudes in the form of institutional prose: the teacher's "policy" does not, as he claims, foster "deeper understanding," as he puts it, "displaying small evenly arranged teeth" "between the generations" (476). The broken syntax calling attention to a fragment and a linking preposition creates a gap that bodes ill for the promise of "understanding." As the story proceeds, the teacher's "understanding" of Mrs. Malby proves limited, as is that of everyone else who tries to help. Mrs. Malby observes that people no longer "converse" but rather "communicate" (477).

The central irony is that Mrs. Malby struggles to be just like everyone else—in a story antagonistic toward the idea of conformity. Advertisements develop simplistic categories encouraging conformity. Indeed, the commercial world thrives on conformity, categorizing people according to simplistic stereotypes, such as "good kids from broken homes." The teacher puts the elderly woman and the juvenile delinquent invaders in the same category of those "we're trying to help" (476). He sees himself in the category of "helper," a position that grants him power and authority.

Mrs. Malby is herself vulnerable to thinking in terms of "types." Seeing the teacher as a type very different from herself, she notes that "Nowadays you saw a lot of men like this" (475). Her view of the students "shouting obscenities" (476) at Tite Comprehensive contradicts the teacher's view of them as suffering from societal ills and needing to work at something worthwhile.

The teacher indeed aggravates Mrs. Malby's worst fear of "becoming senile" (477). Unaware that his "volunteer" do-gooder worries about not hearing or understanding what others say, the teacher repeats himself "as if she hadn't heard a thing he'd been saying" (476), much to the old woman's "horror." Her distress is agonizingly clear. She succumbs to the teacher's demands because she is insecure and because she believes in "human conscience" (477); she agrees with the teacher's philosophy that "we all [have] a special duty where such children were concerned" (476).

Loosing the "hooligans" (484) from Tite Comprehensive, the teacher directs them to Mrs. Malby's home. They proceed to paint her kitchen (without permission) a color Mrs. Malby hates, thoughtlessly descending on her and flippantly engaging her in a discussion about whether they have "come to the wrong house" (480). Mrs. Malby is then placed in the peculiar position of explaining they are not in the wrong house, but she fails to convey her feelings that what they plan to do is "wrong." Her inability to communicate surely owes to the agony she feels over being thought of as "wrong" or hearing things "wrong" because she is elderly and making mistakes that will inevitably force her to relinquish her home.

The powerlessness of the aged woman was never more clear. When she tries to stop what seems to her the destruction of her home—not to mention her memories of her loved ones associated with the décor of her home—the adolescent painters even threaten the desperate woman's identity by renaming her Mrs. Wheeler. Then they refuse to take orders from the poor woman they misname. They declare, "Only *he* [the nameless teacher] gives instructions" (481).

Perhaps Mrs. Malby's impotence has to do with the impotence we all suffer when trying to escape the barrage of commercial messages that invade and diminish our private worlds. The invaders in this story wear badges promoting the "Bay City Rollers" and "Jaws" (479)—T-shirts declaring, "I Lay Down with Jesus." Symphony is reduced to "sound" when Mrs. Malby shuts off the radio and one of the young painters demands, "Where's the sound gone?" (480). The commercial world of slogans, jingles, and tunes—worse, "a tuneless twanging"—also displaces music with a "blare" (480).

Sexuality is reduced to biological drive. Mrs. Malby flees from the boy and girl who violate her bed because they "needed sex" (482). She weeps and then escapes to the window overlooking Agnes Street and watches the "people [who] passed by on bicycles, girls from the polish factory returning home to lunch, men from the brickworks" (482). This helps her to "feel better . . . more composed, and more in control of herself" (482).

The activity of bustling life in her neighborhood reassures this wise old woman so aware that she lingers on in life as a shadow of her past. Her fear of being isolated with other such shades in the "Sunset Home" does not undermine her sense of community. Institutional care of the elderly is in fact another thriving business replacing the family and the community. Even though Mrs. Malby hates the "communal jolliness" (477) of the elderly and isolated groups she finds threatening to one's sense of individuality, still she seeks community. She goes out to buy bread from Len Skipps, a man of 62 whom she remembers being born. She nods at the Kings and meets other neighbors she has known for years. Her humanity is here suggested.

Mrs. Malby does not grow bitter, even though she suffers from those who victimize her as well as from Mr. and Mrs. King, who see themselves as her rescuers. Mr. King does chastize the boys and girls, but then his insensitivity is clear when he complains that this disaster "wasted two hours of his time" (484) and declares "thunderously" that the delinquents "could have killed an eighty-seven-year-old stone dead." In response to the blatant articulation of her worst fears, "Mrs. Malby stood up" (485), resisting also the "help" Mrs. King offers by placing "a hand under her elbow" (485). Mrs. King further assumes "that all would be well because a sum of money would be paid" (485), a grievously inadequate response to Mrs. Malby's plight.

The décor of her home—all that remains to affirm Mrs. Malby's identity and to remind her of lost loved ones—has been destroyed. The old woman is abandoned by her neighbors, the do-gooder, and the adolescent hooligans, all of whom leave her to grieve over her loss and her diminished sense of self-worth. In a daydream she reenacts the death of her sons, the "double wound" suffered so long ago, and the reader shares her grief.

Whether or not it seems appropriate to end this study with these comic stories is debatable. Some say that poetry is more important than the short story, drama more important than the novel, unambiguous tragedy more moving than tragicomedy. Critics may find more flaws in these stories, especially if they apply standards other than those appropriate to short stories *and* to tragicomedy. But these stories are the most likely to achieve catharsis through laughter, to cut to the quick of communal flaws "of our time." The value of participating in the carnivalesque of life cannot be overestimated, nor can the redeeming and warm humor of Trevor's tragicomic tales. The intensity of the shadows in Trevor's work does not eclipse the hope and compassion, even in the darkest of tales. Trevor's mastery of the poetic passage, the drama of dialogue, the invariably human character—at times tragic, at times comic, at times tragicomic—deserves far more critical attention in America than this study can possibly achieve, not least because even his tales of suffering offer "abundant compensations ... steadily concerned with human feeling"; we find everywhere in his stories "the faintly rising scent of laughter."[32]

Conclusion

The voices of extraordinary writers like William Trevor are almost as quickly recognizable as those of great singers. . . . Any lover of song will know Pavarotti. . . . The genuinely sizable writers of fiction announce their presence almost as early. Some, like Conrad or Hemingway, speak in timbres distinctive enough to declare their makers in a single sentence. (Price, 27)

After making these comparisons hinting at Trevor's greatness, Reynolds Price, reviewing Trevor's *Collected Stories* in the *New York Times Book Review*, takes issue with what he calls "the recent claims of literary *couturiers* that Mr. Trevor is now the premier storywriter in the language" (27). Trevor's limitations, Price contends, have to do with the fact that his stories lack "hope, the clear stream however slight and easily stemmed that runs on past private loss and ruin in the world of writers even as near desperation as Kafka and James Joyce, Mr. Trevor's huge predecessor" (25).

I cannot agree with those who find Trevor's work dour; instead I side with the many who appreciate the comic aspects of his best stories, not to mention those—Graham Greene, for example—who compare him favorably with Joyce. The *New York Times Book Review* in 1991 called Trevor's work "among the most subtle and sophisticated fiction being written today," and a 1993 *New Yorker* profile of the author claims that he "is probably the greatest writer of short stories in the English language."

The photographs of Trevor published to date do not capture the author's warmth and spirit. Trevor's best stories are brilliantly witty even though they belong to a serious modernist tradition focused on the divided self struggling for a secure identity in a complex world. This tradition especially tends toward the grotesque—and Trevor indeed develops grotesqueries. His best stories, however, capture the promise of humanity as well—promise expressing the human capacity for love, for example, in characters such as Dukelow, a nurturing father figure in "A Choice of Butchers"; Mrs. Ashburton, a community mother in "Matilda's England"; Bridie, the devoted daughter in "The Ballroom of Romance"; Dervla, the self-sacrificing lover in "The Wedding in the Garden"; and the charitable Mrs. Malby in "Broken Homes."

Trevor's genius has not yet been fully appreciated for either his stories' tragic bass ("Attracta," "The Raising of Elvira Tremlett," "A School Story," "A Happy Family," "The Blue Dress," "Kathleen's Field") or their comic treble ("Mulvihill's Memorial," "The Day We Got Drunk on Cake," "Lovers of Their Time," "An Evening with John Joe Dempsey," "The Forty-seventh Saturday"). It was not the tragic tales that inspired the remarkably large number of outrageously comic titles for reviews of his work and interviews. These titles stand as further testimony to the importance of Trevor's contagious humor.

Trevor's comic tales are truly memorable, sparkling with neon signs and hilarity as they rigorously demythologize the commercial enterprise but ultimately expose a more essential solipsism than the narcissistic discourse of ballrooms and billboards. Trevor's stories and novellas are devoted to fashioning a full and compassionate vision of humanity. This requires that he invariably expose not only psychic splits between the Jekyll/Hyde parts of the self but also male/female, parent/child, mind/body, British/Irish, Protestant/Catholic, and community/individual splits. Trevor's modernity is explained by this dividedness rather than the ad men and shysters, pubs and hotels, that form the fabric of his work. Trevor's masterpieces of short fiction will most certainly earn him his proper place as a major writer in the modernist tradition.

Notes to Part 1

1. This story might have been included in this first group of stories; however, it ultimately represents the long-term suffering of childhood and adolescence rather than focusing more intently on the effort to master a particular crisis in a shorter span of time, the primary focus of this chapter.

2. *The Stories of William Trevor* (London: Penguin, 1983), 704. All stories from this collection are hereafter cited in text by page number alone.

3. The post-Freudians Otto Rank and Joseph Campbell and the Irish intellectual Erich Neumann (*The Origin and History of Consciousness* [New York: Bollingen, 1954]) explored the importance of ritual and myth in human development as it related to trauma and suffering.

4. For example, the "predatory" Timothy Gedge is a close relative of Williams and appears as an antagonist to various members of the community in *The Children of Dynmouth*, a 1976 novella that won the Whitbread Prize for Fiction.

5. France Morrow points out that only 1 percent of the world's property is owned by women; see *Unleashing Our Unknown Selves: An Enquiry into the Future of Femininity and Masculinity* (New York: Praeger, 1991).

6. Freud never meant to imply that children literally want to "possess" the parent in a sexual way but rather that children want the attentions of the mother exclusively.

7. Freud disdained the popularization and distortion of the term *narcissism*; I mean it as Freud used it to refer to the return of powerful infantile feelings based on primitive instincts.

8. Jessica Benjamin, "A Desire of One's Own: Psychoanalytic Feminism and Intersubjective Space," *Feminist Studies* 8 (1982): 78–101; hereafter cited in text.

9. Fyodor Dostoyevski, Edgar Allan Poe, E. T. A. Hoffmann, and Flannery O'Connor exploit the idea of a "figment" voice in their tales of double figures and madness.

10. R. D. Laing, *The Divided Self: An Existential Study in Sanity and Madness* (Harmondsworth, England: Penguin, 1969), 105.

11. Interview with the author, August 1989.

12. According to Bonnie Kime Scott, *Joyce and Feminism* (Bloomington: Indiana University Press, 1984), in Ireland "the ideal peasant woman is a submissive virgin destined for marriage, who can do menial, charitable, or clerical work . . . [women are] expected to be dependent, self-sacrificing 'angels of the house'" (189).

13. Carolyn G. Heilbrun, *Toward a Recognition of Androgyny* (New York: Harper & Row, 1973), 154.

14. Dorothy Dinnerstein, *The Mermaid and the Minotaur* (New York: Harper & Row, 1976), 40.

15. Suzette A. Henke, *James Joyce and the Politics of Desire* (London: Routledge, 1990), 13.

16. In a 1988 interview Trevor declared this story as most important in establishing his reputation in Ireland: "I am known there as the man who wrote 'The Ballroom of Romance'" (Geordie Greig, *Sunday Times*, 29 May 1988, G9).

17. Trevor's narrators are often unreliable and vulnerable to the discourse of routine—perhaps a third-person perspective reflecting the internal landscape of an adolescent "naif," a drunken ex-husband, or, as in this case, a vulnerable young woman. Bridie's limitations are more evident because Trevor alternates between an indifferent, third-person point of view and an omniscient third-person point of view, dramatically rendering Bridie's feelings, her limited viewpoint then serving as window to Trevor's fictive world.

18. M. M. Bakhtin, *The Dialogic Imagination*, ed. Michael Holquist, trans. Caryl Emerson and Michael Holquist (Austin: University of Texas Press, 1981); *Problems of Dostoevsky's Poetics*, trans. R. W. Rotsel (Minneapolis: University of Minnesota Press, 1984).

19. Elaine Showalter, ed., *The New Feminist Criticism* (New York: Pantheon, 1985), 243.

20. Annette Kolodny, "A Map for Rereading Gender and the Interpretation of Literary Texts," in *The New Feminist Criticism*, 147.

21. In "On the Zattere" Trevor develops another crippling father-daughter relationship.

22. Margot Norris "Stifled Back Answers: The Gender Politics of Art in Joyce's 'The Dead,'" *Modern Fiction Studies* 35, no. 3 (1989): 489.

23. T. S. Eliot in *The Waste Land* uses the story of Philomena as a classic case substantiating the abuse of women throughout the ages.

24. James Joyce, *Stephen Hero*, cited by Brown.

25. "The Property of Colette Nervi," in *The News from Ireland and Other Stories* (Harmondsworth, England: Penguin Books, 1986), 101; page references to this collection hereafter cited in text.

26. "Wedding in the Garden," in *The News from Ireland and Other Stories*, 262; my italics. Page references to this collection hereafter cited in text.

27. Trevor's dismay over modern fantasy as represented in the commercial world was evident during an interview: "The whole world of the poster and the advertisement [is a] pretend world of dark chocolate and turkish delight. . . . I'm quite serious in my attacks on it" (*Transatlantic Review* [London] 53–54 [1976]: 10).

27. Mark Mortimer, *Contemporary Irish Writers*, Series 15, Bulletin of the Department of Foreign Affairs no. 1031, September 1986.

28. Doris Betts, "William Trevor: Still Stories Run Deep," review of *Beyond the Pale*, *Washington Post Book World*, 21 February 1982, 3.

29. Valentine Cunningham, *Times Literary Supplement*, 24 October 1975, 1255. In a review of *Lovers of Their Time* and *Angels at the Ritz* the *Community Mirror* (Ireland) argued that "sympathy for the admittedly dreary side of life emerges. . . . If you can

bear to look at the human condition without rose-tinted spectacles, then you will enjoy and remember reading [these stories]."

30. Post-Freudians (even those who throw the baby out with the bathwater by presenting Freud in the light of only his weakest theories) rightly point out that memories of the helplessness of infancy and discomfort associated with the mother cause both men and women to feel pleasure when in positions of authority or control over other women.

31. Reynolds Price, "A Lifetime of Tales from the Land of Broken Hearts," review of *The Collected Stories, New York Times Book Review,* 28 February 1993, 26; hereafter cited in text.

Part 2

THE WRITER

Interview, 1992

Suzanne Paulson

Ultimately, you have to celebrate the human condition.[1]

William Trevor's wife, Jane, beamed lovingly at her husband while we discussed the inordinate number of interviews this author has been subjected to. "Hundreds," she said glowingly. William Trevor Cox looked embarrassed and smiled: "Ah no, not hundreds." That moment deepened my respect for this author's stories about women. He has dedicated almost all of his books "To Jane."

Do such moments that might occur during an interview really matter? If I had not interviewed the subject of this study, I would still have eventually realized, for example, that his work is a tribute to the women in his life; still, the fantasies that all interviewers spin as they try to represent an author are better forestalled by direct experience with their subject.[2] Despite Trevor's warnings about his difficulties with being interviewed, he *does* indeed try to communicate his perspective on his art. Critics and readers everywhere should appreciate his generosity.

❖

INTERVIEWER: One of the more interesting aspects of your stories is that sometimes they make the reader laugh despite disturbing events—say, in a story like "Mulvihill's Memorial" involving the sudden death of an ad man who secretly watches pornography, or "The Day We Got Drunk on Cake."

TREVOR: I simply write the stories as I see them. If they're funny in places, then they're funny in places. If there's tragedy, then there's tragedy, which I think is like life itself.

INTERVIEWER: The reader gets a glimpse of the humanity in your characters and then feels pain—even though laughing a moment before.

TREVOR: I have a great fear of analyzing why and how one writes. There is a considerable element of mystery. One does not *know* how the magic of a good story works. When you "talk" about writing, you turn yourself into another person—an academic talking about the raw material, but this is not really you talking. The writer talking is the story itself.

INTERVIEWER: Many of your characters suffer terribly traumatic experiences. Do you consider how contemporary life aggravates their woes?

TREVOR: No. There is perhaps more pressure in human relationships in contemporary times, but my stories are set in contemporary times because I happen to live in the late twentieth century. That is the material, the stuff around me, from which I select. The stories may possibly be set in the thirties, forties, or fifties, but I'm not really interested in reflecting these periods. I'm more interested in people, who don't change all that much.

INTERVIEWER: Many reviewers have noticed that you render the commercial world in great detail—ads, billboards, songs, slogans, and so forth.

TREVOR: Yes, there is a sort of backdrop, but it is simply there because it exists in reality. Two things interest me: one is real life, the other is people.

INTERVIEWER: Does that backdrop of the commercial world affect those relationships between people?

TREVOR: I don't think so, or if it does create special problems, these are essentially superficial problems. Humanity tends to tackle the same problems, even though the contemporary world may appear to contradict that.

INTERVIEWER: Talking about the way you develop relations between men and women, you once said you were most "appalled" about "the terrible vacuum, in which no effort is made to communicate" by two people supposedly in love. Your characters seem so disjointed from one another: "Death in Jerusalem" depicts the destructive relationship of two brothers; in "A Choice of Butchers" two father figures clash over who should be recognized for parenting a young boy. Are these men—the aggressive butcher-father and passive butcher's assistant–adoptive father, Dukelow—opposites?

TREVOR: Patterns like opposites may emerge in the telling of a story, but they don't suggest any answers. I don't have any answers, just questions.

INTERVIEWER: In such early stories such as "The Raising of Elvira Tremlett" and "A Choice of Butchers"—or later in "Her Mother's Daughter"—parents impose an overpowering will on a child and try to mold the child into a mirror image of themselves—what the critic John T. Irwin calls a "procreative double." The demand is that the child accept his or her destiny according to the parent's conception of it.

TREVOR: I don't entirely understand that, but it's an interesting idea. Many of my stories start with ideas like this, but the philosophy behind it doesn't interest me at all. I simply tell people's stories for them.[3]

INTERVIEWER: When the demand to follow in the father's footsteps seems important, you tend to focus on the child's viewpoint.

TREVOR: My stories are often written from the child's point of view.

INTERVIEWER: On the other hand, "August Sunshine" is written from the parent's perspective—a good parent suffering from the bad behavior of a narcissistic, rebellious daughter. "Matilda's England" also provides positive parental models. Mrs. Ashburton mothers Matilda. Although not Matilda's mother, she influences her in a profound way. One of my freshman students saw Mrs. Ashburton as the villain responsible for Matilda's decline.

TREVOR: I think the sympathy in that story is with Matilda.

INTERVIEWER: At the start Matilda seems so vulnerable, but as she matures she seems cruel. Her own suffering hardens her to the suffering of others.

TREVOR: I think it's interesting that your student should see Mrs. Ashburton as a kind of villain. She did impose on Matilda a certain sequence of ideas, but she's simply being herself. People—sometimes very good people—can actually harm others without fully meaning to. It has nothing to do with Mrs. Ashburton's nature, which is certainly benign. She harmed by chance, like Miss Havisham in *Great Expectations*.

INTERVIEWER: I can't help but prefer old Mrs. Ashburton to the mature Matilda. This frail, old, aristocratic woman invites the children of her hired hands over for afternoon tea. She gets everyone in the community together during that last tennis party.

TREVOR: Mrs. Ashburton wasn't a disruptive, and I believe that there are people who simply are disruptives—people who disrupt human relationships all the time. She was just caught up in circumstances, and Matilda caught something from her. It's almost like someone having a disease—a cold passed on to someone else, who then develops pneumonia and dies. It's no one's fault.

Part 2

INTERVIEWER: Matilda doesn't follow Mrs. Ashburton's example of bringing people together.

TREVOR: No, she doesn't, but this story is really a study of Matilda's imagination. Her imagination was sparked by her own idea of Mrs. Ashburton. Imagination is often a burden, I think, and it did a lot of damage to Matilda. If Mrs. Ashburton hadn't been there, something else might have damaged her in the same way. The story is a record of circumstances, and I write quite a lot about circumstances affecting people.[4]

INTERVIEWER: Circumstances or your characters' own distorted view of circumstances? Sometimes it's difficult for the reader to decide whether an event is actually happening or whether it is strictly happening in the character's imagination. "The Blue Dress" starts realistically enough with an image of imprisonment, but the narrator's daydreams and nightmares eventually overwhelm the reader with puzzlement. The reader may feel trapped by the narrator's perspective because he or she is left questioning whether or not Dorothy meant to kill her friend.

TREVOR: That story, "The Blue Dress," is about the way in which a fiction writer—or a journalist of the kind portrayed here—recognizes truth immediately. Some fiction writers very easily spot lies because they spend so much time relating truth to lies. If, in what they're writing, people say the wrong thing, writers recognize it instinctively. People make excuses accepted by others but not accepted by the sort of journalist in that story. He—like the fiction writer—is so used to making certain that the jigsaw on the page really works that he separates truth from falsehood when it creeps into real life.

INTERVIEWER: So the narrator in that story is truly perceptive in terms of other people? His view of Dorothy as murderer is valid?

TREVOR: Yes, it is valid.

INTERVIEWER: And of course the irony is that he's lonely, and she appears to be the ideal woman he has always wanted.

TREVOR: Yes, but he also spots something. He feels something isn't quite right. There's something funny about this family, and that keeps nagging him. He tends to regard people with a particularly beady eye. And this—although with a journalist, not a fiction writer—is what is happening in that story. Real life is the raw material of the fiction writer. People you meet, gossip you hear. And since people after all are your "meat," you do look at them with a beady eye.

INTERVIEWER: In "The Blue Dress" the cohesiveness of Dorothy's family is interesting. There's a sense of togetherness that is almost ominous. They all look alike. The brothers are twins. They know each other's minds. They even share their dreams every morning. Where does this interest in imagination and dreams come from? Did you ever read the psychologists or philosophers on dreams and the imagination?

TREVOR: Being interested in dreams and the imagination is simply part of me. I have no interest whatsoever in what psychologists or philosophers have to say on the subject. Dreams come into my stories quite often because people dream. We all do. I include my character's dreams just as I include details about what clothes someone is wearing. It seems to me a very natural thing to do. If I see someone in a blue dress, I want the reader to see someone in a blue dress. I want the reader actually to see that image. Every fiction writer has a relationship with the reader. I imagine something, and I want that to work in the reader's imagination. I like writing that way—writing for the page or for radio. It's different with television or the cinema, for which I write also, because the images are created by a camera. I much prefer the no man's land of literature where the reader's and the writer's imaginations are entwined.

INTERVIEWER: You mentioned in another interview that you were curious about how a person gets to the point of being capable of murder. Some of your stories like "Attracta" represent grotesque events, but most are not about horrible crimes but rather crimes that involve basic human flaws like talking too much about yourself at a party as in "Raymond Bamber and Mrs. Fitch." Or else you focus on the terrible circumstances that drive a character to desperate acts. But sometimes—and now I'm thinking in particular about Williams in "A School Story"—we aren't given any circumstances explaining the character's grotesque behavior. Instead we've got motiveless malignity. Are there exceptions to your statement that "there may be evil people in the world, but I am reluctant to put them down on paper. I think it's more likely that we all are touched sometimes by what we could call evil, but it can happen to anyone"?

TREVOR: The trouble with statements like that is they're off the cuff. It is true that some people in certain circumstances can do evil things even though they are not truly evil. If a terrorist plants a bomb and kills people, you have to assume that he is "evil," but I'm curious about what makes this person evil. I'm curious about why someone would plant a bomb knowing that innocent people will be harmed. I write in order to try to find out. I write out of such curiosity.

INTERVIEWER: Much of the time when you present what you call "disruptives" readers can see the trauma or understand why they are that way because you present difficult circumstances that have forced them to desperate action. But in "A School Story" you don't provide any background to explain Williams's vicious nature.

TREVOR: Williams's story is based on the notion that people like Williams do occasionally exist. I think the structure of my stories, though, is a lot simpler than it seems. When you first finish a story, it seems quite complex. In that story a boy appears to be capable of what you call "evil." That's enough for me to wonder about. I used to teach boys that age. I never met anyone quite like Williams, but it's very believable that one might.

INTERVIEWER: I'm interested in your settings focused on the boarding school run for profit and on urban offices or rural businesses—the ad agency, the butcher shop, the auto garage, the pub. "The Ballroom of Romance" is a complex story focused on relationships, yet it also develops a "commercial" setting—an unpromising place for romance.

TREVOR: I wouldn't think of that story in terms of the commercial world, although the commercial world does come into some of my stories. One I suppose is "Mulvihill's Memorial."

INTERVIEWER: Have you read any of the modern philosophers' objections to the materialistic aspects of modern life?

TREVOR: I have no interest in philosophy whatsoever.

INTERVIEWER: Anyone thinking about human experience is dealing with the same material to some degree. If authors are true to human nature and philosophers are true to human nature, shouldn't there be some concordance?

TREVOR: I am an instinctive fiction writer. I am not an intellectual. I distrust the purely intellectual approach to experience. To me, the kind of intellectualism of philosophers seems tied up with anthropological examination and theory, which I find particularly boring. I prefer human nature to sociology. I just like people.[5]

INTERVIEWER: If a writer doesn't read psychology or philosophy but reads novelists or poets steeped in modernist thought, that's bound to have an effect. Freud wrote about the compulsion to repeat; Dostoevsky represented it, Golyadkin in *The Double*, for example. I think I see in your characters the drive to master trauma developing like Freud explains it—as a repetition compulsion.

TREVOR: I'm very aware of repetition in the stories. People do repeat themselves. And we all have obsessions, which crop up in various conversations. This obsessive side of people is sometimes revealed by repetition.

INTERVIEWER: Markham in "A School Story" tells the story of his mother's death over and over again. Your traumatized characters seek refuge in routine, in repetition. A reviewer has complained about your "studiously repetitious style," but I wonder if it isn't a technique for conveying psychological distress—not meant to be "translated" line by line?

TREVOR: Yes, that is certainly true. The routine, the feeling of repetition, suggests a kind of consolation.

INTERVIEWER: This also involves a mechanical response to life.

TREVOR: Yes. But of course you have to return to normal, and the return to normal after a terrible event is itself interesting. I write about what fascinates and interests me: to me, the story is very important. I don't read the critics anymore. They sometimes read into the stories a lot which doesn't seem to me apposite, but then again they may read a lot into it which I wouldn't have thought of but does seem apposite.

INTERVIEWER: If eight out of ten critics come up with the same observation.

TREVOR: Then there's probably something to it.

INTERVIEWER: You are a master at compassionately representing neurosis and psychological pain. I think of "A Happy Family," "The Mark-2 Wife," "Beyond the Pale."

TREVOR: The BBC has just made a film of "Beyond the Pale," and I believe you would learn more from looking at that film than talking to me. The film is very different from the story. I wrote the script myself, and what I had to do was to find the heart of the story, and then retell it very economically, because on television you can't have a woman going on so for as long as the wife does at the end of the story.

INTERVIEWER: "Beyond the Pale" is one of your best stories about women who suffer quietly. You represent quite a few men who fear women in your stories—perhaps rightly so given aggressive women like Hilda in "Lovers of Their Time" and Mrs. da Tanka in "A Meeting in Middle Age." But these women are the minority case.

TREVOR: The relationship between men and women is a particularly meaty one: there's an awful lot to be said about it. There are many variations of it in my stories, and there is also repetition. "A Meeting in Middle Age" about Mrs. da Tanka and "Raymond Bamber and Mrs. Fitch" are very similar. Writing short stories is a repetitious business anyway if you write, as I do, in order to experiment, and I consider myself, like all fiction writers, an experimentalist. I find that in a lot of my stories I'm investigating the same theme to see what happens a second or third, even a fourth or fifth, time. I would liken that to a Renaissance painter who painted over and over again the Virgin and Child or the Nativity.

INTERVIEWER: I'm still wondering about the characters like Raymond Barber who feel so distanced from women and yet are so very lonely. Why are these characters like this?

TREVOR: I think the honest answer is I don't know. There are a lot of them. I suppose it's just an interesting piece of ground to cover. . . .

INTERVIEWER: In "The Blue Dress" Terris longs for the perfect woman. Dorothea seems almost ethereal. So much of modern literature suggests a discomfort with the body.

TREVOR: That comes into the story about Dolores in "The Property of Colette Nervi." Dolores's whole life centers on the fact that she has to use crutches. Her existence centers on her bodily imperfections.

INTERVIEWER: The ethereal woman in "The Blue Dress" is in a different world from one allowing bodily imperfections to occur. She represents an escape—unlike Norman's wife in "Lovers of Their Time," whose sexual demands are threatening. Then there's "The Introspections of J. P. Powers," a grossly overweight man whose underarm hair is "a growth that sours." He seems repulsive physically. Yet his wife still loves him.

TREVOR: I think maybe Powers just wasn't a very attractive man. He was a big, heavy man whose body was a bit of a burden to him. Whether in the end, however, the story actually is about what I wanted it to be about is another matter. You may well be right. It may have ended up being about something else. But it was meant to be about someone doing a job he hates and the way this affects that particular man in that story. That is what interested me.[6]

INTERVIEWER: I must confess that I worry when male authors take on the perspective of a young girl or a woman. You've changed my mind in this regard, when I think of Bridie, for example, or "The Mark-2 Wife." You are very brave to write from the perspective of a young girl's initiation into womanhood, a barren wife, or from the perspective of an old woman worried about senility as in "Broken Homes."

TREVOR: I think there are women like that everywhere. I write about women because I'm not a woman. I write about girls because I'm not a girl. The relationship between a boy and his father doesn't fascinate me in the same way; I know too much about it. I was a boy who had a father. But at the same time, all fiction is rooted in autobiographical experience: the fiction writer is like a piece of litmus paper. He or she experiences pain, or distress, and that personal experience is his yardstick. I can't really know what another person's physical pain is, so I have to use my own.

INTERVIEWER: Yet actually you do have some firsthand experience with the perspective of girls and women. You have a sister. You have a wife. And in your early schooling in the convent and elsewhere, you were a minority boy. Weren't most of the children in your classrooms girls?

TREVOR: In one particular classroom, when I was six.

INTERVIEWER: So you had some special opportunities to observe the girls and their interactions with each other, or their interactions with boys?

TREVOR: That's a rather interesting idea—that after such a long time, before I wrote at all, I was observing this and remembering it. It's interesting, but in my case, I don't think it's true. As far as I can remember, I wasn't an observant child. It is the passing of time between childhood and now that allows me to dwell naturally on childhood images.

INTERVIEWER: Americans want to read adventures about boys, the initiation into manhood, what Leslie Fiedler calls the "male-male marriage," or war—although I think this is changing. I for one teach Carson McCullers's *Ballad of the Sad Café*, a woman's view of the male-male marriage. D. H. Lawrence of course is the major English writer concerned with marriage and sexuality. Has Lawrence been any sort of an influence?

117

TREVOR: No. The major influence was detective stories. I still read thrillers and mysteries, and I think I sense the form of the detective story as a pattern in my work.

INTERVIEWER: One thing so amazing about your stories is your ability in the first few sentences to get the suspense going.

TREVOR: Well, there you are. Other influences are not as strong. Other people are always battering away at detecting influences in my fiction, and sometimes they mention writers I haven't ever read. Often they do that.

INTERVIEWER: They mention Joyce.

TREVOR: Yes. I'm very fond of *Dubliners* and *Portrait of the Artist*, but I don't much like *Ulysses*.

INTERVIEWER: There is of course word play in your work—that's Joycean—but Chaucer, Shakespeare, and Dickens were also masters of wordplay. And don't most writers work at it?

TREVOR: I'm unaware of wordplay in what I write. That's something that gets into a writer's work by accident. Many of Joyce's "puns" were mistakes in the manuscript. Joyce retained typographical errors just for fun, I think. But I'm very fond of Shakespeare, and if a writer is fond of someone, that's going to be an influence. I have a feeling Dickens is an influence. On the other hand, I'm very fond of Jane Austen and George Eliot, and I don't see any influence there.

INTERVIEWER: Jane Austen and George Eliot also wrote about women. There may be a coincidence of ideas without any direct influence because poets, authors, philosophers, and psychologists are dealing with human existence in a certain time.

TREVOR: Parallel lines do exist. The great influence for me didn't come from books but from people I know or knew.

INTERVIEWER: It seems that much of your work develops parallel lines that coincide with book knowledge despite your objections. That's true of writers with insight.

TREVOR: But quite often authors may cite certain works as influences and be wrong. It's a very difficult thing.

INTERVIEWER: Sometimes there's one particular work a writer says, "This is what got me going, this is what I always go back to."

TREVOR: Well, I read and reread more than any other book *The Diary of a Nobody* by George and Weedon Grossmith.

INTERVIEWER: I know you've spent most of your adult life in England, but since you were born and raised in Ireland, some people might look for the influences of Yeats or Irish folklore on your work.

TREVOR: I would say none. It's very hard to say if, for instance, I had been born in another country, say France, whether I'd write the same kind of stuff or not. It's very hard to say what makes it what it is. I have written short stories which are set in Irish villages, but the essentials could be found—or might once have been found—in rural Italy or France.

INTERVIEWER: Is there a particular short-story writer you like?

TREVOR: I like Katherine Mansfield.

INTERVIEWER: What about the Russian influence?

TREVOR: I haven't read enough of Russian literature to say that there's any influence at all. I don't like reading languages which are not English. I rarely read anything in another language. I don't trust translations.[7]

INTERVIEWER: All of this raises extremely difficult issues about authorial intention and consensus.

TREVOR: All art creates argument, not agreement. If critics express a strong dislike for a story, sometimes that means it works. You have to upset rather than please. Many readers write to me and have the wrong end of the stick but appreciate the story. If there is bland agreement, this kills it. There is no uniformity. If you don't raise hackles, you're not a good writer.

Notes

1. Geordie Greig interview, *Sunday Times*, 29 May 1988, sec. 2, pp. G8–9.
2. Trevor ghosts fabricated by interviewers and reviewers include the "literary leprechaun . . . dangerously in touch with the nether Kingdom of the trolles" (Richard Mayne's review of *The Love Department*, "The World of Books," BBC transmission, 4 October 1966); the "Gentle Gerontocrat" (W. L. Webb's profile of the early play "The Elephant's Foot" [*Guardian*, 1 May 1965]); the "age sage" (interview of William Trevor, *Observer*, 4 July 1965); "Distiller of the Extraordinary" (*Times*, 15–21 March 1987); "The Irish Raj" (John Naughton's review of *The Silence in the Garden*, 31 July 1988, 26); "The Irish Maupassant" (John Fowles's review of *The News from Ireland, Atlantic*, August 1986, 89–91); an Irish writer with a "gentle Cork lilt [who] became strangely animated" so that "one could almost hear the click of creation"

119

(Hugh Montgomery-Massingberd interview, *Sunday Telegraph*, 21 January 1990, 38); "A Gentleman of Substance" wearing a "tweed jacket," gazing at others with "immediately trustworthy blue eyes . . . a Mr. Chips set loose in New York" (Gail Caldwell, interview, *Boston Globe*, 30 May 1990, 37–44); and "a teller of fairy tales in a small-town library," "an Irish housekeeper humming to herself as she makes beds," and "a boy liberated from study hall to play once again among the characters he loves" (Stephen Schiff, "The Shadows of William Trevor," *New Yorker*, 28 December 1992–4 January 1993, 159). This last impression Trevor corrected: "No, no, no . . . writing is a serious business with me, and there isn't much play there. Writing's a killer. It's difficult and obsessive. It's possessive. It's heartbreaking."

3. A sculptor in the early days of his career, Trevor abandoned this pursuit because "the absence of people was upsetting me. I still don't like pictures without people in them" (Amanda Smith, "PW Interviews," *Publishers Weekly*, 28 October 1983, 80).

4. Trevor declares during an interview that he is "very interested in the sadness of fate, the things that just happen to people" (Smith, 80).

5. Reynolds Price rightly notes that "Trevor's knowledge—despite his disclaimer—proves deeper, broader and longer winded than Joyce's, yet far less showy in its calm refusal to follow Joyce in the strangling pursuit of a handmade new tongue able to do more than language can. And the language of Mr. Trevor's best work, of whatever length, proves its modest but entire adequacy in telling us all he seems to know or means to tell us" (review of *The Collected Stories*, *New York Times Book Review*, 28 February 1993, 26).

6. In the Smith interview Trevor says, "What interests me most of all about writing is the relationship between you and the unknown reader and the sort of link you have with that person, the way in which that person actually picks up something which isn't in the story. . . . Some people pick up [what the author intended]; other people don't get it at all. It's like looking at a picture which you don't like. Somebody else comes along and adores it. There's that odd, peculiar relationship, I think, between writer and reader. It's not in any way a personal one. It's purely people on the same sort of wavelength" (81).

7. Trevor's stories have been translated into Japanese, Chinese, Bulgarian, Czechoslovakian, Hebrew, French, Spanish, Portuguese, Flemmish, Dutch, German, Italian, Romanian, and Russian—all of the Western European languages and Scandinavian languages.

Interview, 1989

Mira Stout

INTERVIEWER: What did you do after leaving university?

TREVOR: When I left Trinity Dublin, I tried to get a job, and it was very difficult in those days—in the 1950s in Ireland. Eventually I found an advertisement in a newspaper that said someone's child needed to be taught. "Would suit a nun," it suggested at the end of it, which was interesting, and I actually got that job. So I used to leave Dublin every day on the bus, go about twenty-five miles into the country, and teach this rather backward child. Her mother brought in the neighbor's children, and a little academy was formed.

INTERVIEWER: Why had they asked for a nun?

TREVOR: Because nuns sometimes have time on their hands. It was half a day's work, which was enough to live on, and this went on for about a year. I wasn't interested in writing in those days. I left that job when I got married, and then worked in a school in Northern Ireland for about eighteen months, before the school went bankrupt. We had to leave Ireland after that because I couldn't get another job. I taught in a school in England for two years or so—in the Midlands near Rugby—before deciding to try and make a living as a sculptor. I came down to the west country and set myself up, rather like Jude the Obscure, as a church sculptor, and existed like that for seven years. Then, when our first child was about to be born, it was clear that the money couldn't be spread between three people, so I gave that up, and got a job writing advertisements—which I was very lucky to get because I knew nothing about it. I was thirty. We moved to London, and I wrote advertisements for some years, always on the point of being sacked.

INTERVIEWER: Why?

From "The Art of Fiction CVIII," *Paris Review* 110 (1989): 118–51. Reprinted by permission of the *Paris Review*.

TREVOR: Because I was extremely bad at it. It was then that I began to write short stories. . . . I've always had an uneasy relationship with employers.

INTERVIEWER: Did you enjoy any aspect of working in an ad agency?

TREVOR: Only in retrospect. But all experience is good for writers—except physical pain. Office life is interesting. People behave quite differently from the way they behave at home with their families. I had to visit a factory near Birmingham, I remember, that manufactured screws. I'd never have met people who made screws otherwise, and I happen to be particularly interested in the work people do. And I was always seriously frightened that I was going to be sacked, and that, too, is a useful feeling to remember.

INTERVIEWER: Did you produce good copy?

TREVOR: Oh, no. I produced very bad copy. I found it difficult to write convincingly about boat propellers or beer or airlines. I could never think of slogans. But advertising wasn't a very big part of my life—I was a teacher for just as long, and if ever I had to earn a salary again I'd prefer to teach, I think.

INTERVIEWER: What did you teach?

TREVOR: More or less everything really. I liked teaching math best because I don't have a natural way with figures and therefore had sympathy with the children who didn't either. And I greatly respected the ones who did possess that aptitude. My skill in art and English made me impatient, and I found those subjects rather dreary to teach as a result. "Why are the art room walls covered with pictures of such ugly women?" a headmaster asked me once. "And why have some of them got those horrible cigarette butts hanging out of their nostrils?" I explained that I had asked the children to paint the ugliest woman they could think of. Unfortunately, almost all of them had looked no further than the headmaster's wife. I like that devilish thing in children.

INTERVIEWER: When you wrote *The Old Boys*, were you friends with other writers and artists?

TREVOR: Up to that time my friends were mostly from the art world rather than from the world of literature; I didn't really know any other writers. But I've never gone in for the business of belonging to sets of people. . . . I have friends because I like them. I hate the idea of groups. . . .

INTERVIEWER: Do you think of yourself as being part of an Irish literary tradition?

TREVOR: I always call myself an Irish writer. I'm one of the few Irish writers who actually likes the phrase. Since I am an Irishman, I feel I belong to the Irish tradition. I don't really feel that being Irish is the important thing. What is important is to take Irish provincialism—which is what I happen to know about because it's what I come from—and to make it universal.

INTERVIEWER: Then there isn't something special about Ireland, some peculiar quality about it that drove you away with all the other famous exiles?

TREVOR: No. The only thing that drove me away from Ireland was the fact that I couldn't get work there. I didn't want to leave Ireland. I would have stayed there. I wasn't ambitious to go away in order to "see Ireland correctly from a distance"; it's just that the accident of going away has caused me to see it. . . .

INTERVIEWER: Did growing up as a Protestant in southern Ireland make you examine religious belief in an intense sort of way?

TREVOR: No. What is now apparent to me is that being a Protestant in Ireland was a *help*, because it began the process of being an outsider—which I think all writers have to be—and began the process of trying to clear the fog away. I didn't belong to the new, post-1923 Catholic society, and I also didn't belong to the Irish Ascendancy. I'm a small-town Irish Protestant, a "lace-curtain" Protestant. Poor Protestants in Ireland are a sliver of people caught between the past—Georgian Ireland with its great houses and all the rest of it—and the new, bustling, Catholic state. Without knowing any of this, without its ever occurring to me, I was able to see things a little more clearly than I would have if I had belonged to either of those worlds. When I write about, say, a Catholic commercial traveler, I can almost feel myself going back to those days—to an observation point. And when I write about the Ascendancy, I am again observing. Elizabeth Bowen writes of her family employing boys from the local town, Mitchelstown, where I was born, to stand round the tennis court collecting the balls. I would have been one of those little Protestant boys, had I been the right age.

INTERVIEWER: You've spoken about religion in a social context, but not about religion as religion.

TREVOR: I didn't come from what you'd call a particularly religious background. But Ireland is a religious country, and in those days everyone went to mass or church. It was just all taken for granted. It didn't really impinge in any sort of way, except that one felt different as a Protestant.

INTERVIEWER: There are a lot of priests in your books.

TREVOR: There are a lot of priests in Ireland—and a lot of nuns. The first school I went to was a convent, and I liked the nuns very much. I had quite a lot to do with the Catholic Church, although I've never been seriously tempted to join it. English writers like Graham Greene, for instance, and Evelyn Waugh, became Catholics because they were frustrated. But Ireland being a religious country, the religious side of people is satisfied more naturally than it is in England.

INTERVIEWER: Are you religious?

TREVOR: I don't really think of myself as religious . . . I only go to church in Ireland. I don't like the Church of England. I feel much more drawn towards Catholicism when I'm in England—not that I'd do anything about it. I always feel that Protestantism in England is strangely connected with the military. All the cathedrals here are full of military honors. It's part of an establishment with the armed forces, tombs, rolls of honor, that sort of thing. It's a strange combination. The Protestant Church of Ireland is a shrunken, withered little church that I'm quite attracted by.

INTERVIEWER: There is a strong element of faith in your work, of people coping, enduring, of being borne along in their lives. Is it humanist or spiritual faith?

TREVOR: I don't think it is humanist; I think it is just a kind of primitive belief in God. . . . I'm always saying that my books are religious. Nobody ever agrees with me. I think there is a sort of God-bothering that goes on from time to time in my books.

INTERVIEWER: What's the difference between an Irish eccentric and an English eccentric?

TREVOR: That's difficult to say—it's like asking what the difference is between English humor and Irish humor. It's a dry quality that you get with English eccentricity at its best; Irish eccentricity is much more outlandish. Crazier. English eccentricity is something you hardly notice until all of the sudden you realize that you're in the presence of an eccentric mind. It's not like that at all with an Irish eccentric; you know about it all very easily and quickly. English eccentricity has a suburban quality—it's like a very neatly-trimmed garden in which you suddenly realize that the flower beds aren't what they seem to be. There's a kind of well-turned-out quality about English eccentricity, whereas the Irish equivalent is higgledy-piggledy, and sometimes even noisy. . . . I've never quite believed in the obvious English eccentric, the man who comes into the pub every night and is known to be a dear old eccentric. What I do believe in is the person who scarcely knows he's eccentric at all. Then he says something so extraordinary and you realize he perhaps lives in a world that is untouched by the world you share with him. . . .

INTERVIEWER: Do you think your Irish stories differ fundamentally from your English and Italian stories?

TREVOR: Yes, I do. There is a sense of community in the Irish short stories that doesn't exist in the others. In the Irish stories people tend to talk to each other, whereas in the English ones people talk *at* each other. The English are much more oblique; we Irish are more direct. . . . A huge amount of what I write about is internal, a drifting back into childhood, based on a small event or a moment. By isolating an encounter and then isolating an incident in the past you try to build up an actual life, and you cannot build up a life without using time in that sense.

INTERVIEWER: Is time a destroyer or a preserver?

TREVOR: Both. It both heals and destroys, depending on the nature of the wound; it actually reveals the character. There is either bitterness or recovery; neither can take place without time. Time is the most interesting thing to write about besides people—everything I write about has to do with it. Time is like air; it is there always, changing people and forming character. Memory also forms character—the way you remember things makes you who you are. People struggle to share a very private side of themselves with other people. It is that great difficulty that I often write about. . . .

INTERVIEWER: If I may reduce your work to being *about* something, it seems to be about people coming to terms with things. I wonder if you think that's right, first of all, and if you think that is the ultimate thing that can be done with what we have, a coming to terms, or an acceptance?

TREVOR: Do you mean a sort of settling for second best?

INTERVIEWER: Sometimes that *could* be the way it's taken, but at other times indeed much more than that, that it is in fact a tremendous act of bravery to accept in this way.

TREVOR: Yes, I suppose that does come in a bit. I don't think on my part it's a conscious conclusion. I don't think I ever think like that when I'm writing the piece of a story which implies that people come to terms with something. I'm still working out what they would do. . . .

INTERVIEWER: Do you agree with what some critics have called a sense of "hopelessness" in your characters?

TREVOR: Well, some characters are pretty hopeless in themselves. Others find themselves in hopeless situations. There doesn't seem to be very much going for them, as it were; that's also true. But generally speaking that's true in life. There is a certain amount of hope, not an endless supply. It's not as rose-tinted a world as most people would like it to be. But the people in my stories and novels are not ragingly desperate; they have, as you said a moment ago, come to terms, and coming to terms in itself is quite an achievement. There's not a total absence of hope there. It's not an entirely pessimistic view, I think. In fact, it's even faintly optimistic.

INTERVIEWER: I read somewhere that you describe yourself as a melancholic; how does this manifest itself? Is it a state, a temperament through which you write?

TREVOR: I don't ever recall referring to myself as a melancholic. . . . I don't think you can write fiction unless you know something about happiness, melancholy—almost everything which human nature touches. . . . I doubt that an overwhelmingly jolly, optimistic person has ever been an artist of any sort. If I were purely a melancholic I don't think I'd write at all. I don't think writers can allow themselves the luxury of being depressives for long. Writers are far less interesting than everyone would have them. They have typewriters and will travel. They sit at desks in a clerk-like way. We are outsiders; we have no place in society because society is what we're watching and dealing with. Other people make their way in the world. They know ambition, they seek power. I certainly don't have any ambitions, nor am I in the least interested in power. I don't think fiction writers tend to be; their needs are different. Personally, I like not being noticed. I like to hang about the shadows of the world both as a writer and as a person; I dislike limelight. . . .

INTERVIEWER: Do you think literature has been much diminished by the glare of TV, cinema, video, and by entertainment hunger?

TREVOR: I think there is a danger of that. In a way it depends on your mood how you answer that question; if you're cross about it then you tend to say, "I wish there was more seriousness about." And by serious writing I mean everything from Thomas Hardy to P. G. Wodehouse, from Chekhov to Sean O'Faolain. Instead of that, there's now the pressure of fashion in literature, and I imagine that is something that's demanded by your entertainment-hungry public. Fashion belongs on a coat hanger. In literature—in any art—it's destructive. Some of the prizes that have crept on to the British literary scene have made rather a circus of literature. It's nice to win them, and all money freely given to the arts is a good thing. But prizes and best-seller lists and fashion tend to *tell* people what to read, and it's discovering what to read for yourself that lends reading half its pleasure. Glamour and glossiness are not what literature is about. Literature is Thomas Hardy, who wasn't fashionable in the least. He ate his guts out in Dorset, and was miserable, and produced marvelous books; in the end, only the books matter. Nowadays, books tend to be shoveled into a chat-show wheelbarrow, more talked-about than read.

INTERVIEWER: Has there been any time when you've been able to figure out what it is that you want to *do* as a writer, what you're aiming at?

TREVOR: Well, to be completely honest, I wouldn't have any such aim at all. I don't have any general ambition. I don't really want to make any statement. I see the writing of a story as creating an impression, and that impression is going to communicate itself to somebody else. That's all I seek to do.

The Irish Short Story

Art has its own way of defying both definitions and rules, and neither offer much help when examining, more particularly, the short stories of Ireland. In putting this anthology together, I was driven back, again and again, to a consideration of the part that storytelling has played, and continues to play, in Irish life. An Irish flair in this direction has long been recognized as a national characteristic. Stories of one kind or another have a way of pressing themselves into Irish conversation, both as entertainment and as a form of communication. For centuries they have been offered to strangers, almost as hospitality is: tall stories, simple stories, stories of extraordinary deeds, of mysteries and wonders, of gentleness, love, cruelty, and violence. And side by side with speculation about their source, the question has always been: why are they so delighted in, why do they so naturally form part of Irish vernacular? . . .

The desire to introduce listeners to people they don't know—which is somewhere near the heart of all storytelling, anecdotal or otherwise—isn't something that disappears simply because passing time brings changes. It remains a strong desire in Ireland, and it continues to be satisfied. . . . [I]t required little perception to pinpoint the Irish passion for peopling bus stops or any other mundane setting with colorful characters, and for retailing, with innate ease, episodes of interest. "Wait till you've heard this." And when you've heard it: "Isn't that the quare one?" . . .

It is against this background of a pervasive, deeply rooted oral tradition that the modern short story in Ireland must inevitably be considered. "A young art," Elizabeth Bowen rightly observed, "a child of this century." Joyce in Ireland and Chekhov in Russia turned the antique inside out: the larger-than-life figures enacting highly charged drama in a mystic past were sent packing. With revolutionary abruptness, the stories that now pressed for attention appeared to be about nothing at all. Added to which, they often dealt in underdogs—what Frank O'Connor called "small men"—and increasingly as the century wore on, in hard-done-by women.

From *The Oxford Book of Irish Short Stories*, ed. William Trevor (Oxford: Oxford University Press, 1989), ix–xv. Reprinted by permission.

The novel had seized upon the heroics that for so long had distinguished the fiction of the myths, the sagas, and the parables. The modern short story grew out of what remained, but it was a growth so fruitful that its emergence as a literary form could not be denied. Its newness was not dissimilar to the newness of the Impressionists and the post-Impressionists. Its intensity left behind an echo, a distinctive imprint on the mind. It withheld as much information as it released. It told as little as it dared, but often it glimpsed into a world as large and as complicated as anything either the legend or the novel could provide. Portraiture thrived within its subtleties.

What was happening internationally suited Ireland particularly well, and the Irish contribution to this very different kind of story was destined to be as generous as that same contribution has been to the older form. It is occasionally argued that the Irish genius for the short story is related to the fact that when the novel reared its head Ireland wasn't ready for it. This is certainly true. In England, for instance, the great Victorian novel had been fed by the architecture of a rich, stratified society in which complacency and hypocrisy, accompanied by the ill-treatment of the unfortunate and the poor, provided both fictional material and grounds for protest. Wealth had purchased leisure and a veneer of sophistication for the up-and-coming middle classes; stability at home was the jewel in the imperial crown. In Ireland there was disaffection, repressed religion, the confusion of two languages, and the spectre of famine. The civilized bookishness of writing novels, and reading them, was as alien in an uneasy, still largely peasant society as timeless afternoons of village cricket still are in the busy, aspiring Ireland of the late twentieth century. While in England readers waited impatiently for another episode of *The Old Curiosity Shop* or *David Copperfield*, in Ireland the cleverness of a story, or the manner of its telling, still persisted as a talking point. The roots of the antique tale continued to grow, and with hindsight they did so to the advantage of the modern art. . . .

Far more important for the new generation of writers was the heritage of an audience for whom fiction of brief duration—irrespective of how it was offered—was the established thing. The receptive nature of this audience—a willingness to believe rather than find instant virtues in scepticism—allowed the modern story to thrive, as the old-fashioned tale had. Stories, far more than novels, cast spells, and spells have been nurtured in Ireland for as long as imperial greed has been attempting to hammer its people into a subject class. The Irish short story has come to appeal to audiences far beyond its home, but the confidence born of instinct and familiarity has encouraged the art of the spell to continue. The understanding of a mode of communication is not easily abandoned. The Irish delight in stories, of whatever kind, because their telling and their reception are by now instinctive. . . .

English fiction writers tend to state that their short stories are leavings from their novels. In Ireland I have heard it put the other way around.

The Novelist's World

Novelists create worlds: the Dickens world, the world of Jane Austen, Cranford, Brickfield Terrace. They're private, exclusive worlds, with laws and a language of their own, populated by people who are at one with their environment and could healthily live in no other. Pickwick in Hartfield would be a silent fellow and Emma would feel as uneasy in the Laurels as Bertie Wooster would in the presence of Buck Mulligan. Nor would one care to contemplate the fate of Widmerpool in Greenland. It is that sense of people being right for the world around them, whether it's Wonderland, Puritania, Nighttown, or anywhere else, that gives good fiction its gloss of success. It's a sense of correctness and aptness, painlessly achieved when the novelist's world grows naturally from seeds of reality. . . .

The simple point is that beneath all the normality of lace curtains and porter and Mass and hurling matches, eccentric events do tend to occur in small Irish towns, and the talk that goes with them is often as wild as Goon-talk. Language is shaped by a craziness which has nothing to do with the darker depths of madness but which, through a misty Celtic twilight, has often been seen as the inspiration of an art form. . . .

In Ireland today there is, understandably, very little laughter in novels, short stories, and plays. If only for that reason and no other, it's good to enter again the George Birmingham world, to be reminded that Ireland, for all its tragedy, can be happily funny too. It's good to laugh and often to marvel, to share in an endless flow of enthusiasm for the comic, and constantly to sense the gentleness of a writer who loved his people.

From the introduction to *The Search Party*, by George Birmingham (London: Bodley Head, 1973), i. Reprinted by permission of the Peters Fraser & Dunlop Group Ltd.

131

"Too Blasé for Rape"

I hadn't, until now, read [Paul] Smith. "A passionate naked realism," one reviewer remarks on the dust-jacket of *Come Trailing Blood*, which is a new title for his first novel published as *Esther's Alter* in 1959. "He writes . . . with compassionate intensity, with sorrow and with a terrible slow-burning anger" suggests another of the dust-jacket voices, and someone else adds that the like of this hasn't come our way since Thomas Wolfe. O'Casey, Joyce, Dickens and Dostoevsky are mentioned in passing. "He is quite possibly the finest writer Ireland has ever produced," proclaims an anonymous raver from the *Spectator*.

To be compared with O'Casey, Joyce, Dickens and Dostoevsky doesn't mean that a writer is in the same class as any of them. It means that here and there in his work there's an echo of literary worlds we already know, that a whiff of an original compound floats now and again through the reader's awareness as he passes from chapter to chapter. In the same way it is far from being preposterous praise to state that a novelist performs with naked realism, though what is meant by nakedness in this context I'm not sure. And clichés like "compassionate intensity" and "terrible slow-burning anger" are so meaningless that they're not worth bothering about. But the cry from the *Spectator* is simple, and huge in its claim.

The reader who has not read Mr. Smith before must therefore approach this present novel with the expectation that he's possibly going to discover in it something more memorable than either the wit of Wilde or the lyricism of Yeats; something more arresting than the invention of Joyce, the language of Synge, the polemics of Shaw, the comedy of Goldsmith, or the passion of Swift. The list goes on, and the longer it gets the harder it seems on poor Mr. Smith, who naturally can't be blamed for other people's silliness. Unfortunately, though, extravagant claims tend to damage a writer in a way that the harshest criticism never can. A novel stands on its own two feet, its style and content defending it whenever they have to. It is much more difficult to live down excessive adulation.

From "Too Blasé for Rape," review of *Come Trailing Blood*, by Paul Smith, *Hibernia* [Dublin], 29 April 1977. From the Bodley Head files.

So, extracting Mr. Smith from his entanglement with our entire literary heritage, what exactly does he offer us? Here's a piece of him, chosen at random:

> Unresigned to what he knew was prepared Jeremiah shoved the bedclothes off and slid his feet to the floor cringing back the way he always did from the icy flags while against his crackling ankles and uncertain shanks the boneless furred body lashed and clawed. Wanting to get back to the warm place from which he had been flung Jeremiah swore and tried to kick the cat off, but it stayed an unmovable weight against him—and then in the open door—as if to demonstrate an emotional life of its own—stood with its nose raised to sniff and test the outer darkness of the passage with the quivering antennae of senses beyond which it refused to budge.

It's a difficult kind of prose, dense, a little fussy, often confusing: the novel itself is rather similar. Set in Easter Week, 1916, it revolves around a group of working-class Dubliners, the inmates of a single house. A young man is killed—clearly destined for that end from the beginning—but apart from that, the butchery on the streets hardly impinges on the house's small array of personal worries and preoccupations. There isn't a plot, and what mainly happens instead is that women's thighs tremble with urgency and men for the most part take advantage of this circumstance. . . . What may have shocked censorious Dublin in 1959 wouldn't cause a maiden aunt to raise an eyebrow now. We've had more than our fill of sex on the printed page. Blasé, we sigh over incest and rape; four-letter words are a bore.

Yet there remains a very great deal to be said for this novel. If it is over-written, it is also, for page after page, vivid and alive. If its broth-of-a-boy rumbustiousness begins to feel like a tourist trap, the vigor from which it overflows is, in its calmer moments, a considerable tonic. And the tenderness that keeps breaking through the hard, sometimes bitter, shell is never sentimental. Certainly you have to persevere, but the rewards are there to make up for the effort. Novels are rarely perfect: warts and all, Paul Smith is a much better writer than some of the vanities on his dust-jacket suggest.

Part 3

THE CRITICS

Introduction

> [Trevor's] excellence comes from a happy marriage of central values in both the Irish and English traditions. Art of this solidity and quality cannot be written from inside frontiers. It is, in the best sense of the word, international.
>
> —John Fowles[1]

> Well written, meticulously observed, ingeniously constructed, generously conceived—deserving to be treated as classics of the form.
>
> —Auberon Waugh[2]

Literary criticism helps readers see how a particular writer's work relates to the great minds of the age, to understand sociocultural and historical contexts, and to analyze craft, "how a poem or story means." Although writers and critics today question whether literary works mean anything at all, scorning the idea of consensus and scoffing at those who "essentialize," reading criticism of every sort hones our sensitivity to literature and life. Some consensus is necessary for the discipline of literary criticism to speak in a coherent way to students, to those in other disciplines, and to the poets and writers whose works become targets for analysis rather than important reflections of human consciousness, human creativity, and shared experience.[3] If we consider life, we must essentialize, especially when dealing with literature as complex as Trevor's stories, as complex as the related works of other modernists.

Modern works are indeed admired for their complexity—the multiplicity of meanings they inspire. Trevor's work is no exception. The Trevor umbrella encompasses a motley crew, a wonderful multiplicity of circumstances, and a comprehensive view of life. An eclectic critical approach does seem appropriate. Specialized approaches (gender criticism, narrative theory) also seem appropriate, as long as critics do not assume theirs is the only approach. I believe that critics to some extent should let the work declare *itself* as to the best approach—whether its formal aspects, an analysis of voice, considerations of gender, development of social and historical contexts, or a combination of these. No one approach to a particular work seems adequate to me.

And yet Trevor critics and reviewers thus far do not demonstrate the full range of critical approaches that have so enriched and polarized the profession. What follows, then, is a brief but necessarily limited gathering of critical excerpts on Trevor's work, arranged chronologically. My selection offers representative views of critical judgments of Trevor's stories. I hope to forge a few pathways in a TrevorTrevorland with very few streets and to encourage many more critics in America and elsewhere to write about William Trevor's art from various angles.

Notes

1. From the dust jacket of *Lovers of Their Time*.
2. From the dust jacket of *The Ballroom of Romance*.
3. For a wonderful assessment of current conflicts between writers and critics, see Jay Parini, "The Theory and Practice of Literature: a New Dialogue," *Chronicle of Higher Education*, 9 September 1992, sect. 2, B1–2.

Robert Nye

Critics have been known to compare the short stories of William Trevor to condensed novels. I can see the sense of that—Mr. Trevor does indeed pack sufficient richness into his delineation of character to suggest that his people could easily be extended and their doings made to occupy chapters instead of paragraphs. However, the idea of Trevor as a novelist-in-miniature seems to me the wrong way of looking at his specific skill in the short story form. The opposite is about true. He is more nearly a poet of brief fictions. Each of his stories is like a poem, an incident, an experience, a situation, which he has captured in words and drawn out to just the length it will tolerably sustain. His is a very rare skill: that of knowing when to start, and when to stop. His stories have more *shape* than those of any other contemporary practitioner of the difficult art.

The twelve examples collected in *Angels at the Ritz* display him at his best. Whether he is writing about a wedding party, the consequences of an attempt to dispose of a corpse in a block of flats, or a fabricated case of haunting, Mr. Trevor is invariably specific and shocking and matter-of-fact. The shock comes in the irony of his matter-of-factness. He tells you the most outrageous things in the most pleasant manner, hardly ever raising his voice, and you believe him for as long as it lasts. The occasional bizarre detail does not obtrude, rather it adds a certain verisimilitude. I was reminded more than once in reading this delightful collection of the lines in Robert Graves' poem, "The Devil's Advice to Story-Tellers": "Nice contradiction between fact and fact / Will make the whole read human and exact."

Mr. Trevor aims for that kind of realism, not the obvious sort. And in doing so, he leaves the reader with some pleasant headaches. Is there really a ghost in "Mrs. Acland's Ghosts," for instance? Or are we meant to infer some disturbance just this side of madness, as in Henry James' "The Turn of the Screw," which has caused what looks like ghosts? The reader is left *haunted*—and perhaps that is how it should be with a successful tale in this genre. . . . [Trevor] writes of ordinary people pitched momentarily into extraordinary situations but never quite stepping out of what

From "Trevor: Storyteller with a Poet's Feeling," review of *Angels at the Ritz, Christian Science Monitor*, 16 June 1976, 23. Reprinted by permission of the *Christian Science Monitor*, © 1976 by the Christian Science Publishing Society. All rights reserved.

we know to be true of the possibilities of human nature.

About the manner of these stories, I noted a marvelous skill with dialogue—especially whimsical and inconsequential conversations—and sometimes approaching a poet's feeling for words and phrases. Which brings me back to my first point. Mr. Trevor is in his shorter fictions more like a poet taking a deep breath and expanding upon the kind of people and events crystalized (say) in a few stanzas by Philip Larkin, than like a novelist condensing acres of information to a few thousand words. More than one of these stories made me think of the beauty and skill of Larkin's poem "The Whitsun Weddings," which also ends on just that note of vaguely affirmative but unsentimental ambiguity which Mr. Trevor favors. However you like to characterize it, *Angels at the Ritz* is a most entertaining and enjoyable book, and no one who cares for decent writing will wish to ignore it.

V. S. Pritchett

The excellent short story depends so much on alerting immediate doubts and acute expectations; we are alerted by a distinctive style and self; yet there are one or two writers who cunningly insinuate an abeyance of the self, a quiet in the inquiry that, for the moment, calms the nerves. To this class William Trevor belongs. He is one of the finest short story writers at present writing in the Anglo-Irish modes. His people are those who, in the course of their lives, are so humdrum in their ordinariness, so removed from the power of expressing themselves that he has to efface himself in order to speak for them. They appear to be confused by experience and in moral judgment, but they live by an obscure dignity and pride which they are either too shy or too unskilled to reveal at once: his art is to show they have their part in an exceptional destiny and even in a history beyond the private. Impartially, he will justify them.

In one of his Irish stories, a bustling tippling priest speaks half pityingly, half in exasperation, of his brother, the timid manager of a provincial hardware store: the man is fatally married to the memory of his domineering mother—a banal and common Irish dilemma—yet the timid, inarticulate man is in the midst of a momentous, devastating religious crisis. The two brothers have made the ritual visit to Jerusalem and the timid one experiences a violent shock not only to his faith but to his understanding and conscience. For him the early Christian legend and especially the sight of the Stations of the Cross in the Via. Dolorosa are unimaginable, meaningless outside the Irish Christianity of Co. Tipperary. He has become a victim of the indignity of History.

The mother of the two men dies while the brothers are away. The timid one will not recover his faith unless he gets back home at once to the proprieties of his mother's funeral. A petty, pathetic dilemma? No, for him an earthquake. And there is more to it than that: for it was he, he now knows, who was by nature a priest; it was the bustling priest, the organizer of Catholic pilgrimages, who has the devious habits of the shopkeeper. This is a story of frustration, and on such a level it may seem dim even in its pathos; but notice—the timid brother will become the master; his

From "Explosion of Conscience," review of *Lovers of Their Time*, *New York Review of Books*, 19 April 1979, 8. Reprinted by permission of the *New York Review of Books*. © 1979 by Nyrev, Inc.

conscience is reborn. He forces his priestly brother to give up the tour and return: Galilee and Bethlehem are travesties.

In nearly all Trevor's stories we are led on at first by plain unpretending words about things done to prosaic people; then comes this explosion of conscience, the assertion of will which in some cases may lead to hallucination and madness. In that disordered state the victim has his or her victory; these people are not oddities but figures crucified by the continuity of evil and cruelty in human history, particularly the violent history of, say, the wars and cruelties of the last sixty years of this century. Theirs is a private moral revolt. The point is important, for Trevor has sometimes been thought of as the quiet recorder of "out of date" lives living tamely on memories of memories, as times change.

Tragically (comically too) he is aware of the seismic shock that history, even the ignorance of it, has prepared for the dumb or the successful. The obvious ironies are not laughed off; he goes deeper and more ruthlessly than that. The Irish in him—one would guess—faces the horrors, the English the plain dismays of having to accept circumstance by putting on the best face available. . . .

Trevor quietly settles into giving complete life histories, not for documentary reasons, but to show people changing and unaware of the shock they are preparing for themselves. . . .

As his master Chekhov did, William Trevor simply, patiently, truthfully allows life to present itself, without preaching; he is the master of the small movements of conscience that worry away at the human imagination and our passions.

Patrick Skene Catling

A good short story, like a good poem, exists only in its expression. Its essence is irreducible and immutable. As William Trevor has written (in a review in praise of one of the writers of short stories he most admires, Sean O'Faolain), "the better the short story, the less easy it is to re-tell." By this criterion, among others, Trevor's short stories are among the best in English. . . . I have just re-read 59 of Trevor's stories and I cannot imagine how any of them could be improved by any alteration. Every story seems as perfect (as Philip Larkin might put it) as an egg.

Perhaps his most important virtue, rare among all sorts of people, especially writers, is that he acknowledges without condescension the value of every human life, no matter how restricted, distorted or embittered: even the outwardly most ordinary person feels extraordinary; everyone is unique and marvellous and awful, alone at the center of his world.

Trevor's subjects are home, family, love, duty, pride and other difficulties and torments that make life, even with alcohol, seem so long. Behind the face of a benign, anxious, philosophical humourist, with his generous nose, quizzical eyes in their pouches of experience, eye-brows slightly raised and forehead corrugated as though in mild surprise, there must be a carefully controlled intelligence of a high order, perhaps even a certain cunning.

He is an inexorable yet usually merciful observer of major weaknesses and minor vices, some not so minor. He is a keen appraiser of the surfaces and depths of people and things. He is a diligent listener, sometimes an eavesdropper, with an ear as accurately retentive as a tape recorder and with the artistic sensibility and skill to edit the recordings to achieve, beyond verbatim realism, a heightened sense of the oddities of different manners of speech.

His calm, evenly weighted, ostensibly dispassionate style makes eccentricity seem normal and normality bizarre. He makes few comments—few are needed; there are no nudges or winks. He presents his observations with such subtle imbalance that he gives an impression of fairness. His malefactors can be understood and sympathised with and their poor, fool-

From "The Genius of William Trevor," review of *The Day We Got Drunk on Cake*, *The Ballroom of Romance*, *Angels at the Ritz*, *Lovers of Their Time*, and *Beyond the Pale*, *Spectator* 249 (1982): 25–26. Published with permission of the *Spectator*.

ish victims can be forgiven. He depicts tragedy without mawkishness, absurdity without ridicule.

"Absurdities," he once told a Dublin interviewer, Clare Boylan, "are the great literary bridge because people recognize them and they are always tragic. I have used my own experience and people I know in my work: every writer does—though not recognizably. Whenever there is an absurd figure in my stories it is me."

He is compassionate but not sentimental, ironic but not cynical. He is a moralist who only implies morality. He never preaches sermons to people when they are down, or even when they are up. He simply offers readers opportunities to perceive aspects of themselves—punishment enough. He also provides the healing Irish consolation of the sort of humor that would enable you to smile if you slipped and twisted your ankle in a graveyard in the rain. He would have made an excellent priest.

John J. Stinson

Although not the recipient of much scholarly attention, William Trevor is yet another Irish writer who has proven himself a master of the short story form. . . . Most of these readers soon feel that if Trevor does not rank near the very top of the list of twentieth-century British and Irish short story writers, that comparisons to such artists as A. E. Coppard, Frank O'Connor, Elizabeth Bowen, Liam O'Flaherty, and V. S. Pritchett are not presumptuous or embarrassing, but are, in fact, reasonable.

The accolades of reviewers for Trevor's short story collections are nearly universal and unabated, but the stories have met with almost total neglect from academic critics.[1] It is possible, though, that this neglect may soon be remedied. . . . In his front-page review in the *New York Times Book Review* of the *Stories* and Trevor's almost simultaneously released novel *Fools of Fortune* (Viking Press), Robert Towers began by remarking that "Trevor's reputation as a major literary presence should by now be secure. . . ." Various tokens of Trevor's recognized stature are just now beginning to circulate; one might note, as a single example, that in the fifth edition of *The Oxford Companion to English Literature* (1985), Trevor is not only included, but actually given an entry larger than those accorded to Frank O'Connor, Liam O'Flaherty, or Edna O'Brien.[2]

Part of the reason for the scholarly neglect of Trevor until recently might well lie in the fact that he is not easily categorized. Most centrally, some uncertainty as to whether Trevor might more properly be classified "British" or "Irish" is probably just enough to discourage the publication of some scholarly studies in academic or critical journals. It seems increasingly clear now, however, that Trevor is an Irish writer. . . . Trevor's readers will note too that in the last few years he has generally been moving away in his fiction from the southwestern districts of London and the peculiar inhabitants he manages to find there, and moving back toward Irish themes, characters, and locales. . . .

[Trevor emphasizes] the oddities of social relations, the vagaries of fate, and the pecularities of our common human nature. Environment is only background, symbolic background, where, through a congeries of history,

From "Repilicas, Foils, Revelation in Some 'Irish' Short Stories of William Trevor," *Canadian Journal of Irish Studies* 11, no. 2, 1985: 17–26. Reprinted by permission of the *Canadian Journal of Irish Studies*, University of Saskatchewan, Canada.

inherited disposition, and even fate, conditions are ripe for the writer to throw some light upon human nature and the human condition. Trevor's eccentric Londoners are, by only slight permutation, all of us. And Ireland is for Trevor, as he himself says it is for Edna O'Brien, "a microcosm of the world as it always is."[3]

The essential loneliness of the human spirit and feelings of imprisonment of the human heart can be effectively shown when fictional characters are deftly placed within environments that are dull, stagnant, or oppressive. Ireland comes almost ready-made for the literary artist who wishes to reflect a primordial dilemma of the heart that lies too deep for ordinary words. Castigation of some aspect of Irish social life is not what many writers are primarily about when they produce fictions that appear merely "negative" about Ireland. For writers such as Trevor, Ireland is very much the Ireland of "reality," a product of its own troubled and peculiar history, but it is also true that in the works of these same writers some process of artistic filtering of the "real" is bound to occur. Thus, a number of Trevor's Irish stories are heavy with an oppressive atmosphere that is characteristic of much Irish short fiction from George Moore and James Joyce all the way through to writers of the present such as James Plunkett and John McGahern. Melancholy or frustrated figures move glumly, stoically, or mechanically in these fictions through stultifyingly dull or constricted worlds that wither the soul and weigh down the heart with the burden of unfulfilled desires. . . .

Trevor achieves a wealth of implication by employing character replicas and foils. The latter technique, foil characterization, is, of course, widely discussed and its meaning commonly known: the inclusion in a literary work of a figure whose characteristics differ sharply from those of another (usually the main) character, thus setting these characteristics out in bold relief because of the starkness of the contrast. It is surprising, though, that no commonly agreed-upon term exists for the inverse of this technique, i.e., emphasizing some salient traits or a conflict existent in a character by the inclusion of another character who has some of the same traits or conflicts. The term *doppelgänger* clearly does not always serve since the mirroring character need not necessarily be an alter ego; even the term *double* does not quite do because even that suggests a psychological depth and resonance that need not always be present. "Mirroring technique," "replication technique," "doubling," "twinning," "paralleling characters" are terms that have been occasionally employed by the relative few who have mentioned the technique. I will simply, then, refer to certain characters as foils, replicas, or reflectors. What is important is the depth, subtlety, and economy Trevor achieves with these techniques. . . .[4]

A kind of epiphany that should occur for each of Trevor's readers, however, is that his characters are so elementally human that they provide reflections of an important part of each of us, that the reverberative echoes ring deeply in our souls. The people of the small Irish towns, villages, and farms are all of us.

Notes

1. The inside front of the dust jacket of *Angels at the Ritz* (New York: Viking Press, 1976).

2. Margaret Drabble, ed., *The Oxford Companion to English Literature*, Fifth Edition (Oxford: Oxford University Press, 1985). The entries are alphabetically arranged.

3. William Trevor, "O'Brien, Edna," in *Contemporary Novelists*, Third Edition, ed. James Vinson (New York: St. Martin's Press, 1982), 504.

4. Gitzen in a short comment on the stories of *The Ballroom of Romance*, correctly observes that "in nearly every story the central figure is confronted by another person whose situation parallels or highlights his own" (62).

Murray Bramwell

Amidst the profusion of new fiction and the apparently endless experimentation with narrative and structure, the fiction of William Trevor can be, and for too many readers still is, overlooked as commonplace and, certainly, unfashionable.

That is not to say that Trevor has gone unregarded—King Penguin published his *Collected Stories* several years ago, and a number of his stories have become memorable television plays—"The General's Day," . . . "Access to the Children," and the remarkable BBC production of "The Ballroom of Romance" with Cyril Cusack.

However, in the stampede to celebrate the various manifestations of post-, neo- and anti-fiction, too few have reiterated the simple fact that William Trevor is a superb prose stylist, who invites comparison with Chekhov, Maupassant, and Joyce. In many respects it is precisely his fearlessness that has made his achievement apparently invisible. At a time of crisis in defining the boundaries between fiction and therapeutic compulsion and where a failure of artistic nerve has led to minimalism or almost parodic self-consciousness about the legitimacy and nature of fiction itself, William Trevor continues to write in a way that reminds us that fiction is first and foremost for readers and not to serve as fodder for theorists in narratology.

This is not to imply that Trevor is "reactionary" or old hat but simply that he gets on with the business of writing stories which are formally and thematically profoundly satisfying in their assurance and because Trevor is unfazed by the undeclared taboos of recent writing. He writes about women and men in society with a cool objectivity that requires no appended political or ethical tub-thumping—the stories speak, he inhabits character effortlessly and vividly and encompasses major themes with commendable understatement. . . .

In his most recent collection of stories, *The News from Ireland*, he is in characteristic form. As ever, what is striking is the variety of circumstance, location, and character—it is as though his invention is such that no two stories ever seem remotely alike. His themes of disillusionment and regret

From "Irish Eyes Have It," review of *The News from Ireland*, *Adelaide Review*, 18 September 1986, 6. Reprinted by permission.

are everywhere identifiable of course, as are the preoccupations with the tyrannies of personal and political history particularly in Trevor's native Ireland. . . .

It is Trevor's Irish settings which continue to acquire, in successive volumes of stories, that combination of humanity and mordant satire that one associates with Joyce . . . that kind of paralysis of spirit that Joyce defines in *Dubliners*. The echoes are strong, but Trevor's accomplishment is such that he can move so close to the masterly work of Joyce and not seem derivative.

Ariel Daigre

William Trevor began to write only in 1958 after a distinguished career as a sculptor. Since then, in 10 or more novels and five collections of short stories, he has continued to enrich our knowledge of and love for Ireland. Born near Cork in 1928, Trevor studied at Dublin before settling (a long time ago now) in England. Being distanced from his country—it is such a common phenomenon that we do not need to stress it—has only distilled, and thereby increased tenfold, his power to evoke the Irish countryside and its people. Even though we must acknowledge this, still he is in no way a regional novelist, and he proves it once again in this new collection of stories. Whether the characters he portrays are Irish or English, whether the stories take place in Ireland, England, or elsewhere, we find the same ability to fashion characters and settings that distinguish his purely Irish stories, which finally are not purely Irish because the author avoids exploitation of those possibilities available to him. A lesser writer would certainly have taken advantage of such possibilities. . . .

In "The Property of Colette Nervi" we find ourselves in a desolate hamlet—a single house at the crossroads, one that serves as pub, grocery, and post office. A little farther along there is an archaeological site that a few scattered tourists visit from time to time. Retail trade is handled by a widow and her lame daughter, Dolores, who has to spend long hours lying down and whose only mental stimulation comes from her dreams—a husband, perhaps someday; you must not count on it—and a stack of westerns that she inherited from her father and reads all day long. The monotony of this daily routine is broken by a visit from a couple of French tourists, the Nervis. Colette Nervi leaves her purse, which contains jewelry, on the roof of her car, and it disappears mysteriously. Dolores is not involved in any way, but her life is nevertheless about to take a new turn: a young man becomes interested in her and gives her a necklace as an engagement gift. Dolores guesses where it comes from but says nothing and wears it proudly on her wedding day. Guess how it all turns out. Will Colette Nervi, who promised to come back again in case her purse was found, burst into the church and demand her necklace? That is the ending we

From a radio review of *The News from Ireland*, French Language Service, BBC World Service Radio, broadcast 19 December 1987. Translated from the French by Edith Farrell, University of Minnesota, Morris. Reprinted by permission.

expect, but it is not what happens. The story's ending is much simpler, much more realistic, much sadder.

The title piece, "The News from Ireland," is the longest and most ambitious of the collection. The story takes place during the great famine of the 1840s and shows us two communities: a well-off Protestant family settles in Ireland and, despite the very best of intentions, cannot seem to understand that the good that they do is not enough to break down the barriers that separate them from the rest of the community, which is steeped in poverty. The rich and poor alike live an alienated existence; only distance might bring them together.

Alienation, the despair of people who are not at home anywhere, is a constant theme throughout these dozen stories. The influence of [James] Joyce, whom one critic takes as [Trevor's] model, is clear. . . . From this brief overview one might suppose that all of these stories are sad and demoralizing. That is far from the truth because the author includes in his dialogue and characters humorous touches that delight readers.

Kristin Morrison

William Trevor writes about political and historical matters from a cosmo-
logical perspective: events remote from each other in time, or space, are
linked in such a way to suggest that the apparent barriers of past and present, as well as of physical distance, are illusory, that connections exist
among the various parts of his universe which make it a cosmos, an
orderly (though often damaging) series of mutual interrelationships.
According to the basic concept which seems to dominate his work, past
and present are actually the same moment; apparently separate realms (the
public and the private, for example, or the political and the domestic)
inevitably overlap; all the various elements of space and time are intrinsically interrelated, comprising an elaborate and powerful "system of correspondences" which shapes the world. This mode of thought is very like the
academically familiar one described by E. M. Tillyard in *The Elizabethan
World Picture*, though not as neat and regular: not now kings and suns and
eagles and whales all conjoined by their rulerships of their respective
realms, but English and Irish, lovers and haters, planters and dispossessed,
the well-fed, the starving. . . . And although now, in the twentieth century,
there are some who see political and moral spheres as quite different, in
Trevor's system of correspondences (as also, indeed, in that medieval and
Renaissance one) questions of good and evil are unavoidably bound up
with political and secular issues. If the king was wicked, the land declined,
the people suffered, inevitably. So, too, now in Trevor's world, the immoral
behavior of individuals necessarily wounds the whole social fabric; and,
conversely, rottenness in the body politic has its inevitable analogue in private lives and personal character. In Trevor's fiction, the relatedness of
microcosm and macrocosm is not a quaint concept from the past but a very
real fact of human life in the present, to be taken quite seriously by readers
of his work.

Where is the source of the evil? As always in Trevor's work, far, far in
the past. In *The News From Ireland*, the governess tells her charge the Legend of the True Cross: that a seed falling into Adam's mouth sprouted from
his body when he died and grew into a great tree on which, centuries later,

From "William Trevor's 'System of Correspondences,'" *Massachusetts Review* 28
(1987): 489–96. Reprinted by permission of the *Massachusetts Review*. © 1987 by the
Massachusetts Review, Inc.

Christ was crucified (11, 21 ff). This ancient legend presents a classic paradigm of the kind of thinking which is behind the correspondences inherent in Trevor's fiction. It is not enough that the act of original sin in the Garden of Paradise and the act of redemption centuries later in Palestine should both have been merely *associated* with trees. No, these trees must themselves be related to each other, intrinsically connected, just as the Savior and the Sinner are connected. Jesus is called the new Adam because there is a profound metaphysical connection between him and the first Adam (as St. Paul puts in 1 Corinthians 15:22: "For as in Adam all die, even so in Christ shall all be made alive"). . . . Christian tradition, liturgy, and poetry extends this equation: "As sin and death had entered the world by the Tree in the Garden, so by a Tree the redemption of the world was achieved. Nay, the Tree of the Garden had been miraculously preserved, and from its wood, by the poetic justice of God, was formed the Cross, that Tree which bore a better fruit for the healing of nations."[1] . . . Trevor himself suggests by his repeated reference to the Legend of the True Cross that he wants his readers to associate such correspondences with the events in this story. Indeed, the governess herself seems to recount her telling of the legend to the butler as if it were a correlate of his story of the starving child, as if this religious legend and that political event were intrinsically connected, just as in another context she matches story with story "because the subjects seemed related."

In the public world of famine a child is marked with the wounds of Christ. In the private world of domestic privilege the governess speaks of the cross on which Christ died. These two events of present starvation and past crucifixion are not more remote from each other in time and space than are the events of Christ's passion and Adam's sin. The whole point, in fact, of that ancient Christian legend is to annihilate time and space, to show the cross of salvation and the tree of transgression to be significantly one. And now, by this same mode of thinking, this starving population in Ireland in the nineteenth century is also one with Christ crucified, not in some vague poetic metaphorical sense, but in a quite powerful, intrinsic one.

The conjunction of these two stories (about the stigmatic child and about the True Cross) clearly establishes this connection between various supposedly separate worlds in Trevor's skillfully structured narrative. So, too, does the grim pun accompanying these accounts. In its etymology, the word "starve" means "to die" and is found thus in many medieval poems and carols which refer to "Christ who starf on rood." The word eventually became restricted to one specialized form of death, the meaning we now use, to die from lack of food. Thus the pun makes all the more appropriate Trevor's association of starvation in Ireland with the death of Christ. . . .

It is precisely this kind of association, with its implied correspondences, which at times makes Trevor's work seem grotesque to some modern readers: often in reviews his characters and situations are described as too bizarre to be generally appealing. But the whole point is that these conjunctions which seem odd are, in fact, pertinent: that there does exist an old and abiding tradition, a view of the universe which asserts that acts in one realm reverberate in another—that, for example, the physical damage of one person is re-created in the spiritual damage of a second, or vice versa.

What is striking in all Trevor's work is how frequent and elaborate these various connections and analogues are, so pervasive that it does not seem an overstatement to call them a *system* of correspondences. In "Beyond the Pale," Cynthia, the English visitor who "is extremely knowledgeable about all matters relating to Irish history,"[2] makes her companions uncomfortable by discerning the past alive in the present of the Antrim coast where they so blindly and blithely holiday: "'Can you imagine,' she embarrassingly asked, 'our very favorite places bitter with disaffection, with plotting and revenge? Can you imagine the treacherous murder of Shane O'Neill the Proud?'" (704). When a suicide occurs at their idyllic hotel, she will not let its implication be ignored: the violence, the terrorism, the murder which precipitated that suicide are not "beyond the pale" of this garden resort but are a symptom of its very existence, a present manifestation of evils going back to the "Battle of the Yellow Ford . . . , the Statutes of Kilkenny. The Battle of Glenmama," and so on through a long recital (704). Their landlord's furious rejection of her associating past events with present realities is itself unwittingly phrased in terms which suggest connection: "You are trying to bring something to our doorstep which most certainly does not belong there" (708). Yes, this is a metaphor, but one which in context seems almost palpable: a real "something," a real "doorstep," just as there was and still is an actual "pale" holding back the starving from the well-fed, protecting the complacent from the desperate, suggesting deceptively that private worlds of vacationing adulterers can be kept discreetly separate from the grander cruelties of history.

Events and persons are not isolated from each other despite spatial or temporal separation. Things unspeakable, "beyond the pale," cannot be kept at bay with physical or social or psychological barriers. The "body politic" is indeed one body, and the health or decay of each member affects the others. Original sins, whether by Adam or Edward, mar the fortune of all, always and everywhere.

Notes

1. F. J. E. Raby, *A History of Christian-Latin Poetry from the Beginning to the Close of the Middle Ages*, 2nd ed. (Oxford: Clarendon Press, 1953), 88.

2. From *Beyond the Pale and Other Stories* (1981) in *The Stories of William Trevor*, 696.

Michael Ponsford

William Trevor, who has emerged as one of the most significant—and one of the most prolific—contemporary writers, is preoccupied with truth. . . . This is noted by Julian Gitzen in his astute survey of Trevor's fiction. . . . Gitzen contends that Trevor's characters invariably respond to an unpalatable truth in one of two ways; "some accept the truth, while others find illusion the only bearable remedy." Gitzen emphasizes, however, those characters who "display strength in accepting or reconciling themselves" to "unpleasant truths," finding that "Trevor repeatedly demonstrates that acceptance of truth requires resoluteness and the power of forgiveness."

But Trevor's world, I think, is darker than this emphasis allows. The short stories, whose narrow scope throws the features of Trevor's longer fiction into strong relief, can certainly depict characters who accept the truth, but the consequences of such an acceptance are never very welcome. Rather than accepting, the characters are more frequently forced to acknowledge a truth, but there are many others for whom the truth is elusive or for whom the discovery of truth can mean only unhappiness. To intensify this negative focus, Trevor chooses as his agents of truth characters who are somehow apart from the rest of society and whose conveying of truth can only pass on a sense of alienation. Trevor's characteristic perception of truth is twofold: either the truth is ineffectual, or it effects only misery and despair. It is just as much the denial as the acceptance of truth that demands resoluteness.

Trevor's art—though it is concerned with the way in which a society is built on deceptions and treats this theme with some measure of comedy—is not exactly satirical: the truth never reforms manners or draws order out of society's chaos as it does in pure satire. For Trevor's sad-comic world is peopled not by reformers or malignants but by a variety of innocents, ingenues for whom the truth never dawns [such as "Raymond Bamber and Mrs. Fitch"]. But most are not so fortunate, and far more numerous than the perceptual innocents are those for whom the acknowledgment of truth means alienation and the loss of stability. Trevor has a particular

From "'Only the Truth': The Short Stories of William Trevor," review of *The Stories of William Trevor*, *Eire-Ireland* 23 (1988): 75–86. © 1988 by the Irish American Cultural Institute, St. Paul, Minnesota. Reprinted by permission of the publisher and Michael Ponsford, Marlborough College, Marlborough, Wiltshire, England.

fondness for stories about children—innocents shocked by a perpetrator of the truth into a world of deceit and lies. He thus finds the exposure of hypocrisy and deception—the insistence on the truth—as an essentially destructive impulse. An encounter with truth can yield only misery, at best a bewildered frustration, at worst the madness of insight.

Death in Trevor's stories is frequently a breeder of truth. A death can force a concealed truth to the surface . . . or it can compel survivors to recognize a further truth about themselves and those around them. The theme is rich in possibilities for Gothic treatment, and several of the stories would fit a broad definition of Gothic—their hints of the horrific, their portrayal of a bizarre existence on the fringes of normal society.

The invalidity of truth underscores the bleakness of William Trevor's world. All the institutions upon which people depend to shape existence and give it meaning are illusory. Human relationships break and fail. Intimate friends, lovers even, have no real knowledge of each other's inner selves. It is because of their reluctance to face up to such a society that Trevor's characters inflict deceptions upon themselves and others; such blindnesses are a natural defense mechanism against a hostile existence.

Robert E. Rhodes

Prior to the 1986 collection, *The News from Ireland and Other Stories*, William Trevor had published five collections of short stories. The first collection (1967) contained a single Irish story, "Miss Smith." The four succeeding volumes had an average of four Irish stories each. In *News*, seven of the twelve are Irish: the title story, "The Property of Colette Nervi," "Bodily Secrets," "Virgins," "Music," "Two More Gallants," and "The Wedding in the Garden." Published almost simultaneously in the *New Yorker* were two thus far uncollected Irish stories, "The Third Party" and "Kathleen's Field," and not many months later, "Events at Drimaghleen" appeared in *Grand Street*.[1]

In these recent Irish works, Trevor has dropped a former major preoccupation, stories of the contemporary Troubles seen largely from an Anglo-Irish perspective, though the title story of *News* is an Anglo-Irish story, telling of the Great Famine and exploring something of the antecedents for the modern conflict. But for the most part these recent stories continue the types of settings, characters, and themes that are familiar to Trevor's regular readers: class and religious stress, rural isolation and loneliness, provincial drabness, thwarted love, the persistent intrusion of the past into the present, imaginations fed by films and shallow fiction, the vanity of human wishes.

On the whole, most reviewers of *News* found the collection admirable and frequently singled out one or more of the Irish stories for something that distinguishes them from the English stories. Virtually alone amongst the reviewers, John Dunne had serious reservations, noting that "generally [Trevor's] work ambles along in a pleasant nondescript manner which, for me at any rate, seldom elicits any emotional response at all."[2]

It is true that Trevor's stories are usually understated. For example, one will search in vain in *News* for striking or even memorable tropes, their stock being pretty much depleted by the following: "His hair was like smooth lead," "his face . . . exploding like a volcano," "The moon that was Thelma's face," "his rounded hill of a stomach," and "short hair as spiky as a hedgehog's." Nor is Trevor the exegete's dream in being a technical

From "'The Rest Is Silence': Secrets in Some William Trevor Stories," in *New Irish Writing*, ed. James D. Brophy and Eamon Grennan (Boston: G. K. Hall, 1989). Reprinted by permission of the author.

experimenter in point of view, for example. He's almost always in total charge as narrator and takes us where we need to go either through omniscience or through easy access to the consciousness of one character or another, with occasional irony deflecting a straightforward view of things. The reader seldom has problems with structure: Trevor stories ordinarily begin in a present and move without interruption to a conclusion; sometimes they open in a present and return to a past; sometimes they alternate between the present and the past; but very seldom do they give us difficulty in knowing where we are and when and why we are there.

But this very lack of difficulty—what Dunne calls "a pleasant nondescript manner"—a certain reticence on Trevor's part, leads, upon consideration, to an important motif that ties these several stories together—his use of secrets as a plot device and as a means of directing our attention to his most important fictional concern: the mystery of human personality, behind which may also preside some assumptions, conscious or otherwise, about dimensions of the Irish personality. Thus, "plot" and "character" and "style" are somewhat congruent and work together toward the presentation of theme.

Secrets are of course not exclusive to Trevor, nor are they new to these stories; a quick review of Trevor's earlier Irish stories turns up, for example, "Autumn Sunshine," "Beyond the Pale," "Saints," "Attracta," "Mr. McNamara," "The Raising of Elvira Tremlett," "The Time of Year," "Miss Smith," "Death in Jerusalem," and "Teresa's Wedding," among others that are activated by secrets. But their persistence in the present set of stories finally claims extended attention and a firm reason for reading Trevor more carefully than may have been the case in the past.

On the face of it, "secrets" are basic to almost any story; indeed, simple plot hinges upon secrets—we keep reading because we want to know what happens next. Not every story has secrets—more ordinarily considered—kept or disclosed by characters. Those that do, however, probably involve readers more than those that do not; as insiders, when a secret is shared with a character or characters or the reader, there is compelling dramatic irony, and the tension that is part of the story communicates itself readily to readers. Certainly secrets in a story can generate tremendous energy by giving, for example, an added erotic charge to the secrecy of a love affair. And secrets may be part of the dramatization of deceit, discretion, or indiscretion, the role of knowledge, the problem of communication, the conflict of illusion and reality.

To go an important step further, they add to the stories something of the mystery of human character, a quality that is at the heart of . . . "The News

159

from Ireland" and "Events at Drimaghleen," both works that probe the difficulty and perhaps the impossibility of one's ever truly penetrating the enigma of others, especially, perhaps, if the others are Irish. . . .

"Kathleen's Field," a title richly evocative of the possibilities of an allegorical reading for a story predicated on a characteristic Irish land hunger, tells of the innocent Kathleen, held hostage to the lechery of her employer by her fear that revelation of his lechery will mean that her father will forfeit the land he covets. . . . In "The Property of Colette Nervi," Trevor reprises his familiar Irish rural isolation and emotional deprivation, and ends with a marriage under the shady circumstances of secrets kept about the stolen property of the French tourist, Colette Nervi, whose brief intrusion into an Irish backwater precipitates events. With a strong subtext of class and religious differences as the source for secrecy, "The Wedding in the Garden" sees maid Dervla remaining in the service of the family of her lost love after he marries another so that she may haunt his happiness with her daily presence and the secret of what had been between them. Like "The Wedding in the Garden," "Bodily Secrets" has deterrents to marriage in religious and class differences, but they are overcome by the middle-aged couple's maturity, intelligence, and determination, traits that also enable them to negotiate secrets and to secure a workable conspiracy of silence over the husband's hidden homosexuality and Norah, the wife's, unwillingness to expose her aging body's loss of beauty.

In all of these stories, by having secrets remain concealed, Trevor has sacrificed at least one dramatic confrontation scene in each that might have eventuated in climax, resolution, and easing of conflict. Instead, secrets—Kathleen's guilty one, for example, or Norah's vain one—remain intact; we share Kathleen's silent despair and perhaps Norah's relief, and whatever tension is generated by the secrets becomes all the more powerful for remaining untold. . . .

In stories where secrets are revealed, Trevor gains some of the dramatic confrontation scenes and sense of climax that he sacrifices when secrets remain concealed. . . . [But] revelation of secrets is no more of a guarantee of a happy ending than their being kept intact, a conclusion that accords with Trevor's persistent rueful appraisal of human affairs. . . .

In several stories, the truth behind secrets is either known to readers almost from the outset or is eventually plainly displayed or can be divined with some certainty. . . . Readers have an obligation to remain alert and to join Trevor in his pursuit of what is elusive in human experience.

For the writer who is more interested in people than in, say, plot, and who likes to take chances by "cutting things" and chancing that readers will involve themselves, stories in which secrets are revealed give us one level for probing and pondering. Stories in which secrets remain unrevealed by an omniscient narrator and/or by characters and/or lack of evidence force us to some deeper level of thought and, if the chance has succeeded, some profounder sense of human personality and conduct. Perhaps we might say that by mystery . . . Trevor wishes to illustrate by technique the enigma of human personality that is at the heart of the stories' substance. . . . Questions multiply and we touch more deeply than if we were not required to ask because we have been told. Beneath the ordinarily unadorned and plain style of Trevor's stories there are often human enigmas that might give up revelation to those who take Trevor's dare.

The persistence of secrets—of several kinds and at different levels of interpretation—in Trevor's Irish stories leads inevitably to the question: Does Trevor mean that there is something in the Irish personality that is more predisposed to secrecy than in that of other peoples or something in Irish circumstances that create this predisposition?

One possible answer is that Trevor does not find the Irish any more inclined to secrecy than any other people. . . . Trevor has made some effort to claim universality for at least some of his Irish stories. For example, in an "Author's Note" to *The Distant Past and Other Stories*, Trevor's own selection of his Irish stories, he says of one of them, "Miss Smith," that it "might perhaps have come out of anywhere, but in fact is set in a town in Munster."[3] . . . Similarly, in a 1985 *Sunday Tribune* interview, he addresses a story that seems quintessentially an Irish story of isolation, deprivation, and loneliness: "Even 'The Ballroom of Romance,' and this might sound strange, I don't consider a particularly Irish story—the film [of the story] seems to have gone down just as well in places like Israel and Norway. It has a universality." And there are traits of jealousy and possessiveness, for example, everywhere, and Ireland has no corner on stultifying provincial towns or the yen for more land.

On the other hand, the particular circumstances of some of the stories place them ineluctably in Ireland. Some facts of the Great Hunger may be similar to those of other famines, but some of the facts of Ireland's and its consequences are intractably Irish. . . . It is typical strictly of the Irish-English relationship that a Hetty Fortune would invidiously attack the rural Irish; or that Protestants in Ireland occupy a position utterly unique; or that Ireland's geography and the history of land ownership are sufficiently singular to have created exceptional attitudes toward ownership.

Furthermore, despite what might appear as Trevor's at least implicit wish for a kind of universality to his characters, and even without an extensive analysis of the Irish personality in search of a penchant for secrecy, we can draw briefly on a handful of commonly held views of the Irish and their uses or nonuses of language to suggest that "secrecy" in its many forms is engrained in the Irish nature.

For example, we can draw on the very fact of the physical isolation of many Irish communities, families, and individuals as a means of explaining . . . a kind of tribal reticence that does not readily yield up its secrets even to other Irish. Carried a step further, it is a commonplace that the Irish as a whole, as a people so long dominated by the British, have been driven to a conspiratorial mode of life in dealing not only with the British but with one another. . . .

Taking an antithetical but complementary tack, we can observe that rather than being characterized by reticence, the Irish are more often and more traditionally marked by their loquacity, and loquacity not merely as small talk and chatter, though it is often enough that, too, but as a wondrous if sometimes manipulative way with words, a trait that often manifests itself in talk as performance. . . . Irish loquacity, in some of its flights of fancy often takes the form of indirectness, obfuscation, obscurity, ambiguity, innuendo, exaggeration and/or understatement—to say nothing of outright lies—all with the same practical effect of secrecy more strictly conceived.

In a fascinating 1982 essay, "Irish Families," in the collection *Ethnicity and Family Therapy,* a compendium of studies designed to assist therapists in dealing with family problems by introducing the therapists to the characteristics of different ethnic families, Monica McGoldrick writes:

> The paradox of the general articulateness of the Irish and their inability to express inner feelings can be puzzling for a therapist who may have difficulty figuring out what is going on in an Irish family. . . . Family members may be so out of touch with their feelings that their inexpressiveness in therapy is not a sign of resistance, as it would be for other cultural groups, but rather a reflection of their blocking off inner emotions, even from themselves. Thus, although the Irish have a marvelous ability to tell stories, when it comes to their own emotions, they may have no words. . . .[4]

It would probably be unwise for a literary study to pursue too far—to say nothing of uncritically accepting—the clinical implications and conclusions of these observations, at least for Trevor's stories, but there is no escaping that a study such as McGoldrick's helps us to understand how and why . . . Trevor has infused so many of his characters and situations

Michael Heyward

There can be few living writers of English with so sure a touch as William Trevor. He is a master of nuance, of the flick of the wrist that seems to disclose everything. His sense of pace and timing, of the balance between dialogue and description, is flawless. The humor in his work is dark and unforgiving, though he also knows how to be simply funny. His formal understanding of the story is traditional, but he tampers with structure and point of view. He hears the speech of his characters exactly. He never panders to the reader, yet his prose is direct, as supple and spare as a blade of grass. He is the kind of writer whose achievement we are inclined to underestimate because his work does not draw attention to itself and because the mysteries of his technique are not easily visible in the effects he creates. He may write in an unassuming style, but whoever tackles his work in quantity becomes aware of an accumulating richness. . . . His fictional resources are immense and his output since his first novel, *The Old Boys* (1964), has a kind of Victorian abundance about it; there's a new book every year or so. In an age of magical realism, of mannerisms hankering to invigorate the language, Trevor comes from another tradition of writing entirely; his literary ancestors include Chekhov, Joyce (in *Dubliners*), and Katherine Mansfield, who in their different ways all practiced an art intent on exposing the hidden codes of conduct and the subtleties of a confined world.

From "Domestic Terror," review of *Family Sins, New Republic*, 1 October 1990, 40–41. Reprinted by permission of the *New Republic*. © 1990 by the New Republic, Inc.

John Banville

Some years ago British television filmed an adaptation of William Trevor's short story "The Ballroom of Romance." It was a grim little drama, set in one of those concrete and galvanized-iron dance halls which sprang up at crossroads in rural Ireland in the 1940s and 1950s. The story centered on a woman, no longer young, who comes every week to the dance in a last-ditch and ultimately vain search for a husband who will take her away from her bleak life of toiling on her widowed father's farm, to which the circumstances of the time have condemned her.

The film was a fine, understated, moving production by the Irish director Pat O'Connor and a cast led by the marvelous actress Brenda Fricker. When it was broadcast, critics in Britain praised it highly, but threw up their hands in horror at the portrait (an accurate one) it gave of rural Irish life in the 1950s. In Ireland for the most part the response was the same. Before long, however, voices were raised in defense of those crossroad dance halls as meeting places for people living lives of quiet desperation in isolated and often dying rural communities. Under the cry of "Bring back the ballrooms of romance!" there ensued a lively debate of the values of rural life, on chastity and marriage, on the place of women in an agricultural society, on the flight from the land, and so on.

Whatever the affair may tell us about modern Ireland and its conception of itself, certainly it illustrates one of the main characteristics of William Trevor's writing, which is its ambiguity, the way in which it so expertly and cunningly avoids any hint of the judgmental. It also shows the broad appeal of Trevor's work, although his is among the most subtle and sophisticated fiction being written today. . . .

What remains consistent throughout Trevor's work is its tone; his inimitable, calmly ambiguous voice can mingle in a single sentence pathos and humor, outrage and irony, mockery and love. It is, to my ear, a wholly Irish voice, even when it speaks of things far from Ireland, and can even rise at times to Swiftian or Beckettian power . . . and although Trevor has something of Dickens's inventiveness and skewed comic vision, he has none of the great Victorian's sentimentality. . . . It is a measure of Trevor's

From "Relics," review of *Two Lives: Reading Turgenev and My House in Umbria, New York Review of Books*, 26 September 1991, 29–30. Reprinted by permission of the *New York Review of Books*. © 1991 by Nyrev, Inc.

skill that he conducts his stately dance along the very edges of sentimentality without a trip. . . .

Trevor speaks in a gentler voice than Beckett, say, or Céline, but his
vision is no less dark, and no less unflinching, than theirs. He is almost
unique among modern novelists in that his own voice is never allowed to
intrude into his fiction; never do we see the face of William Trevor behind
the lovingly fashioned mask of his style. Yet the work is never impersonal,
or cold. A sensibility reigns here which is at once inquisitive and loving.

Dean Flower

Trevor's fiction [stresses] that storytelling itself is dangerous. And everyone has a story to inflict on someone else. Each story in *Family Sins* involves someone's coercive narrative, some reductive and destructive fable.

In "Kathleen's Field," for example, Kathleen Hagarty's father wants to buy a rich pasture adjacent to his impoverished little farm in Ireland. The bank won't loan him money, and he can't raise enough by selling his prize bullocks. But the Shaughnessys are affluent and want a slavey to keep house for them in town; they loan Hagarty the money in exchange for Kathleen. She is so plain, everybody knows she'll never marry. And besides, all the other children have moved away—except for the eldest male who will inherit a better farm and marry well if Kathleen sacrifices fourteen years of her life. Never mind that Mrs. Shaughnessy is critical and impatient and lazy, or that Mr. Shaughnessy finds a subtle way of tyrannizing Kathleen sexually. It's all for the good of the family. "You're a great girl," her father says, unaware that he's forced his daughter into a form of prostitution.

Trevor makes such powerful material work by systematic self-effacement. His techniques may seem old fashioned at first, permitting leisurely exposition and switching from one point of view to another. But soon you realize that no judgments come from the author, that the style conforms to each character, and objective-sounding information is really subjective, frequently verging on indirect discourse. Hagarty for example sits in the pub "with a bottle of stout to console him," telling himself that since he's already paid to have the bullocks penned, "he might as well take full advantage of it by delaying a little longer." Trevor's indebtedness to the James Joyce of *Dubliners* is especially apparent here; both are masters of the subjective third-person and the ironic nuances of indirect discourse. Here's a choice moment, from "In Love with Ariadne," where Trevor shifts from direct to indirect:

> "If there's a man in Dublin that knows his bricks and mortar better than Ned Sheehy give me a gander at him."

From "The Reticence of William Trevor," review of *Family Sins*, *Hudson Review* 43, no. 4 (1991): 686–90. Reprinted by permission of the *Hudson Review*. © 1991 by the Hudson Review, Inc.

Barney said he didn't think he could supply the old woman with such a person, and she said that of course he couldn't. No flies on Ned Sheehy, she said, in spite of what you might think to look at him.

Joyce ends "Ivy Day in the Committee Room" with the exquisitely ironic anticlimax, "Mr. Crofton said that it was a very fine piece of writing"; Trevor ends "Kathleen's Field" with an equally crushing use of the device, "her mother would say again that a bargain was a bargain."

Sometimes Trevor will switch from direct to indirect discourse five or six times in a short scene. It's all so swiftly and compactly done you hardly notice the narrator's voice is absent. Trevor also switches quickly from one character's mind to another, untroubled by Jamesian conventions, yet the effect is never omniscience. In "A Husband's Return" the first four paragraphs convey four different minds, without any "author" there at all; in "A Trinity" the irritations of husband and wife interweave so inconspicuously we hear them both thinking and taking neither side: "The trouble with Keith was, he always sounded confident, as though he knew something she didn't"; and then "[Keith] wished she'd leave the talking to him." Trevor also likes to intercut dialogue with remembrances. In "The Third Party" and "August Saturday" conversations go on in the present while the main character's attention keeps lapsing and escaping into the past. Eventually memory becomes the more powerful storyteller. Often too Trevor will embed a letter or fragments from a journal in a story so as to complicate and extend a seemingly simple point of view. What all these techniques have in common is the author's disappearance from the text. You never quite hear Trevor's own voice. Even stories that sound like autobiography—"A Choice of Butchers" (1972), "Matilda's England" (1978), *Nights at the Alexandra* (1987)—turn out to be just first-person fictions, about different Irish childhoods that may or may not resemble the author's. For decades now the dust jackets have informed us simply that Trevor was born in County Cork and "lives in Devon with his wife and two sons." His reticence is just about flawless.

I do not mean to suggest that Trevor never adopts a storyteller's expository "once upon a time" role. He often begins in this seemingly authoritative old mode, e.g., the first story in *Family Sins*: "Nothing as appalling had happened before at Drimaghleen; its people had never been as shocked." And he sometimes ends stories with a George Eliot–like summation (e.g., "The Wedding in the Garden," 1986). But in these roles he reveals no trace of performative ego. Even when he's onstage he's off: the words are someone else's.

One reviewer complained a few years ago that Trevor was prudish about sex, assuming from the opening words of "Mulvihill's Memorial" (1981) that the author had to be squeamish to describe details in a pornographic film with such dowdy language as "petticoat," "further underclothes," and "divested himself." In fact the description amusingly reflects the quaintly inhibited prurience of a middle-aged bachelor, Mulvihill himself. . . .

The truth is that Trevor does not want to tell his own stories; he wants other people to tell theirs. Curiosity about others . . . impels him to write. He is fascinated by other people's worlds, especially by their ability to invent coercive fictions or to be victimized by them. Apparent in Trevor's earliest work (e.g., "The Table," 1967), the theme has become noticeably darker in recent years. . . . Old injuries, old resentments and grievances harden into the fictions that rule our lives. We keep uttering them to ourselves and others not to find absolution or escape but to justify ourselves after all. To have the last word. To impose our truth no matter what.

When communities and nations do this, Trevor suggests, the costs are even more unbearable.

Chronology

1928	William Trevor Cox born 24 May at his home in Mitchelstown, County Cork, Ireland, the second child of Gertrude Davison Cox and James William Cox, both Protestants. Trevor's sister June is the elder by five years. Adventures with his younger brother, Alan, are developed in autobiographical pieces. His grandfathers on both sides are farmers.
1933–1943	Because his father's career as a bank official requires frequent relocations, Trevor attends a dozen or so different primary and secondary schools in Ireland, including the Loreto Convent in Youghal, County Cork; the Tate School in Wexford; and the Sandford Park School, Dublin.
1943–1946	Introduced to sculpture by Oisin Kelly while a student at St. Columba's College.
1946–1950	Attends Trinity College, Dublin, where he meets his wife, Jane Ryan.
1950	Receives B.A. in history from Trinity University, Dublin.
1951	Takes first job after Trinity: answers ad for private tutor ("would suit a nun"), then teaches in a home 25 miles outside of Dublin.
1952	Marries Jane Ryan in County Armagh, Northern Ireland, where they settle for 18 months. Leaves job as tutor and works as a schoolteacher; leaves, however, when the school appears on the brink of bankruptcy (school eventually closes).
1953–1955	Emigrates to England and teaches in the Midlands at a preparatory school, Bilton Grange.

1955–1959	Works as a full-time, independent sculptor in the village of Greenham, Southwest England (near Wellington, Somerset). Also works as a visiting art master for various schools in the area.
1956	Has successful exhibition of sculpture at the Dublin Painters' Gallery.
1958	First novel, *A Standard of Behavior*, published under the name "William Trevor," which the author begins using professionally.
1960	First son, Patrick, born. Takes job writing advertisements. While at ad agency publishes stories in the *Transatlantic Review, London Magazine,* and other periodicals. A Bodley Head editor notices these stories and asks for a novel.
1963	Son Dominic born.
1964	*Old Boys* wins Hawthorndon Prize for literature.
1965	Quits ad agency.
1966	The story "A Meeting in Middle Age" is adapted for BBC television as the play *A Night with Mrs. da Tanka*.
1980	*The Children of Dynmouth* wins Whitbread Prize for Fiction.
1981	*Beyond the Pale* wins the Giles Cooper Award for the best radio play.
1983	*Fools of Fortune* wins Whitbread Prize for Fiction.
1991	Wins *Hudson Review* Bennett Award. *Two Lives* is short-listed for the Booker Prize.

Selected Bibliography

Primary Works

Story Collections and Novellas

The Day We Got Drunk on Cake and Other Stories. New York: Viking, 1967; Harmondsworth, England: Penguin Books (Bodley Head), 1969.

The Ballroom of Romance and Other Stories. Harmondsworth: Penguin Books, 1972.

Angels at the Ritz and Other Stories. Harmondsworth: Penguin Books, 1975.

Lovers of Their Time and Other Stories. Harmondsworth: Penguin Books, 1978.

The Distant Past and Other Stories. Harmondsworth: Penguin Books, 1979.

Beyond the Pale and Other Stories. Harmondsworth: Penguin Books, 1981.

The Stories of William Trevor. Harmondsworth: Penguin Books, 1983.

The News from Ireland and Other Stories. Harmondsworth: Penguin Books, 1986.

Nights at the Alexandra. Harper Short Novel Series. New York: Harper & Row, 1987.

Family Sins and Other Stories. Harmondsworth: Penguin Books, 1990.

The Collected Stories of William Trevor. New York: Viking, 1993.

Two Lives: Reading Turgenev and My House in Umbria. Harmondsworth: Penguin Books, 1991.

Novels

The Old Boys. Harmondsworth: Penguin Books, 1964.

The Boarding-House. Harmondsworth: Penguin Books, 1965.

The Love Department. Harmondsworth: Penguin Books, 1965.

Mrs. Eckdorf in O'Neill's Hotel. Harmondsworth: Penguin Books, 1969.

Miss Gomez and the Brethren. Harmondsworth: Penguin Books, 1971.

Elizabeth Alone. Harmondsworth: Penguin Books, 1973.

The Children of Dynmouth. Harmondsworth: Penguin Books, 1976.

Other People's Worlds. Harmondsworth: Penguin Books, 1979.

Fools of Fortune. Harmondsworth: Penguin Books, 1983.

The Silence in the Garden. London: Penguin Books, 1988.

Prose Pieces

"Leaving School." *London Magazine* 3 (1966): 68, 82.

"Involvement: Writers Reply." *London Magazine* 8, no. 5 (1968): 5, 19.

"Some Notes on Writing Stories." *London Magazine* 9, no. 12 (1970): 11–12.

"Where the Old Grow Older: Sussex-by-the-Sea Out of Season," *New Statesman*, 27 February 1970, 287–88.

Introduction to *The Search Party*, George A. Birmingham. London: Penguin Books, 1973.

"Saying Good-bye to Elizabeth: Writers at Work." *Author* 84 (1973): 107–9.

"A View of My Own." *Nova*, September 1974, 98.

"A Writer's Day." *Society Magazine*, April 1976, 7.

"Too Blasé for Rape." Review of *Come Trailing Blood*, by Paul Smith. *Hibernia* (Dublin), 28 April 1977. From the Bodley Head files.

Review of *The Collected Stories of Elizabeth Bowen*. *Times Literary Supplement*, 6 February 1981, 131. Reprinted in *Elizabeth Bowen: A Study of the Short Fiction* (Boston: Twayne Publishers, 1991).

"Frank O'Connor: The Way of a Storyteller." *Washington Post Book World*, 13 September 1981, 1–2.

Introduction to *David's Daughter Tamar*, by Margaret Barrington. Dublin: Wolfhound Press, 1982.

"O'Brien, Edna." In *Contemporary Novelists*, 3d ed., edited by James Vinson, p. 504. New York: St. Martin's Press, 1982.

A Writer's Ireland: Landscape in Literature. New York: Viking, 1984.

Introduction to *Oxford Book of Irish Short Stories*. Edited by William Trevor, ix–xv. Oxford: Oxford University Press, 1989.

"Child of the Century." Review of V. S. Pritchett's Stories. *New York Review of Books*, 13 June 1991, 8–10.

Children's Book

Juliet's Story. Dublin: O'Brien Press, 1991.

Plays

The Last Lunch of the Season. London: Covent Garden Press, 1972.

Scenes from an Album. First presented at the Abbey Theater, Dublin, 13 August 1981. Dublin: Irish Writer's Cooperative, 1981.

Secondary Works

Biography

Bruckner, D. J. R. "Stories Keep Coming to a Late Blooming Writer." *New York Times,* 21 May 1990, sec. C, p. 11.

Drabble, Margaret, ed. *The Oxford Companion to English Literature,* 5th ed., p. 997. Oxford: Oxford University Press, 1985.

Halio, Jay L., ed. *British Novelists since 1960. Dictionary of Literary Biography.* Vol. 14. Detroit: Gale Research, 1983.

_____. *Contemporary Authors.* Vol. 4. Detroit: Gale Research, 1981.

MacKenna, Dolores. "William Trevor." In *Contemporary Irish Novelists,* edited by Rüdiger Imhof. Tübingen, Germany: Gunter Narr Verlag, 1990.

Wakeman, John, ed. *World Authors: 1950 to 1970,* pp. 1441–43. New York: H. W. Wilson, 1975.

Interviews

"Age Sage." *Observer* (London), 4 July 1965.

Aronson, Jacqueline Stahl. "William Trevor: An Interview." *Irish Literary Supplement* 5, no. 1 (Spring 1986): 7–8.

Battersby, Eileen. "William Trevor: Chronicler of Everyday Agonies." *Irish Times,* 4 June 1988.

Caldwell, Gail. "A Gentleman of Substance." *Boston Globe,* 30 May 1990, 37–38, 44.

Firchow, Peter, ed. "William Trevor." In *The Writer's Place: Interviews on the Literary Situation in Contemporary Britain.* Minneapolis: University of Minnesota Press, 1974.

Greig, Geordie. "Guarded Celebrant of the Human Condition." *Sunday Times,* 29 May 1988, G9.

Hayman, Ronald. "William Trevor in Interview." *British Book News,* June 1980, 13–14.

Hubert, Hugh. "Love among the Ruins of War." (Manchester) *Guardian,* 23 April 1983, 10.

Hunnewell, Susannah. "Characters Always Come First." *New York Times.*

Ingrams, Richard. "Treasure Ireland." (Dublin) *Independent,* 2 June 1988.

"An Irish Humour Man." (Edinburgh) *Scotsman,* 7 March 1964.

Lean, Derek. "Writer Has to Avoid the View." (London) *Western Morning News,* 12 December 1975.

Leonard, Hugh. "In a Pastel World Where Passion Is Usually Spent." *Sunday Independent,* 23 March 1986, 12.

Selected Bibliography

Montgomery-Massingberd, Hugh. "An Unassuming Lapidary in Words." (London) *Sunday Telegraph*, 21 January 1990.

Nettell, Stephanie. "Sadly Comic or Comically Sad?" *Books and Bookmen* (May 1965): 22, 58.

Profumo, David. "Tower of Fable." *Harpers*, November 1988, 226–28.

Ralph-Bowman, Mark. *Transatlantic Review* (London) 53–54 (1976): 5–12.

Schiff, Stephen. "The Shadows of William Trevor." *New Yorker*, 28 December 1992–4 January 1993, 158–63.

Smith, Amanda. "PW Interviews: William Trevor." *Publishers Weekly*, 28 October 1983, 80.

Stout, Mira. "The Art of Fiction CVIII." *Paris Review* 110 (1989): 118–51.

Webb, W. L. "Gentle Gerontocrat." (Manchester) *Guardian*, 1 May 1965, 7.

Criticism and Articles

Allen, Bruce. "William Trevor and Other People's Worlds." *Sewanee Review* 101, no. 1 (1993): 138–44.

Bragg, Melvin. "William Trevor—the Most English of Irishmen." *Good Housekeeping*, December 1984, 64–65.

Brophy, James D., and Raymond J. Porter, eds. *Contemporary Irish Writing*. Boston: Twayne Publishers, 1983.

Dawe, Gerald, and Edna Longley, eds. In *Across a Roaring Hill: The Protestant Imagination in Modern Ireland*. Belfast: Blackstaff Press, 1985.

Fitzgerald-Hoyt, Mary. "The Influence of Italy in the Writings of William Trevor and Julia O'Faolain," *Notes on Modern Irish Literature* 2 (1990): 61–67.

Gitzen, Julian. "The Truth-Tellers of William Trevor." *Critique: Studies in Modern Fiction* 21, no. 1 (1979): 59–72.

Hayman, R. "William Trevor." (London) *Times*, 31 July 1971, 17.

Jeffares, Norman. *Anglo-Irish Literature*. History of Literature Series. New York: Schocken Books, 1982.

Keefe, Joan Trodden. "What Ish My Language?" *World Literature Today* 54, no. 1 (1985): 5–8.

MacKenna, Mary Dolores. "William Trevor: The Moral Landscape." Ph.D. diss., University of Dublin, 1987.

"Master of Malevolence." *Newsweek*, 19 January 1981, 82.

Morrissey, Thomas. "Trevor's Fools of Fortune: The Rape of Ireland." *Notes on Modern Irish Literature* 2 (1990): 58–60.

Morrison, Kristin. *William Trevor*. New York: Twayne Publishers, 1993.

_____. "William Trevor's 'System of Correspondences.'" *Massachusetts Review* 28 (1987): 489–96.

Mortimer, Mark. "The Short Stories of William Trevor." *Etudes Irlandaises* 9 (December 1984): 161–73.

Ralph-Bowman, Mark. "Focal Distance: A Study of the Novels of William Trevor." Ph.D. diss., University of Leicester, 1974.

Rhodes, Robert E. "'The Rest Is Silence': Secrets in Some William Trevor Stories." In *New Irish Writing: Essays in Memory of Raymond J. Porter*, edited by James D. Brophy and Eamon Grennan, 35–53. Boston: G. K. Hall, 1989.

Schirmer, Gregory A. *William Trevor: A Study of His Fiction*. London: Routledge, 1990.

Stinson, John J. "Replicas, Foils, and Revelation in Some 'Irish' Short Stories of William Trevor." *Canadian Journal of Irish Studies* 11, no. 2 (1985): 17–26.

Taylor, Rachel Lillian. "William Trevor: A Critical Study." Ph.D. diss., University of Maryland, 1980.

Reviews

Ackroyd, Peter. Review of *Angels at the Ritz. Spectator*, 8 November 1975, 604–5.

"Aerial Photography." Review of *Mrs. Eckdorf in O'Neill's Hotel. Times Literary Supplement*, 1 October 1969, 1121.

Agar, John. Review of *Angels at the Ritz. Library Journal*, 15 May 1976, 1226.

Allen, Bruce. "Irish Humanism." Review of *The Stories of William Trevor. Saturday Review*, October 1983, 57–58.

Allen, Walter. Review of *Beyond the Pale. Irish Press*, 12 November 1981.

Bailey, Paul. "Living Dolls." Review of *Elizabeth Alone. New Statesman*, 26 October 1973, 611.

Banville, John. "Cultured Pearls." Review of *Family Sins. London Evening Standard*, 25 January 1990, 2B.

———. "Relics." Review of *Two Lives: Reading Turgenev and My House in Umbria. New York Review of Books*, 26 September 1991, 29–30.

———. Review of *Lovers of Their Time. New Republic*, 5 May 1979, 37–38.

Beards, Richard D. Review of *The Stories of William Trevor. World Literature Today* 58, no. 3 (1984): 416–17.

Beatty, Jack. Review of *Lovers of Their Time. New Republic*, 5 May 1979, 37–38.

———. Review of *Other People's Worlds. New Republic*, 7 February 1981, 38.

Becker, Alida. "Two Women: One Mad, One Bad, Both Wise." Review of *Two Lives: Reading Turgenev and My House in Umbria. New York Times Book Review*, 8 September 1991, 3.

Benedictus, David. "Beware the Puff-Adder." Review of *The Silence in the Garden. Punch*, 3 June 1988, 44–45.

Betts, Doris. "William Trevor: Still Stories Run Deep." Review of *Beyond the Pale. Washington Post Book World*, 21 February 1982, 3.

Binnie, Connie. "Haunting Tale." Review of *Fools of Fortune. Auckland* [New Zealand] *Star*, 10 September 1983.

Blake, Robert. Review of *The Stories of William Trevor. London News* 271 (July 1983): 68.

Blom, J. M., and L. R. Leavis. Review of *Beyond the Pale. English Studies* 63 (1982): 437.

Bradbury, Malcolm. "Dubliners." Review of *Mrs. Eckdorf in O'Neill's Hotel. New Statesman*, 3 October 1969, 462–63.

Bramwell, Murray. "Irish Eyes Have It." Review of *The News from Ireland. Adelaide Review* (Australia), 18 September 1986, 6.

Bricklebank, Peter. Review of *The News from Ireland. Library Journal*, 1 April 1986, 164.

"Briefly Noted." Review of *Angels at The Ritz. New Yorker*, 12 July 1976, 104–05.

Broderick, John. "Socialites." Review of *Angels at the Ritz. Hibernia*, 31 October 1975, 20.

Broyard, Anatole. "Radical Comes from ' Root.' " Review of *The Ballroom of Romance. New York Times Book Review*, 31 October 1972, 43.

Buitenhuis, Peter. "Prufrock Updated." Review of *The Day We Got Drunk on Cake. New York Times Book Review*, 11 February 1968, 38.

Campbell, Peter. "People Who Love People Who Love Somebody Else." *London Review of Books* 25 (January 1990): 19.

"Castle Heartrent." Review of *The Old Boys. Times Literary Supplement*, 6 May 1965, 345.

Catling, Patrick Skene. "The Genius of William Trevor." Review of *The Day We Got Drunk On Cake, The Ballroom of Romance, Angels at The Ritz, Lovers of Their Time,* and *Beyond the Pale. Spectator* 249 (1982): 25–26.

Champlin, Charles. Review of *The Stories of William Trevor. Los Angeles Times Book Review*, 2 October 1983, 1.

Chapin, Victor. "Rooms for Misfits." Review of *The Boarding-House. Saturday Review*, 26 June 1965, 39.

Clemons, Walter. "Dickensian Evil." Review of *Other People's Worlds. Newsweek*, 19 January 1981, 82.

Cole, William. "Gloom, Gloom." Review of *Elizabeth Alone. Saturday Review Book World*, 9 February 1974, 42.

Conarroe, Joel. Review of *Family Sins. New York Times*, 3 June 1990, sec. 7, p. 9.

Connelly, Steve. Review of *A Writer's Ireland: Landscape in Literature. Eire-Ireland: A Journal of Irish Studies* 20, no. 2 (1985): 144–47.

Core, George. "Wanton Life, Importunate Art." Review of *Angels at the Ritz. Sewanee Review* 85, no. 1 (1977): iv–v.

Cox, Shelly. Review of *The Stories of William Trevor. Library Journal*, 1 September 1983, 1722.

Craig, Patricia. "Gulled, Lulled, and De-hoodwinked." Review of *The News from Ireland. Times Literary Supplement,* 11 April 1986, 382.

_____. "Backwaters Tale." Review of *Nights at the Alexandra. Times Literary Supplement,* 30 October 1987, 1192.

_____. "The Shape of Past Iniquities." Review of *The Silence in the Garden. Times Literary Supplement,* 10 June 1988, 643.

_____. "The Pressure of Events." Review of *Family Sins. Times Literary Supplement,* 1 February 1990, 87.

Cunningham, Valentine. "Sinking Fund." Review of *Angels at the Ritz. Times Literary Supplement,* 24 October 1975, 1255.

Curley, Thomas. "Without Pretense." Review of *The Old Boys. Commonweal,* 18 September 1964, 645–46.

Daigre, Ariel. Review of *The News from Ireland.* BBC Literary Service.

Davenport, Gary. "The Novel of Disrupted Maturity." Review of *Fools of Fortune. Sewanee Review* 93 (1985): 321–29.

Davies, Russel. "Wombs and Carrier Bags." Review of *Elizabeth Alone.* (London) *Observer,* 28 October 1973, 38.

_____. "Tiny Tim." Review of *The Children of Dynmouth. New Statesman,* 9 July 1976, 152.

De Mott, Benjamin. "British to the Core." *Atlantic,* May 1979, 92.

Duchene, Anne. "The Decencies Observed." Review of *The Children of Dynmouth. Times Literary Supplement,* 18 June 1976, 731.

Dunne, John. "Good and Averagely Good." Review of *The News from Ireland. Books Ireland,* September 1986, 157.

Dyer, Geoff. "On Their Mettle." Review of *The News from Ireland. New Statesman,* 4 April 1986, 25–26.

Eder, Richard. Review of *The News from Ireland. Los Angeles Times Book Review,* 4 May 1986, 3.

_____. Review of *Two Lives.* 20 May 1990, 3.

Emerson, Sally. Review of *Beyond The Pale. Illustrated London News,* October 1982, 63.

_____. Review of *The Stories of William Trevor. Illustrated London News,* July 1983, 68.

Esmonde de Usabel, Frances. Review of *Beyond the Pale. Library Journal* 106 (1981): 2408.

_____. Review of *The Stories of William Trevor. London News,* July 1983, 68.

Farren, Ronan. "Separate Worlds." Review of *The Children of Dynmouth. Irish Independent,* 24 July 1976.

Fitzgerald-Hoyt, Mary. Review of *Two Lives. Irish Literary Supplement* 2, no. 1 (1992): 12.

Selected Bibliography

Flower, Dean. "Barbaric Yawpes and Breathing Lessons." *Hudson Review* 42, no. 1 (1989): 133–40.

———. "The Flavour of Failure." *Times Literary Supplement*, 26 October 1973, 1299.

———. "The Reticence of William Trevor." Review of *Family Sins*. *Hudson Review* 43, no. 4 (1991): 686–90.

Fowles, John. "The Irish Maupassant." Review of *The News from Ireland*. *Atlantic*, August 1986, 89–91.

———. "Central Values." *Irish Press*, 28 September 1978, 6.

Frankel, Haskel. "In Search of Septimus Tuam." Review of *The Love Department*. *Saturday Review*, 28 January 1967, 41.

Fraser, Gerald C. Review of *Mrs. Eckdorf in O'Neill's Hotel*. *New York Times Book Review*, 23 June 1985, 32.

Geng, Veronica. "Geographer of Delusions." Review of *The News from Ireland* and *The Stories of William Trevor*. *New Republic*, 9 June 1986, 28–30.

Glavin, Anthony. "Separate Realities." Review of *The News from Ireland*. *Christian Science Monitor*, 2 May 1986, B5.

Glendinning, Victoria. "Oblique Approach to Major Passions." Review of *Lovers of Their Time*. *New York Times Book Review*, 8 April 1979, 15.

Goldsworthy, Peter. "Flawed Characters Collected." Review of *The News from Ireland*. (Sydney, New South Wales) *Morning Herald*, 23 August 1986.

Gordon, Mary. "The Luck of the Irish." Review of *Fools of Fortune* and *The Stories of William Trevor*. *New York Review of Books*, 22 December 1983, 53–54.

Gorra, Michael. Review of *Fools of Fortune*. *Boston Review* 8 (December 1983): 33.

———. "Laughter and Bloodshed." *Hudson Review* 37, no. 1 (1984): 151–64.

Greenwood, Gillian. "A Fine Anguish." Review of *The News from Ireland*. (London) *Literary Review*, May 1986, 21.

Grieve, James. Review of *The News from Ireland*. (Melbourne, Victoria) *Times*, 26 July 1986.

Grimes, William. Review of *Nights at the Alexandra*. *New York Times Book Review*, 17 January 1988, 24.

———. Review of *Two Lives*. *Washington Post Book World*, 18 August 1991, 1.

Grumbach, Doris. "Hanged by a School-Tie." Review of *The Old Boys*. *Times Literary Supplement*, 5 March 1964, 189.

Halio, Jay L. "Fiction and the Malaise of Our Time." Review of *Lovers of Their Time*. *Southern Review* 17 (Summer 1981): 622–30.

Hanna, Frank. Review of *Beyond the Pale*. *Sunday Tribune*, 27 September 1981, 18.

Harrington, John P. Review of *Family Sins*. *Library Journal*, 1 March 1990, 118.

Harris, Lis. "An Irishman in England." Review of *Lovers of Their Time*. *New Yorker*, 28 January 1980, 99–101.

Harsent, David. "Tiny Tears." Review of *Angels at The Ritz*. *New Statesman*, 24 October 1975, 519.

Hemmings, F. W. J. "New Fiction." *New Statesman*, 7 May 1965, 733–34.

Hepburn, Neil. "Ever Wakeful." Review of *Angels at the Ritz*. *Listener*, 8 January 1976, 30.

Heyward, Michael. "Domestic Terrors." Review of *Family Sins*. *New Republic*, 1 October 1990, 40–41.

Hill, Susan. "Masterly Sprints." Review of *Angels at the Ritz*. (London) *Times*, 15 December 1975, 41A.

Holland, Mary. "Codes." Review of *Beyond the Pale*. *New Statesman*, 13 November 1981, 26.

Hulbert, Ann. Review of *Beyond the Pale*. *New Republic*, 10 February 1982, 39.

_____. Review of *Fools of Fortune*. *New Republic*, 28 November 1983, 593.

Ingrams, Richard. Review of *The News from Ireland*. *Spectator* 9 November 1986, 25.

_____. "Caught at a Crucial Moment." Review of *Family Sins*. *Sunday Times*, 28 January 1990, H6.

Jamal, Zahir. "Silt & Scythe." Review of *Lovers of Their Time*. *New Statesman*, 22 September 1978, 380.

Jaspersohn, William. "Bleak Douse from Trevor." Review of *Lovers of Their Time*. *Christian Science Monitor*, 9 April 1979, B7.

Jefford, A. "Dispossessed." Review of *The News from Ireland*. *Partisan Review* 12 (March 1987): 62.

Johnson, Diane. "Peculiarly Irish Stew." Review of *The Ballroom of Romance*. *Washington Post Book World*, 19 November 1972, 2.

Kakutani, Michiko. Review of *Family Sins*. *New York Times*, 11 May 1990, sec. C, p. 33.

_____. Review of *The News from Ireland*. *New York Times Book Review*, 14 May 1986, 19.

Kemp, Peter. "Grisliness in an Anglo-Irish Garden." *Review of Silence in the Garden*. (Capetown, South Africa) *Star*, 1 September 1988.

Kilroy, James. "Irish Short Stories, Past and Present." *Sewanee Review* 90 (Winter 1982): 89–100.

King, Francis. "Loosening Up." Review of *Beyond the Pale*. *Spectator*, 24 October 1981, 23.

Lemmons, Philip. "The Awesome Power of the Past." Review of *Angels at the Ritz*. *New Leader*, 16 August 1976, 18–19.

Levin, Martin. "A Reader's Report." Review of *The Boarding-House*. *New York Times Book Review*, 20 June 1965, 31–32.

"The Lonely and the Bitter." *Atlantic*, August 1965, 126.

Long, J. V. "New Collections, New Pleasures." Review of *The News from Ireland*. *Commonweal*, 24 October 1986, 570.

Selected Bibliography

Lownsbrough, John. "Daring People on Flying Trapezes." Review of *Lovers of Their Time*. *Macleans's*, 22 January 1979, 43.

Lucie-Smith, E. Review of *The Day We Got Drunk on Cake*. *Listener*, 22 June 1967, 829.

MacMahon, Sean. "Pitiful and Unbearably Funny." Review of *The Children of Dynmouth*. *Hibernia*, 16 July 1976.

Mahon, Derek. "Stoically through the Shambles." Review of *Lovers of Their Time*. *Times Literary Supplement*, 6 October 1978, 1109.

"A Man Who Understands Women." Review of *The Ballroom of Romance*. (Dublin) *Sunday Independent*, 2 July 1972.

Manzo, Fred William. "Fantasy and Its Outcomes in the Novels and Stories of William Trevor." Ph.D. diss., University of California at Santa Barbara, 1987.

Marsh, Pamela. "New Fiction in Brief." Review of *The Day We Got Drunk on Cake*. *Christian Science Monitor*, 11 January 1968, 11.

Massie, Allan. "Perfect Poet of Loneliness." Review of *The News from Ireland*. (Edinburgh) *Scotsman*, 22 March 1986, 11.

May, Derwent. "Fiction: Self-Deceivers Ever." Review of *The Day We Got Drunk on Cake*. *Listener* 77 (1967): 829.

McCabe, Bernard. "Irish Outrage." Review of *The Stories of William Trevor*. *Nation*, 3 December 1983, 574–77.

McCaffrey, Lawrence J. Review of *Lovers of Their Time*. *America*, 26 May 1979, 440.

Mellors, John. "Irish Times." Review of *Lovers of Their Time*. *Listener*, 4 January 1979, 30–31.

_____. "Unbecoming Tales." Review of *Beyond the Pale*. *Listener*, 5 November 1981, 544.

_____. "Going Back to First Love." Review of *The News From Ireland*. *Listener*, 29 May 1986, 25.

"Middle-aged Obsessions." Review of *The Boarding-House*. (London) *Observer*, 2 May 1965, 27.

Review of *Miss Gomez and the Brethren*. (Christchurch, New Zealand) *Press*, 11 March 1972.

Mosher, Howard Frank. "William Trevor: Pictures from an Irish Exhibition." Review of *The News From Ireland*. *Washington Post Book World*, 25 May 1986, 6.

Morrison, Kristin. "The Family Sins of Social and Political Evils." Review of *Family Sins*. *Irish Literary Supplement*, Spring 1991, 20.

Naughton, John. "The Irish Raj." Review of *The Silence in the Garden*. *Listener*, 21 July 1988, 26.

Nettell, Stephanie. "Sadly Comic or Comically Sad?" *Books and Bookmen*, May 1965, 22, 58.

"Notes on Current Books." Review of *Other People's Worlds*. *Virginia Quarterly Review* 57, no. 3 (1981): 102–3.

Nott, Kathleen. "Life at Rock-Bottom." Review of *The Ballroom of Romance. Observer,* 14 May 1972, 36.

Nye, Robert. "Trevor: Storyteller with a Poet's Feeling." Review of *Angels at the Ritz. Christian Science Monitor,* 16 June 1976, 23.

Oates, Joyce Carol. "More Lonely than Evil." Review of *The Children of Dynmouth. New York Times Book Review,* 17 April 1977, 13, 36.

O'Faolain, Sean. "Dire Innocence." Review of *The Children of Dynmouth. Irish Press,* 26 June 1976.

Pacey, Martin. "A Pallid Daydream." Review of *Nights at the Alexandra. Listener* 118 (1987): 29.

"Partitioned Off." Review of *The Ballroom of Romance. Times Literary Supplement,* 26 May 1972, 595.

Paterson, Jennifer. Review of *The Silence in the Garden. Spectator,* 3 December 1988, 35.

"Pathetic Phalluses." Review of *The Ballroom of Romance. Listener,* 4 May 1972, 596.

Paulin, Tom. "Abandoned Prefabs." Review of *Lovers of Their Time. Encounter* 52 (1979): 49.

Perrick, Penny. "They All Go into the Dark." (London) *Sunday Times,* 28 January 1990, H6.

Pollock, Veneita. "New Novels." Review of *The Boarding-House. Punch,* 19 May 1965, 752.

Ponsford, Michael. "'Only the Truth': The Short Stories of William Trevor." Review of *The Stories of William Trevor. Eire-Ireland* 23 (1988): 75–86.

Prescott, Peter S. "Domestic Dilemmas." Review of *Angels at the Ritz. Newsweek,* 14 June 1976, 91–93.

_____. "Small Change." Review of *Beyond the Pale. Newsweek,* 22 February 1982, 74–75.

_____. "The Hound of History." Review of *The Stories of William Trevor. Newsweek,* 10 October 1983, 85–88.

_____. Review of *Nights at the Alexandra. Newsweek,* 7 December 1987, 94.

_____. "Timeless Stories of Oppression." Review of *Lovers of Their Time. Newsweek,* 9 April 1979, 93–94.

Price, R. G. G. Review of *The Day We Got Drunk on Cake. Punch,* 2 August 1967, 182.

Price, Reynolds. "A Lifetime of Tales from the Land of Broken Hearts." Review of *The Collected Stories of William Trevor. New York Times Books Review,* 28 February 1993, 1, 25–27.

Pritchett, V. S. "Explosions of Conscience." Review of *Lovers of Their Time. New York Review of Books,* 19 April 1979, 8.

Raban, Jonathan. "Crow Street." Review of *Miss Gomez and the Brethren. New Statesman,* 15 October 1971, 514.

Selected Bibliography

Rayner, Richard. "Love and Loss." Review of *Family Sins*. *Daily Telegraph*, 27 January 1990, 2B.

Rhodes, Robert E. Review of *The Day We Got Drunk on Cake*. *Irish Literary Supplement* 5, no. 2 (1969): 11.

_____. Review of *Beyond the Pale* and *Scenes from an Album*. *Irish Literary Supplement* 2, no. 2 (1983): 28.

_____. Review of *The News from Ireland*. *Irish Literary Supplement* 5, no. 2 (1986): 11.

Rubins, Josh. "Doing It All." Review of *Lovers of Their Time*. *Saturday Review*, 12 May 1979, 44.

Schirmer, Gregory A. "Revelations and Predicaments." Review of *Family Sins*. *Washington Post Book World*, 27 May 1990, 6.

Shakespeare, Nicholas, "Distiller of the Extraordinary." Review of *The News from Ireland*. (London) *Times*, 15 March 1986, 23

Sheehy, Terence. Review of *The News from Ireland*. *Catholic Herald*, 5 September 1986.

Sheppard, R. Z. "The Banality of Deceit." Review of *Other People's Worlds*. *Time*, 2 February 1981, 82.

_____. "Tales of Lovers and Haters." Review of *The Stories of William Trevor*. *Time*, 10 October 1983, 72.

"The Silence of Forgiveness." Review of *Mrs. Eckdorf in O'Neill's Hotel*. *Time*, 26 January 1970, 80–82.

Solotaroff, Ted. "The Dark Souls of Ordinary People." Review of *Beyond the Pale*. *New York Times Book Review*, 21 February 1982, 7.

Spencer, Elizabeth. "French Lessons While the Neighbors Starve." Review of *The News from Ireland*. *New York Times Book Review*, 8 June 1986, 14.

Stitt, Kenn. "Searching." Review of *The Ballroom of Romance*. *New Statesman*, 5 May 1972, 611.

Sullivan, Walter. "Documents from the Ice Age: Recent British Novels." Review of *The Children of Dynmouth*. *Sewanee Review* 86 (1978): 320–25.

"Summer Reading." Review of *The News from Ireland*. *Time*, 7 July 1986, 60.

Taliaferro, Frances. Review of *The Stories of William Trevor*. *Harper's*, October 1983, 74.

Tallent, Elizabeth. Review of *The Silence in the Garden*. *New York Times Book Review*, 9 October 1988, 12.

Theroux, Paul. "Miseries and Splendours." Review of *The Ballroom of Romance*. *Encounter* 39 (September 1972): 69–75.

Thwaite, Anthony. "Keeping up Appearances." Review of *Angels at the Ritz*. (London) *Observer*, 26 October 1975, 30.

"Timeless Stories of Oppression." Review of *Lovers of Their Time*. *Newsweek*, 9 April 1979, 93–94.

Tomalin, Claire. "An Intruder in Dublin." Review of *Mrs. Eckdorf in O'Neill's Hotel*. (London) *Observer*, 5 October 1969, 34.

_____. "A Gallery of Types." Review of *Miss Gomez and the Brethren*. (London) *Observer*, 17 October 1971, 34.

Towers, Robert. "Gleeful Misanthropy." Review of *The Stories of William Trevor*. *New York Times Book Review*, 2 October 1983, 1.

_____. "Good News." Review of *The News from Ireland*. *New York Review of Books*, 26 June 1986, 32–33.

_____. "Short Satisfactions." Review of *Family Sins*. *New York Review of Books*, 17 May 1990, 38–39.

Tuohy, Frank. "Seeing How the Other Half Lives." Review of *Other People's Worlds*. *Times Literary Supplement*, 20 June 1980, 690.

Tyler, Anne. Review of *Angels at the Ritz*. *New York Times Book Review*, 11 July 1976, 7.

Uglow, Jennifer. "Heart and Mind." Review of *Beyond the Pale*. *Literary Review* (December 1981): 43–44.

"Under Restraint." Review of *The Love Department*. *Times Literary Supplement*, 22 September 1966, 873.

Waugh, Auberon. Review of *Miss Gomez and the Brethren*. *Spectator*, 16 October 1971, 511.

_____. "Brief cases [*sic*]." Review of *The Ballroom of Romance*. *Spectator*, 13 May 1972, 733–34.

_____. Review of *Angels at the Ritz*. (London) *Evening Standard*, 30 December 1975.

Waugh, Harriet. "Skinned Alive but without Malice." Review of *The News from Ireland*. *Spectator*, 5 April 1986, 30–31.

Williams, David. Review of *The Ballroom of Romance*. *Punch*, 3 May 1972, 623.

Young, Vernon. "The Music of What Happens." *Parnassus* 11, no. 2 (1984): 323–35.

Index

187

The Author

Suzanne Morrow Paulson is an associate professor of English at Minot State University in North Dakota. She earned a Ph.D. from the University of Minnesota, Minneapolis, in 1984 and has taught at the University of St. Thomas, St. Paul; the University of Minnesota, Minneapolis and Morris; and the University of Illinois, Urbana. She is the author of *Flannery O'Connor: A Study of the Short Fiction* (1988) and contributed the chapter "Apocalypse of Self, Resurrection of the Double—Flannery O'Connor's *The Violent Bear It Away*" in *Flannery O'Connor: New Perspectives*, ed. Mary Neff Shaw and Sura Rath (1993). Her work has also appeared in *Literature and Psychology*.